THE INDEPENDENT HIGHLAND COMPANIES

'Sir we are prisoners, for I did see many men coming down the rock and rid croses in there bonets' – Statement regarding the Prince 'in the heather', by the servant of Malcolm MacLeod of Brea (Raasay) when he saw the approach of the pursuing Independent Companies (1746), from *The Lyon in Mourning*, vol. III, by Robert Forbes, Bishop of Ross and Caithness, 1746–1775.

'Fancy sees clansmen bound over the heath,
Pibrochs loud screaming,
Tartans wide streaming,
Far rolls the shout of the slogan of death.'
— Sir William Allan

THE INDEPENDENT HIGHLAND COMPANIES 1603–1760

PETER SIMPSON

Foreword by Godfrey, Lord Macdonald

JOHN DONALD PUBLISHERS LTD
EDINBURGH

ISBN 0 85976 432 X

British Library Cataloguing in Publication Data
A catalogue record for this book
is available from the British Library

Phototypeset by WestKey Ltd., Falmouth, Cornwall
Printed and bound in Great Britain by Bell & Bain Ltd., Glasgow

Foreword

I feel very honoured to have been asked to write a few words as a preface to this fascinating book. As a direct descendant of Sir Alexander Macdonald I have always been rather mystified by his role in this period of our history. However, thanks to the painstaking researches of Peter Simpson the part played by my ancestor and other prominent Highlanders of the time is now much clearer. I can appreciate that they were men of vision and could see the dangers of openly supporting an 'affair of the heart'. They had to play a very dangerous game, and thanks to Captain Simpson another vital element of this turbulent time is vividly described and explained most clearly.

The Independent Companies and especially those raised from the two main clans from the Isle of Skye (Macdonalds and Macleods) obviously had a major effect on the outcome of the '45 Rising.

Had they not intervened on behalf of the government of the day and instead joined forces with Prince Charles Edward Stuart it is more than probable that the history of the British monarchy would have been changed for all time.

Godfrey, Lord Macdonald
High Chief of Clan Donald

The detailed drawing of dress and arms on the front cover is reproduced by courtesy of the United Services Museum, The Castle, Edinburgh, with the collaboration of Captain E.A. Campbell and Major I.H. Mackay-Scobie.

The following maps, gratefully acknowledged to Caroline Alder of San Francisco, and to C.J. Simpson, appear on preliminary pages xiii–xvi:

Districts at the time of the Jacobite Risings
Road systems: Wade and Caulfield
Scotland at the time of the Jacobite Rising, 1745
The flight of Prince Charles after Culloden.

Contents

Foreword   v
Ruling Dynasties, 1603–1760   viii
Introduction   ix
Extract by Bernard Fergusson   xii
Maps   xiii

Part I – The Highlands in the 17th Century   1
 1 The State of the Highlands 1603–1760   3
 2 The Clan System   8
 3 The Highland Soldier   15
 4 Garb of Old Gaul   20
 5 Highland Weapons   25
 6 Highland Lawlessness   34

Part II – The Independent Highland Companies   41
 7 The Years Before the Union   42
 8 The Early Days of the Independent Highland
    Companies (1603–1660)   48
 9 Between the Restoration and the Glorious Revolution
    (1660–1688)   57
10 Killiecrankie, Cromdale and Glencoe (1688–1700)   76
11 The Act of Union, Sherrifmuir and the Risings of
    1708 and 1715 (1700–1717)   91
12 General Wade to the Rescue (1717–1739)   101
13 The Great Raising of the Companies and the Road to
    Culloden (1740–1746)   118
14 The Prince in the Heather (1746)   137
15 The Bloody Aftermath (1746–1760)   148
16 Epilogue   153
Appendices   165
Acknowledgements   221
Bibliography   223
Manuscripts   228
Other Material   229
Index   230

Ruling Dynasties (1603–1760)

Second or Lennox House of Stewart

James VI of Scotland and I of England (son of Mary I and Henry Stewart)	1603–1625
Charles I (son of James VI & I)	1625–1649
Charles II (son of Charles I)	1649–1651

Commonwealth

Oliver Cromwell (Protector)	1651–1658
Richard Cromwell (Protector)	1658–1659

House of Stewart

Charles II (restored)	1660–1685
James VII of Scotland & II of England (brother of Charles II)	1685–1688 1685–1688

House of Orange

Mary II (d. of James VII & II) & William II of Scotland and III of England	1689–1702

House of Stewart

Anne (sister of Mary II)	1702–1714

House of Hanover

George I (Great grandson of James VI & I)	1714–1727
George II (son of George I)	1727–1760

Introduction

The first Independent Highland Companies were raised from clan sources by order of the Government from 1603 onwards to help 'keep the Peace in the Braes' and were last mustered in 1760 after a period of social unrest in the Highlands which in turn followed the rising in 1745/6 and the punitive measures imposed mainly on the clans loyal to the Stewart cause.

During this period of some 150 years, which encompassed possibly the most violent and turbulent period in Scottish history, the Independent Companies were mustered and disbanded many times. This largely depended upon the state of peace or disorder at any specific time and so often upon the whim of the ruling cliques whether located in Edinburgh or London. Originally they were raised as local gendarmerie forces from among the dominant Whig clans primarily to curb cattle 'lifters', to maintain peace among the feuding clans and to act as guides to the regular crown armed forces. In later periods, however, they were used to dissuade clansmen from joining the Young Pretender in 1745/6 as well as taking an active part in the many skirmishes and pitched battles which occurred during this period – including Auldern, Killiecrankie, Haughs of Cromdale, Sherrifmuir, Glenshiel, Inverurie, Prestonpans, Falkirk, The Rout of Moy, Dornoch and even Culloden itself.

These Independent Companies were the true progenitors of the Highland Regiments which became world-famous in subsequent times beginning with the raising of the Black Watch (Royal Highland Regiment) in the early 18th Century and followed by others throughout that century. Following the example and the success of the Black Watch at Fontenoy, the Highlands were seen to offer a pool of fighting men of outstanding stature, hardiness and bravery who subsequently became part and parcel of the British Armed Forces – the rest is history.

In this research an attempt is made to unravel some facts and factors of the military and social background to the mustering, maintenance and disbandment of these clan forces in this period of just over a century and a half. In the early days from 1603–1660 very little written information is available in military records and it is the clan archives that have revealed what little there is to be known. After the Restoration, however (and the official beginnings of the British Army) the situation has become a little clearer following some partial documentation of these clan/crown forces. From these two basic sources (military records and clan archives) pieced together a story the extent which will probably never be fully known, but which is undoubtedly of great importance in the overall background to Scottish and British military history and the subsequent development of the British Empire.

During this 150 years monumental changes were to take place, unthought of and unwanted in many cases – changes of dynasties; changes in religion; civil wars on a grand scale; union of two countries; intrigues and plots a plenty. A period of great symbolic importance and glamour encompassing the Restoration, the Glorious Revolution; the Massacre of Glencoe; three major uprisings on behalf of James and his son Prince Charles Edward and the last civil war battle fought on British soil at Culloden in 1746.

In this my first essay into history, my interest has been fostered and kept alive by a number of dedicated historians of this period, clan chiefs and archivists who have helped and guided in the compilation of this story behind the most famous regiments in the world.

Some twenty clans supplied captains and lesser officers for these Independent Companies from 1603 onwards and all chiefs and their archivists/historians have been approached with reference to the background history and family ties of these commanders. While most of the major clans have generally well organised and specific records going back to well beyond the 17th century, other clans have only minimal archives. Their records have unfortunately either been irretrievably lost, destroyed or sold abroad over the years. Continuity of family history, detail of actions or commissions is often difficult to trace.

However, some fifty or sixty percent of these captains have been traced with varying degrees of detail uncovered.

In some cases, clans who were generally in favour of the Jacobite cause supplied captains to the Independent Companies. These captains were then paid by the Government and commissioned to act against the very clans to whom they belonged. It was reasonably common to find families divided amongst themselves in terms of loyalty to either the Stewart or the Hanoverian cause – many clan

Introduction

families, including such notables as the Duke of Atholl, hedged their bets with a son in each camp.

Captains and other officers were drawn mainly from an officer class which had its roots in the lesser gentry of the clan; often the close blood relation of the chief; from tacksman who were the large tenant farmers and from professional soldiers many of whom gained their military knowledge from having fought as mercenaries on behalf of Continental causes abroad. These commanders, by and large, had been brought up from birth to be the natural leaders of the clansmen; were mostly well trained in military matters and field tactics and were therefore proficient to pass on their military skills to their men with a relatively high degree of fighting competence.

The chapters in Part I dwell on the general state of the Highlands in the 17th and 18th centuries along with a description of the clan system, the Highland soldier, the state of lawlessness. The weaponry and dress of the period are all relevant to the emergence of the Independent Companies and the role they played in the developing history of Scotland until the years just following the tragedy of Drumossie Moor (Culloden) and the 'end of a way of life'.

Part II is devoted to the history of the Companies and their activities within the social and military fabric of the country.

This story has also to be seen against the background of the social history of the period – the grinding poverty, lack of communications, the almost unbreakable ties of a feudal and/or patriarchal clan system, agriculture of the most basic kind and its direct bonding effect to the land.

An Extract From *The Black Watch And The King's Enemies* by Bernard Fergusson, 1950

Highland soldiers have fought with distinction on practically every battlefield of the British Army for the past 200 years, since William Pitt (the future Earl of Chatham) decided after the 1745 rebellion to enlist these fierce turbulent hillmen into the service of the Empire as a whole.

The type has changed. The Jock of to-day comes from the city as often from the hills and the fields. But he still inherits the spirit and traditions of his Highland forbears – the clan feeling, the toughness, the fierceness in assault, the independence of character, the boundless self-confidence in his own powers in all circumstances and conditions. He has also the habit of impressing his own personality on any comrades of other origins while retaining his own, whatever his surroundings.

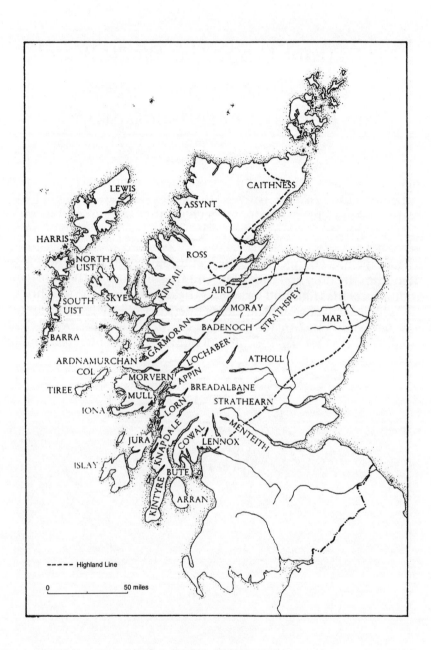

LEWIS

CAITHNESS

ASSYNT

HARRIS

NORTH
UIST

ROSS

SOUTH
UIST

SKYE

KINTAIL

AIRD

MORAY

STRATHSPEY

MAR

BADENOCH

BARRA

GARMORAN

LOCHABER

ATHOLL

ARDNAMURCHAN
COL

MORVERN

APPIN

TIREE

MULL

LORN

BREADALBANE

STRATHEARN

IONA

KNAPDALE

COWAL

MENTEITH

JURA

LENNOX

ISLAY

KINTYRE

BUTE

ARRAN

- - - - Highland Line

0   50 miles

Districts at the time of the Jacobite Risings.

xiii

Road systems: Wade and Caulfield.

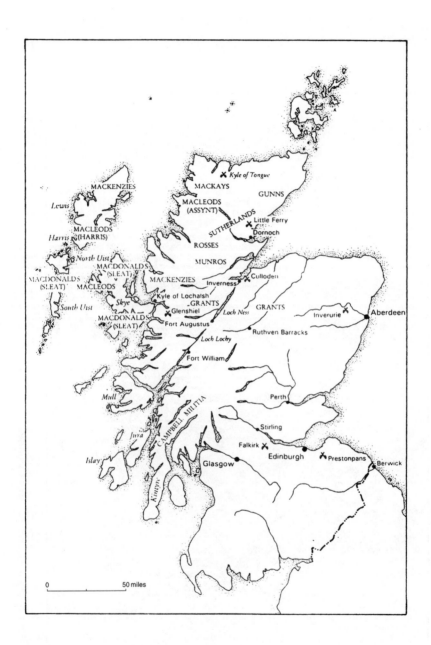

Scotland at the time of the Jacobite Rising, 1745.

XV

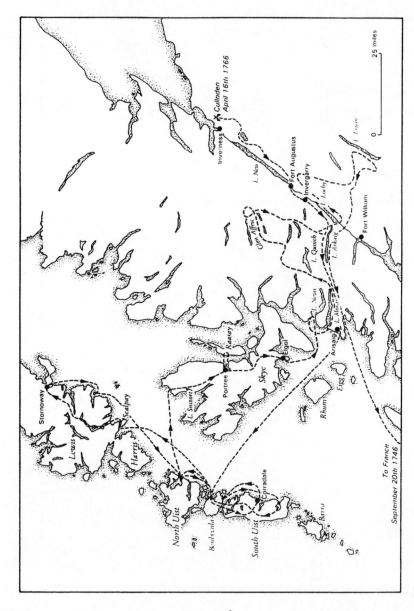

The flight of Prince Charles after Culloden.

xvi

PART I

THE HIGHLANDS IN THE 17TH CENTURY

Heritage
by Lord Ballantrae, Colonel of the Black Watch, Royal Highland
Regiment, 1969–76
Dedicated to the Memory of Scottish Soldiers who died fighting in Past
Times

Another field is fought; a little fight
    Not to be famed in chronicles of war,
Not to be noticed in the News tonight
    Nor cabled eagerly to lands afar.
Only upon the regimental scrolls
    Begun long since, the day of Fontenoy,
Among old skirmishes and lost patrols
    They will record tonight this latest ploy.

Now where today the sun blazed overhead,
    In the cool evening moving to and fro
Their comrades bury the immortal dead
    For ever from the sight of friend and foe.
And round them in the darkness sentries stand
    And watch with tired eyes and straining ears,
Even as long ago in our old land
    Their weary kinsfolk leaned upon their spears.

In old wild days, if one should chance to fall,
    The son caught up the broadsword of the slain,
Girt on the dirk and the accoutrements all
    And saw to it the ranks were whole again;
So now, as sure as when in ancient days
    Brave youth espoused the patriarchal feud,
Still, in the fashion of our modern ways,
    The oath of Aberfeldy is renewed.

We know not yet the comrades who are down,
    Who are the two and who the twenty-four
That shall not see again the country town,
    The pithead or the cothouse or the moor,
From whence they came to fill their father's place,
    To keep the long heroic line unbroke,
The seed, the fruit, the harvest of their race,
    The latest warriors of a fighting folk.

From such small battles was a Kingdom built,
    By such bold forays was a Border held,
By men in hodden gray or tattered kilt
    Who knew defeat, but knew not to be quelled;
And they that fell today were of a blood
    That cannot all be drunk by greedy earth,
And whoso fell in honour where he stood
    Fulfilled the purpose of his warrior birth.

Bernard Fergusson

CHAPTER 1
The State of the Highlands 1603–1760

The other partie northerne ar full of mountaines and verie rud
and homelie kynd of people doeth inhabite which is called the
Reidshankes, or wyld Scottis. They be cloathed with ane mantle,
with ane schirt, going bair legged to the knie.—Extract from
Chronicles of Scotland, 1, XXIV, 4th. ed.

Highland Fewds never dies—*Wardlaw MSS*

Following the Union of the Crowns in 1603 James VI of Scotland
also became James I of England. This joint monarchy allowed him
to link his actions between the two countries and to take advantage
in Scotland of the ceaseless feuding and warfare among the clans.
It is also clear that the clans had no central direction and this lack
of military and political authority meant that there was no real unity
or cohesion in their struggles.

The first list of Highland clans were embodied in an Act of
Parliament in 1587 and a roll of 'the names of the landordis and
baillis of landis in the hielandis and ilis' was drawn up.

In the early 17th century control royal was sought through a
number of agencies – commissions of 'fire and sword', the building
of castles and fortifications and by the appointment of king's
lieutenants via the Gordon earls in the north and east and the
Campbell earls in the west and south. These appointments of
Huntly and Argyll sought to make these all-powerful chiefs responsible for controlling their own kinsmen by a series of rewards and
punishments.

James VI made very determined efforts to end strife among the
clans. He insisted upon the divine right of his kingship, but made
his Highland chiefs responsible for their offending clansmen. He
also insisted that titles of lands should be produced in order to
validate the claims of chiefs to specific land areas 'on pain of
Forfeiture' and that 'broken' clans, who had no clearly defined areas
of land, should ally themselves with another and titled clan. The
clan Macgregor was often quoted as an example of a 'broken' clan

and subsequently paid the penalty for not conforming with the system.

James shrewdly assessed that the most western of the clans and the Island chiefs were the least likely to conform with this new discipline. Accordingly he imprisoned every one of them until they agreed to sign and rigidly abide by the Statutes of Icolmkill or Iona Statutes. (1609)

These statutes tried to introduce certain measures under the guise of civilizing the clans, while at the same time ensuring that the central power of Government extended to all parts of the Highlands. An oath of allegiance and obedience to the King was the central instrument. At the same time he extended and reinforced the power of the church and its ministry, by insisting upon compulsory money payments as well as stipendiary dues. Associated with this latter religious edict was the rather vague statement that 'immorality should be suppressed'. Inns for travellers were also to be set up in order to lessen the abuse of 'sorning' the extraction of food and lodging by threat of force. These were known as 'King's houses' and a number remain to this day, for instance at Balquhidder and Rannoch Moor.

The households of the chief were also to be limited in the belief that many of the traditional hangers-on were in fact armed bodyguards, who could so readily form the nucleus of an armed force in times of inter-clan feuding. The countless numbers of beggars and vagrants were to be outlawed along with the historian bards or 'seanachies', who were to be singled out for special treatment as it was feared that their influence encouraged the warlike behaviour of the clans via the brosnachadh catha or incitement to battle. In addition, the carrying of arms was to be banned as also the illegal trade in wines and spirits. These sanctions, in part or in total, were seen to be most punitive to the Highland way of life: but probably the most effective sanction of all in helping to destroy the old traditions, was the edict that education of the elder sons (and daughters) was to be made obligatory for all the Highland chiefs and tacksmen (the lesser gentry) at Lowland schools, so that the reading and writing of English could be fostered.

In conclusion, the clan chief was also to be held responsible for the absolute obedience to these Statutes by his kinsfolk, dependents and clansmen.

As the chiefs most unwillingly signed the Statutes they claimed 'The grite miserie, barbaritie and povertie unto the quhilk for the

4

present our barrane cuntrie is subject' which 'Hes proceidit of the unaturall deidlie feidis quhilkis hes bene foisterit amangis us this laid aig'.

Undoubtedly the Iona Statutes as they were commonly called, strove to limit the absolute power of the chiefs and to bring some semblance of peace to the ordinary clansmen. It was felt, too that a working knowledge of English, however rudimentary, would aid this process and would help in the fuller understanding of affairs in England and Lowland Scotland.

The Statutes were patently unworkable in total. They were never fully implemented, but they did have a measure of success in that feuding did appreciably decline by around 1615. So while the chiefs and the lesser gentry still clung tenaceously to their considerable authority in purely local affairs, their influence on wider social and political matters began to wane. Correspondingly the power of central Government was increased – for example by holding clan hostages in Edinburgh along with financial penalties and even property forfeiture, in the case of serious demeanours. This use (or abuse) of Royal power plus the partial implementation of the main Statutes, undoubtedly curbed the worst of the clan excesses and lawlessness in the early part of the 17th Century. By 1620 a semblance of order was apparent in the Highlands.

At about this time, additional important groupings of clans broke into the scene. They held and had established feudal titles and the rights of chieftainship – of these the most important were the Mackenzies, Mackintoshes, and the earls of Atholl, although the latter were not strictly chiefs of a clan in that area. The above, along with the already established Campbells and Gordons, held sway over the majority of the Highland land area.

During the remainder of the century the Government renewed commissions and granted authority to the main clan chiefs, thinking that they would represent the Monarchy while keeping the warring factions under some control. The power of these families grew and consolidated under such patronage to such an extent that they became virtually indispensible to any monarchical rule. The Government realised only too well that this extension of clan power meant that while they tended to misuse this increased power for their own ends, they could effect a good measure of control especially in the inaccessible areas of the Highlands where road communication was virtually non-existent.

The Highlands were obviously extremely difficult to manage or control without the absolute backing of the chief and the virtual isolation from the remainder of the United Kingdom meant that it was by-passed in terms of economic and cultural developments evidenced elsewhere. It's survival depended almost wholly on strictly maintained clan units; on the self-sufficiency of these units and their ability to defend themselves from any warlike neighbour. In this type of social situation a strong, tough and warlike race of people, well-versed in military matters had existed for a considerable period.

In the mid-seventeenth century, around the groupings of the five major clans, both Jacobite and Whig principles were strongly supported. In these dissentions the main clans were able to 'come to arms' effectively and easily, chiefly because of the nature of the economy within the Highlands. Also, because of certain changes in their weaponry and military tactics, e.g. the replacement of the 'twa-handit' sword by the smaller and lighter basket-hilt sword along with the development of the fearsome Highland charge with targe and dirk in the hands of the lightly-clad clansmen.

Primarily the Highland economy was largely pastoral and based on black-cattle and sheep in almost equal numbers. While some grain was grown (mainly oats and barley), it was normally insufficient for winter needs and most of the store-cattle had to be sold in the autumn to Lowland Scotland and England in order to buy grain for both human and animal use. This type of agrarian economy allowed men to leave the land for considerable periods of time (apart from early spring sowing and autumn harvest) and thus became available for marauding and skirmishing when the chief so desired. Had more arable land been available for cereal production and settled agriculture, doubtless the clansmen would have been very much less available for fighting duties on behalf of the clan. Furthermore, many of the principal fighting-men came from the tacksmen class who sub-let most of their land holdings to working tenant farmers. In this situation, the tacksmen class became the semi-professional soldiers and did not personally engage in daily farm work. Daniel De Foe in his *Memoirs of a Cavalier*, states of the tacksmen – 'they are all gentlemen and proud enough to be kings.' Even the labouring classes, when called upon for military service, left a great deal of the concentrated spring and autumn cultivation and harvesting to the women-folk and were therefore available for 'hosting' without seriously effecting the farm economy. It was mainly because of this single agrarian fact that the Jacobite risings were possible.

6

James VI died in 1625 and between this date and the rising in 1745/6, there were many military campaigns of note. It was a period of concentrated civil wars, with the Highland chiefs acquiring considerable political importance during this time – more so, indeed, than their wealthier Lowland counterparts.

As an example of how ready the clans were to engage in warfare the number of the main pitched battles, encounters and skirmishes are important to list.

In 1644–5, James Graham, Marquis of Montrose fighting for Charles I won six resounding victories at Tippermuir, Aberdeen, Inverlochy, Auldern, Alford and Kilsyth until he was finally defeated by greatly superior odds at Philiphaugh.

1651 saw the campaign of Charles II which ended so finally at Worcester with many Scots fatalities.

This was followed in 1653–54 by a royalist rising when the Earl of Glencairn rose against the Cromwellian occupation and Lochiel's resistance to General Monk after 1654.

May 1685 saw the abortive rising by the Earl of Argyll. This was followed four years later in 1689 when John Graham, Viscount Dundee, fighting on the side of James VII, completely routed the troops of William III at Killiekrankie.

The first Jacobite rising in 1715 led by the Earl of Mar on behalf of 'King James VIII' fought John, the Duke of Argyll, supporting the first Hanoverian King George I at Sherrifmuir – an indecisive encounter.

Some four years later, in 1719, the second Jacobite rising led to the Jacobite army under the Marquis of Tullibardine of the house of Atholl, being decisively routed by the Government forces at Glenshiel, in the Western Highlands.

Lastly, in the famous rebellion of 1745/6, Prince Charles Edward Stewart (son of James VIII) defeated the Government forces at Prestonpans and Falkirk, but in turn was defeated at Culloden by his cousin the Duke of Cumberland.

So, in little over 100 years, Scotland was almost constantly in a state of war or preparation for war, with many major campaigns – such was the turbulent history of the Highlands prior to Culloden.

CHAPTER 2
The Clan System

This chief does not think this present abject Disposition of his Clan towards him to be sufficient but entertains that tyrannical and detestable maxim – that to render them poor will double the Tie of their Obedience; and accordingly he makes Use of all oppressive Means to that End. Edward Burt: *Letters from a Gentleman in the North of Scotland.*

As those Clans or Kindreds live by themselves, and possess different Straths, Glens, or districts, without any considerable mixture of Strangers, it has been for a great many years impracticable (and hardly thought safe to try it) to give the Law its course amongst the Mountains. It required no small degree of Courage, and a greater degree of power than men are generally possessed of, to arrest an offender or a debtor in the midst of his Clan. And for this reason it was, that the Crown, in former times, was obliged to put Sheriffships, and other Jurisdictions, in the hands of powerful families in the Highlands, who by their respective clans and followings could give execution to the Laws within their general territories and frequently did so at the expense of considerable bloodshed.

But if the Highlanders can be eventually debarred from the Use of Arms until the present generation die out, their Successors, unacquainted with the use of Gun, Sword or Durk, must be harmless to the community of the adjacent Low Countries: and when they can no longer live by Rapine, must think of living by industry. Report by *Lord President Duncan Forbes*

The somewhat cynical but nevertheless penetrating observation by Captain Edward Burt, one of General Wade's engineers is important, in that it came from an outsider looking in at the Highland scene with a degree of shrewd insight in the early 1700s.

The chief was the parent, ruler, landowner and proprietor on behalf of his 'clanna' or children. A combination of pride and race with pride of soil, came to form in Scottish clanship perhaps the most exalted and powerful relationship of people to soil and chief to people which has been evolved as a social system. One in which 'hail people, noct onlie the nobilitie' take an immense pride in clan grandeur 'gentility is of all things esteemed the most valuable in the notions of the people':

> Clannish ties of relationship ran through every rank of Society uniting folk in a homely, heart-warming way that the abstract tenets of democracy can never achieve. *The Clans, Septs and Regiments of the Scottish Highlanders* — Frank Adams, 1908

From the 12th, right through to the 18th century the clan system meant mutual help and defence within the Highlands. The continuing emergence of the feudal system, especially in the 17th and 18th Centuries, helped to establish some clans but hindered others. The principal of military service in return for land and protection, was the mainstay of a feudal system and was an important element in the clan organisation.

Lord President Forbes in 1746 aptly described a Highland clan as a 'set of men all bearing the same surname and believing themselves to be related the one to the other and to be descended from the same commons stock. In each clan, there are several subaltern tribes, who owe their dependance on their own immediate chief: but all agree in owing allegiance to the Supreme Chief of the Clan or Kindred and look upon it to be their duty to support him in all adventures.'

Perhaps the most notorious of those chiefs who wished to retain the status quo was Simon, Lord Lovat in the early 18th Century, although most chiefs, to a lesser or greater degree encouraged this type of control over their clanspeople.

By the early 17th century clanship in it's most basic form increasingly had become a stabilised and recognised part of the 'Highland System'. clanship was indeed synonymous with the very social fabric of the country for the great majority of Highlanders.

The whole organisation of the clan centered around the chief, whether or not he had lost his estate entitlement. The various branches or septs of the clan were in turn led by a chieftan and so on through various levels in this hierarchy. There were four basic levels of classes within the clan structure:

A. *The Chief*
B. *Chieftans* - heads of clan branches or septs.
C. *Gentlemen of close or distant relationships* to the chief. They would either be:

1. Tacksmen
2. Wadsetters
3. Goodmen

This group farmed part of the land and sub-let the remainder. They also generally formed the majority of the fighting force and officered the clan in battle. The 13th Lord Lovat stated 'Gentlemen are appointed to watch and guard the country and therefore ought to live upon marches, skirts and extremities thereof to keep off thieves and sorrorers'.

D. *Clansmen*

They were the working farmers and farm workers and were called upon to support the clan in all it's activities – military or otherwise.

The power of the chief was virtually absolute in most civic, legal and economic matters, backed as it was by the clan council composed largely of the principal men of the clan – the chieftans, lairds and tacksmen.

The very name clan (gaelic *clann*) means offspring or children and this is how the ordinary clansmen saw himself in relation to his chief and in avowing allegiance to his chief in all matters including military service when called upon. He in turn, would expect to be protected within the clan body in all affairs.

This incredibly close knit kinship formed both the basis and inherent strength of the clan.

General Wade in his *Report of the Highlands* in 1724 said that the people owed to their chief 'a Servile and Abject obedience' which in return the chief was accustomed to treat his clansmen 'with great Familiarity', shaking them by the hand whenever he met them.

In the Lowlands, at that same time, all members of the family had the same surname but within the clan structure only the chief and immediate kin used the surname, with ordinary clansmen known by genealogical strings, such as Alister Mac Ian, Mac Sheumas, Mac Ian Beg; 'Mac' denotedly 'son of'. In later times these men assumed the patronymic of the chief or one of the clan septs, but originally it was a social group within a defined district with families actually descended from or accepting themselves as descendants of a common ancestor. If the patronymic was not assumed or the protection of the clan umbrella sought, the clansmen, in effect, became outlaws or 'broken men'.

Undoubtedly many chiefs jealously kept their clansmen in subjugation by denying them access to employment outside the clan system fearing that (again according to Burt) they would lose this:

Slavish Attachment to him and his Family. This he does when downright Authority fails, by telling them how their Ancestors chose to live sparingly and be accounted a Martial People rather than submit themselves to Low and mercenary Employment like the Lowlanders, whom their Forefathers always despised for the Want of that Warlike Temper which they (his vassals) still retained.

It may, for aught I know, be suitable to Clannish Power: but, in general, it seems quite contrary to Reason, Justice and Nature that any one Person, from the mere Accident of his Birth, should have the Prerogative to oppress a whole Community for the Gratification of his own selfish Views and Inclinations: and I cannot but think, the Contented Poverty of a People is, of all Oppressions the Strongest indication to Sedition, Rebellion and Plunder.

Wade also reports that the chief imposed taxes, settled all disputes and called clansmen to arms by sending a Fiery Cross around the clan area. The Fiery Cross (Croish Cran-Taraidh) was constructed of half-burned wood, dipped in goat's blood and in the rough shape of a cross.

The chief although he was judge, leader and prime administrator relied very heavily upon the clan council who, on certain occasions, could countermand his instructions especially where serious benefit or danger to the clan was called into question.

The expenses of the chief were often very heavy in support of the poorer members of the clan and the hospitality he was expected to offer to his family, tenants, and servants. However, as a good proportion of land rents were paid in kind (i.e. farm produce, venison, salmon, grouse, etc.) he was able to maintain a relatively high standard at table but was probably relatively very poor in actual money terms. Indeed most Highland chiefs were deeply in debt during the 17th and 18th centuries and heavily mortgaged for most of the period under review. MacDonnell of Keppoch when asked the amount of his income replied – 'I can call out and command 500 men'.

The essence of clanship was a curious mixture of feudalism and paternalism with feudalism gaining in importance as the 17th Century progressed and as the chief's power was further buttressed by additional powers granted by the Crown. Baron courts which have survived show not only punishment of offenders, but also the settling of many local disputes by the chief. In purely agriculture concerns, the chief not only rented the land but often supplied stock and seed corn – it was often the case that tenant's rents were remitted following poor harvests and feed and seed corn supplied in famine years.

Originally the chiefship of a Highland clan was not a feudal dignity and from the beginning it was based on the customs and local laws of the people within the clan. The land belonged to the people in toto and as feudalism gradually advanced, it did not destroy their interest in the soil nor the right to select one of their body as chief. However, over the passage of time, the chief was granted the feudal rights not initially by authority outside the clan, but solely as a result of his position as head of the clan. The succession of the chief normally followed the essentially feudal principle of primogeniture, but on a number of occasions the clan insisted on their rights of the Celtic Law of Tanistry in order to choose another chief or to depose one who did not have the overall confidence of the clan.

In essence, the clan system meant strong family ties, loyalty to the tribe, plus a feudal obligation to maintain the chief in material terms and to render him military service when called upon.

The purely feudal influence was more noticeable in the eastern Highlands where, for example, the Duke of Atholl (not strictly a clan chief) had almost unlimited power. Generally, in the west, tribal and patriarchal influences were more apparent. In broad terms, however, the rising tide of a more informed feudalism throughout the century, led to increased discipline within the clan, led to direct ownership of land and to the chief insisting upon the concept of primogeniture. However, no title to possession meant anything without an adequate armed force to ensure it's continuity – hence the vital importance of maintaining a sizeable number of armed followers.

Above all, feudalism in it's purest form started with the basic baronial jurisdiction, but when a number of baronies grouped together then regalities, or mini-kingdoms were brought into being. These occurred and were exampled by the Grants of Speyside: Lord Fraser of Lovat: Mackintosh of Mackintosh: the Duke of Argyll and the Duke of Atholl. In the absence of strong central Government the chiefs had almost unlimited power over their clansmen, possessing the sole right of jurisdiction in both civil and criminal cases.

After the Union of Parliaments in 1707, the Scot's Privy Council ceased to exist as immediate superiors to the clan chiefs, and national Parliamentary direct rule took it's place. Also at this time the national alignment of certain clans emerged to form an anti-

Jacobite block. This consisted of the Campbells in the West; the families of Reay and Sutherland along with the Munros and Rosses who in turn allied with the Brodies, Roses and the majority of the Grant and Forbes clans.

The basic geography of the Highland area, with it's many narrow glens and lochs, undoubtedly helped to maintain the clan system as it existed in the 17th and 18th Centuries – isolated by virtue of only very minor roads or tracks criss-crossing very mountainous areas and in the West by lochs and sea meant that much of the area was virtually impassable during the wet and winter months. So the success and continuance of strong clanship was strengthened by this almost total clan isolation, with every clan area becoming in fact an independent state on it's own.

The almost universal use of the gaelic tongue also helped to maintain this isolation from Anglo-Saxon culture, which was quickly spreading to all parts south of the Highland line.

Feudal systems were also controlled to a great extent by the type of land – in areas of good or even adequate soils for crop-growing overlords insisted upon a standard rental system of land utilisation. This occurred mostly in the South and East. However, in the West and North, where peat and upland soils dominated and where only rudimentary agriculture was practical (based on cattle/sheep husbandry), there remained mostly a type of patriarchal/tribal kind of society of a less formal nature.

It is interesting to note how little change took place in the basic clan system during the 16th to the 18th Centuries and this is well examplified in the sayings of Bishop Lesley (16th Century) and Lord President Forbes in the mid 18th Century. Firstly Bishop Lesley writing about the Clan Mackintosh and their chiefs:

> He defends them against invasions of their enemies, their neighbours and he causes minister justice to them all in the manner of their country, so that none should be suffered to make spoil or go in sorning, as they call it, or as vagabonds in the country.

Now, Lord President Forbes in the *Culloden Papers* 1746:

> The inhabitants of the mountains, unacquainted with industry and the fruits of it and united in some degree by the singularity of dress and language, stick close to their ancient idleway of life; retain their barbarous customs and maxims; depend generally on their Chiefs, as their sovereign Lords and masters; and being accustomed to the

13

use of Arms, and injured to hard living, are dangerous to the public peace; and must continue to be so, until, being deprived of Arms for some years, they forget the use of them.

The power of the clan and its inherent strength remained a relatively static feature while the Highlands were in a state of isolation. During the 17th and 18th Centuries the clan (as a social group) survived almost intact providing both obligation and mutual support and in the wild country with it's equally wild climate a tough, self-reliant and warlike people survived who were accustomed to battle and skilled in arms.

It was not until General George Wade began to open up the Highlands in the early 18th Century by building roads and bridges suitable for conventional armed forces and for wheeled transport that the totality of the clan system came under pressure. However, it took the overwhelming tragedy of Culloden and the smashing of the Jacobite military power to bring about its abrupt and sudden demise. From this last civil-war battle on British soil it never recovered.

CHAPTER 3
The Highland Soldier

Were their skill in exercise and discipline proportional to their courage, they would make the bravest soldiers in the world. They are large bodies and prodigiously strong: and two qualities they have above other nations viz hardy to endure hunger, cold and hardships and wonderfully swift of foot. *Daniel de Foe in his* Memoirs of a Cavalier, *a summary of the military virtues of the Highlander.*

The order to attack being given, the two thousand Highlandmen . . . run towards the ennemie in a disorderlie manner, always fireing some dropeing shots, which drew upon them a generall salvo from the ennemie, which begun at their left, opposite to us, and run to their right. No sooner that begun, the Highlandmen threw themselves flat on their bellies; and when it slackned, they started to their feet. Most threw away their fuzies, and drawing their suords, pierced them everie where with ane incredible vigour and rapiditie, in four minutes' time from their receaving the order to attack. – A description of the attack by the Earl of Mar's Highlanders at Sherrifmuir (1715)

After the Union of the Crowns in 1603, which included the Kingdom of Ireland, there ceased to be a need for Scottish military forces, popularly known as 'redshanks', in the Ulster war.

However, Highland mercenaries were very much sought after in Europe with the Privy Council in Edinburgh actively encouraging 'idle men and soldiers' to pass 'to the wars in Flanders and other foreign countries'. A Scots brigade was formed which lasted a very long time indeed up to the War of American Independence in 1782. These clansmen, along with a smattering of Lowlanders, came mainly from the clans of the Macphersons, Macleans, Camerons, Frasers and Macdonalds.

Also during the Thirty Years' War, Scotland contributed many fighting men for Denmark, Sweden and France. Perhaps the most notable clan actively to provide mercenaries was the Clan Mackay, when a whole regiment was formed to fight in the army of Gustavus

15

Adolphus, King of Sweden. They became 'His right hand in battle, brought forward in all dangerous enterprises. Invincible old regiment'.

In 1633 Sir John Hepburn also raised a regiment to fight for Adolphus which later became the famous Douglas Regiment in the French service by 1638. We now know it as the 1st of Foot or the Royal Scots.

The Mackay chief Lord Reay, obtained a license from Charles I to raise 3,000 men for service in Germany. In 1626, 1,000 men were 'his immediate clansmen' from Sutherland. They earned fame for their hardiness, their impetuosity in battle and for the famous Highland charge which until Culloden, against much superior numbers and firepower, was often a most successful and fearsome tactic by lightly clad men against infantry and cavalry alike.

The foreign wars were outlets for the brimming energies of the young Scots, mostly sons of chiefs, chieftains, lairds, tacksmen and lesser gentry: these mercenaries were much sought after for their prowess in arms, and for steadfastness in battle. Many members of the Highland ruling classes were professional soldiers mainly concerned with maintaining the militaristic French monarchy—as an example, the chiefs of Glengarry supported and supplied fighting men for Louis XV.

The experience some of them gained in European theatres of war, stood them in good stead in the Jacobite rising of 1745 and the description by the Duke of Cumberland of the Highlanders 'as a rabble of bare-arsed banditti', belied the fact that they constituted a well organised and ordered armed force, trained and versed in all military matters and tactics – they were also officered by seasoned campaigners. But mixed with so many other 'irregular' clan fighting men, the Jacobite Army was in the end unable prevail over regular troops, regimented and drilled to a higher standard.

Military service offered honourable employment, pay and pride in the bearing of arms: indeed it was a natural state for men who were brought up to consider that what nearly equated with regimental command and discipline, were part and parcel of their normal way of life.

Highland armies under Montrose and Prince Charles Edward Stewart often marched in excess of 30 miles per day on a meagre ration of oatmeal and water (drammach). Such feats of mobility, under very adverse conditions of virtually impassable terrain and lack of support services, enabled them to surprise the opposing factions time and time again. Such monumental marches, sometimes as much as 60 miles per day, were an especial feature in the case of the Montrose campaigns. Sir J. Dalrymple in his Memoirs of Great Britain comments:

> The lightness and looseness of their dress, the habit they had of always going on foot, their love of long journeys but above all, their patience of hunger and every kind of hardship which carried their bodies forward, made them exceed all other European nations in speed and perseverance of march.

In 1745 the British troops who pursued the Jacobite army, in reference to their mobility and meagreness of rations said 'that they lived by sniffing the wind'.

The individual Highland soldier, whether as a tacksman or ordinary clansman, locked as they were into agriculture, had plenty of time to practice military skills and most clan chiefs encouraged their kinsmen and followers in the martial arts whenever possible.

Outdoor sports and hunting played an important part in the everyday life of the clans and was invaluable training for more warlike pursuits. Stalking deer was very little different from stalking the enemy in terms of long, often uphill marches, the use of 'dead' ground plus the final surprise at close quarters.

The state of readiness of the clansman soldier is well illustrated in a description found in Logan's *The Scottish Gael* where he talks of a young chief and his followers.

These groups were called Catharn (sometimes Cearnachs) and were for all intents, fighting units within the clan. A company of soldiers in the Catharn required to be kept in action as the clan were not continuously at war – it was imperative that training kept them at a high degree of readiness and prepared for most eventualities. Hence the frequent forays on Lowland farms – 'to enrich themselves by a valuable creach', i.e. cattle rustling. This being classed as a necessary and therefore honourable pursuit: catharns or cearnachs were reckoned to play a valuable part in keeping the fighting spirit alive – soldiers were often used in plundering stock and 'to revenge old injuries.'

Increasingly after Culloden when Highland soldiers fought in the British army in recognised Highland regiments, it was seen that there was an essential difference between men who served in Highland and English line regiments. Much of this has been ascribed to the volatility and fierce pride of the Celt, as opposed to his more docile and phlegmatic Anglo-Saxon counterpart. Within the English regiments of that time, discipline was incredibly harsh with frequent floggings for minor misdemeanours, although largely this was a result of the preponderance of ex-convicts and pressed men in the ranks. The Highland regiments contained a different type of soldier altogether – a person of independent spirit. Because of his clan background he tended to take his problems and complaints to his colonel or captain, with whom he could talk over issues in a more friendly but still deferential fashion.

In later Highland regiments nearly every man was there by his own choice, as soldiering was considered a most honourable profession. It was not beneath the dignity of a Highland gentleman to serve in the ranks. So discipline was a matter of respect for the regiment and his comrades in it rather than fear of punishment. Colonels or captains took this background into consideration in their dealings with their men.

General David Stewart of Garth in an extract from his *Sketches of the Character, Manners and Present State of the Highlanders of Scotland* (1822) eloquently summarises the character of the Highland soldier of his day:

> In forming his military character, the Highlander was not more favoured by nature than by the social system under which he lived. Raised in poverty, he acquired a hardihood which enabled him to sustain severe privation. As the simplicity of his life gave rigour to his body, so it fortified his mind. Possessing a frame and constitution thus hardened, he was taught to consider courage as the most honourable virtue, cowardice the most disgraceful failing; to venerate and obey his chief and devote himself for his native country and clan: and thus prepared to be a soldier, he was ready to follow wherever honour and duty called him. With such principles and regarding any disgrace which he might bring on his clan and district as the most cruel misfortune, the Highland private soldier had a peculiar motive to exertion . . .
>
> When in a national or district corps, he is surrounded by the companions of his youth and the rivals of his early achievements: he feels the impulse of emulation strengthened by the consciousness that every proof which he displays, either of bravery or cowardice, will find it's way to his native home. He thus learns to appreciate the value of a good name; and it is this, that in a Highland regiment, consisting of men from the same country, whose kindred and connections are mutually known, every individual feels that his conduct is the subject of observation and that, independently of his duty, as

one member of a systematic whole he has a separate and individual reputation to sustain, which will be reflected on his family and district or glen.

In many respects these essential characteristics continued for a long period. The pride in the regiment replaced the pride of the clan in days gone by.

CHAPTER 4
Garb of Old Gaul

*As for their apparel, next to their skin they wear a linnen shirt,
which the great men among them dye of saffron colour. They use
it short, that it may not encumber them when running or travelling.
   To fence their feet they put on Rullions or raw leather shoes.
Above their shirt they have a single coat reaching no farther than
the navel. Their uppermost garment is a loose cloke of several
ells, striped and partly coloured which they girt breadth-wise
with a leathern belt so it scarce covers the knees and that for the
above-mentioned reason, that it may be no lett to them when on
a journey or doing any work. Far the greatest part of the plaid
covers the uppermost part of the body. Sometimes it is all folded
round the body about the region of the belt, for disengaging and
leaving the hands free: and sometimes 'tis wrapped round all
that is above the flank. The trouzes are for winter use: at other
times they content themselves with short hose, which scarce
reaches to the knee.—History of Scots Affairs (1637–1641) by
Robert Gordon of Straloch. Spalding Club.*

The freedom and lightness of the highland dress which 'enabled
them to use their limbs and to handle their arms with ease and
celerity and to move with great speed when employed with
cavalry or light infantry' (General David Stewart of Garth).

Take care to provide a Plaid (tartan), Cloathing and Bonnets in
The Highland Dress for the Non-Commissioned Officers and
Soldiers belonging to their Companies. General George Wade:
Independent Company Edict (1725)

This description by Gordon of Straloch is possibly the best contemporary summary of the Highland garb, which was to remain in this
form and virtually unchanged for the next 100 years. See Appendix
1 for further references on Highland dress.
   At first glance the dress of the Highlander looked quite unsuitable
and even foppish for everyday wear. In fact it was a most functional
outfit, bearing in mind the climate of North Britain, the freedom it
gave to people travelling in extremely rough terrain, the use of the

plaid which could double as a blanket under inclement conditions or if a journey lasted overnight.

In a military situation, it allowed a fleetness in movement especially on long marches; when taking part in the redoubtable Highland charge or 'for running with the cavalry'.

Much has been written concerning the origins and general use of tartan and tartan plaids in the Highlands, but certainly from c1650 onwards the soldier-clansman and the traveller had adopted the 'belted plaid' as a standard mode of dress. The belted plaid, or its modification the kilt, was worn by people of all ranks and it was never exclusively a peasant dress. The exception to this was where people of some standing and who could afford to ride generally adopted trews, 'that is breeches and stockings all of one piece and drawn on together: those who travel on foot dress with the belted plaid'.

The belted plaid (breacan an fhélidh) had superseded its forerunner, the saffron tunic (leine crochach) by around 1600 and remained so until the various Disarming Acts of 1725 and 1746 forbade the wearing of Highland dress, apart from those engaged in lawful military pursuits and certain favoured Whig clans.

General Stewart in his *Sketches of the Highlanders* described the belted plaid as 12 yards plaited round the middle of the body, the upper part being fixed on the left shoulder, ready to be thrown loose and wrapped round both shoulders or firelock in rainy weather – at night the plaid served the purpose of a blanket and was sufficient covering for the Highlander. It is often quoted that the plaid was soaked in water prior to its being used as a blanket and this in fact made it marginally warmer, as it was now more wind-proof.

The hose (or stockings) were generally made of white cloth with red diagonal stripes and seamed at the back – it is almost certain that this design is based on the famous red and white Menzies tartan, because of the influence of this clan in the early formation of the Independent Companies. The hose were held up beneath the knee by a garter wound around the leg. The military clansmen wore black brogues with buckles when on parade, but these were replaced by light heelless shoes of untanned hide (known as curan) when on active duty. The latter were the commonplace shoe of the Highlander and were found to be more suitable in the rough Highland terrain. It is interesting to note that the modern brogue shoe has a pattern of tiny holes in the upper leather. This is a relic of the time when curans were so made to let out the water after

21

travelling in boggy conditions. Edward Burt explains this well: 'They cut Holes in their Brogues, though new made, to let out the Water, where they have far to go and Rivers to pass: this they do to preserve their Feet from galling.'

Clan tartans were not known as such, even by the time of the 1745 rising and it appears that district rather than clan tartans were more likely, in that certain dyes were only available in certain areas of the Highlands. Different districts, sporting a distinctive tartan, indicating that a man might come from Badenoch, Argyll or Lochaber. Definitive and rigid clan tartans or checks were not available until a very much later period, and largely reflecting regular military practice.

In a military context it was not until the establishment of six Independent Companies in 1725 that any attempt was made to establish a standard of dress within these newly installed Highland forces. This edict by General Wade, commander of armed forces in Scotland, stated that 'the Plaid of each Company be as near as they can of the same sort and colour.'

This suggests that a uniform pattern was not on issue, the men wearing their own kilts with most of them coming from the pro-Hanoverian companies and belonging to the Grant, Campbell, Fraser and Munro clans. However, by 1727 a letter from Lord Lovat to the other Company captains, offered a quantity of tartan for those who wished it for their men for 'ye sex companies at 10 pence per yard'. At this stage, it indicated that this pointed to a standard and uniform material now being available.

Clan tartans have long been the subject of intense and often heated debate. It is now widely accepted, however, that although tartan (in its many and basic forms) has been known for many centuries, it was not until the beginning of the 19th Century that the modern precise setts were registered and accepted as being peculiar to particular families and/or clans.

A War Office report of 1709 stated that the Independent Companies' 'peculiar cloathing of plads, tartan coats, trowse and hose was not at all military, but like the cloathing of the natives there, that they might better discover any designs or machinations against the government or the country'.

There was an obvious and important political reason to retain this Highland garb, so men who joined the companies could maintain their cultural links, identity and trust with the ordinary clanspeople. Their clothing was provided by their captains and, as

previously stated, not of a uniform pattern. However, it was apparent that their sombre dress of dark cloth or dark tartan in their
coats and tartan plaids earned them the title of An Freiceadan Dubh
(Black Watch) to differentiate them from the cotaichean or
saighdearan dearg (red soldiers or redcoats), who were part of the
regular British troops in garrison. Other observers have proposed
alternative reasons for the Black Watch name – the most popular
of these being that because their main task in the early days was
to give some protection against the levying of 'blackmail', a system
of enforced 'insurance' against cattle rustling, the name was appropriate. Yet another suggestion arose from the preponderance of
Campbell captains and officers: clan Campbell members were generally known as the Black Campbells because of their allegiance to
the throne and their unpopularity with the Jacobite clans. The same
accolade was then accorded to the Independent Companies. General
David Stewart of Garth remarked that the designation Black Watch
arose from the dark coloured tartans (of their respective commanding officers) which were worn by the Companies. However, 3 out of
the 4 at that time (i.e. Grant, Fraser and Munro) had red as a
dominant colour in their belted plaids. It is obviously impossible to
ever know the truth of the matter but reason would possibly favour
the 'blackmail' or 'black Campbell' explanations as being the more
logical.

The exact uniform pattern for the early Independent Companies
is not known in great detail, but it is generally agreed that they were
dressed in the normal Highland fashion and wearing the tartan of
their district. It has also been documented that they carried a form
of tipstaff to show their authority as Crown forces. However, in the
early to mid 18th Century the black cockade and a red-cross
(attached saltire-wise) were worn in their bonnets.

With the regimentation of the Independent Companies as the
Regular regiment the 43rd of Foot (later to become the 42nd of Foot
or Royal Highlanders) it became necessary to devise a standard
military or Government tartan. Probably because most of the officers
and men in the Companies came either from Campbell, Fraser,
Grant or Munro clans, it became reasonable to adopt a tartan
broadly in line with their current area-clan patterns. Anyway it
seems that the dark, sombre Campbell tartan won the day and a
tartan akin to this clan sett became the new Government or Black
Watch tartan.

Later, as other Regular Highland regiments were formed during the 18th Century they adopted the dark blue, black and green tartan with various coloured overstripes added. The one exception is to be seen in the case of the Cameron Highlanders, who adopted the Cameron of Erracht tartan, but even in this situation if the red and yellow overstripes are removed something like the conventional Forty-Second tartan remains.

The uniform of the Black Watch, when it was embodied from the Independent Companies in May 1740, introduced the scarlet jacket and waistcoat with buff facings and white lace – tartan plaid of 12 ells plaited round the body and held in place by a black leathern belt. The loose end of the plaid was fixed to the left shoulder, ready to be thrown loose and used as a blanket or to protect weapons from rain.

The belted plaid was used for all grand duties, reviews and all ceremonial occasions. On the leather belt round the plaid were held pistols and a dirk. When not on duty, the little kilt (feileadh beag) was worn. The bonnet was blue with a border of red, white and green in small squares with a tuft of feathers or a small piece of black bearskin replacing the 'rid cros' of Independent Company days.

CHAPTER 5
Highland Weapons

In their short hose and belted plaids, armed each of them with
a well-fixed gun on his shoulder, a strong handsome target with
a sharp-pointed steel of about half an ell in length (screwed into
the navel of it) on his left arm: a sturdy claymore by his side and
a pistol or two, with a durk and knife in his belt. *Clan Grant
historian c. 1715.*

Highland furies rushed in upon us with more violence than ever
did a sea driven by a tempest. *Marquis de Stolle after Fontenoy,
11 May 1745*

The onset of the Highlanders was so terrible that the best troops
in Europe would with difficulty sustain the first shock of it: and
if the swords of the Highlanders once came in contact with them
their defeat was inevitable. Chevalier de Johnstone: *Memoirs of
the Forty-Five.*

The short paragraph by the Clan Grant historian provides a most
succinct summary of the arms generally carried by the Highland
clansman of the late 17th and 18th Century. It is, however, worthwhile to go into much detail on weapons and the methods Highland
clansmen used in actual fighting before looking at the way independent companies were armed and fought.

The cumbersome habergeon (coat of mail) and the heavy 'twa-
handit' sword of the 15th and 16th and early 17th Centuries,
(described by the French as 'very large and marvellously cutting')
had been replaced by the shorter, lighter one-handed broadsword,
a targe (or target) to block the bayonet, plus a dirk for close-quarter
fighting.

The musket and pistols were discharged from a distance and once
used, were abandoned in favour of the broadsword and dirk the
deadly slashing and stabbing weapons so dexterously handled by
the Highlander.

The Highland single-edged broadsword (wrongly named claymore
– claidheamh mhor in the gaelic) had a basket-hilt to protect the

holding hand. It was a relatively light sword, only some 42 inches in length including the hilt and because of its lightness, could be wielded for considerable periods without fatigue.

It was truly a fearsome weapon in the hands of a practiced clansman and won for the Highlanders many of the great campaigns of the 17th and 18th centuries. While guards and hilts were often locally produced, many of the blades were imported and the most prestigious of these were Toledo blades (lannan spainnteach). These fine blades were much prized by the clansmen and consequently were much sought after.

The anglicisation of the gaelic claidheamh mhor to claymore should properly refer to the relatively large and heavy two-handed sword which was in general use until the third quarter of the 17th Century. However, the term claymore was applied universally to the basket-hilt broadsword after that time. Perhaps the best description of the essential difference would be the older two-handed claymore and the more modern basket-hilted claymore.

It is worth noting that surprisingly bows and arrows were still in common use in the early part of the 17th Century, along with two-handed swords (the original claymore or great sword), muskets, hagbuts and pistols, Jedburgh staffs and Lochaber axes. However, by the time of the Battle of Killiecrankie in 1689 this list of weaponry had all but disappeared and replaced by more suitable weapons for the new style of warfare – i.e. lightly clad clansmen carrying single handed lighter broadswords, targe, pistol and dirk as well as muskets for initial firing at long range.

The broadsword and target won the day at Killiecrankie and from then onwards until Culloden, these weapons became the standard armament of the now much more-mobile Highlander with his new battle tactics described above.

The Highland dirk was unique in its design and quite dissimilar to all other weapons of that ilk, with its triangular, thick-backed, single-edged blade. It generally had a cylindrical handle with no guard, was shouldered at its junction with the blade and with the grip swelling in the middle. The pommel was often circular and flat on the top.

Along with the broadsword and dirk, the targe or target was invaluable in parrying the bayonet of the opposing Regular infantry and before the sword or the dirk could be brought into play. Caldwell in *Scottish Weapons* gives a very good description of the five-layered Highland targe. Firstly, the inside skin generally of deer-hide. Then a layer of steel with wool 'stuffed in very hard: then cork or tough dried fungus: on top plain well-wrought leather.'

The topmost layer was often adorned with brass studs in the form of a pattern. The account also mentions brass, 'in the form of a Cupelo about 3″ over in the centre within which there is a piece of Horn of the same forme like a cup out of which they drink their usquebagh' [whisky].

This account obviously refers to a rather special targe and the ordinary clanman possibly had a more functional wooden targe, covered with tough leather and sporting a sharp-pointed steel in the centre. This central steel or spike, when not in action, was kept in a leather sheath attached to the inside of the target.

The targe, apart from it's main use in fending off bayonet thrusts acted as a good shield against a musket ball unless fired at almost point-blank range.

The rising of 1715 brought into play a Disarming Act which made it a penal offence for any one to have in his custody or to use or wear 'broadsword or target, poignard, whinger or durk, side-pistol, gun or other warlike weapon'.

It is interesting to note that some of the original Independent Companies regimented into the Black Watch and thereby the British army in 1740, still carried targes in Flanders in 1747 and 48. – They were no longer by then part of general issue weaponry, but many private soldiers still carried them and obviously thought them vitally important in battle.

Pistols were also generally carried, mainly of a Highland pattern with iron or brass stocks and with ram's horn or kidney shaped butts. Those made in Scotland – the town of Doune in Perthshire was an important centre for their manufacture – showed very fine craftsmanship and were very much superior to Army-issue models.

The pistol often hung on a leather strap going over the right shoulder or sometimes tucked into the waist belt. As with the musket, the pistol was fired at a distance and before closing in for hand-to-hand combat.

An outstanding military feature in 17th and 18th Century Scotland was exampled in the marvellous fighting ability and sheer strength of the clansmen. This was, in large, due to the fighting tactics of the Highland charge of lightly clad, but heavily armed men. Initially this was used with great effect against the Government forces at close quarters at Killiecrankie in 1689, and most definitely had a major effect on the fear that British soldiers had for the

Highlander for the next 60 years. The tactic was mostly suited to mountainous country where the clanmen could rush on the enemy from a greater height – it was most effective when used as a guerilla exercise and was certainly not a tactic to be employed in a straight-forward set-piece battle in open country, against disciplined well-trained troops with artillery and/or cavalry support, as at Culloden.

In the charge, the Highlanders, claymore in hand, advanced with their bodies bent forward sheltering behind the targe so as to present as small a target as possible to the opposing musket fire. When the opponents fired they would often drop to the ground – upon rising they in turn would discharge their muskets and/or pistols throwing them to the ground before attacking at the run with fearsome clan war-cries and the dreaded slashing broadsword. (If they were successful in action firearms could be retrieved at some later stage – if they were routed, wounded or killed then the retrieval was a matter of no import!)

At Killiecrankie, General Hugh Mackay's men had old-fashioned matchlock muskets with plug bayonets and the clansmen were upon them before they could fix their bayonets after firing. Following this catastrophic defeat of the Government forces, troops were issued with bayonets which ringed the musket barrel and therefore did not interfere with discharge.

Various written descriptions of the Highland charge speak of it as 'like a living flood' and of the terrifying nature of the Highlanders' war-like 'brawny and purposeful hill-men, once they were let loose, putting the fear of God into any but exceptionally highly disciplined troops.'

The rapidity of movement and the devastating swing of their broadswords, accompanied by their war-like appearance and deep-throated war-cries were just too much for some English and Low-land soldiers at Falkirk and Prestonpans – They made a, blood-soaked shambles of the troops who tried to resist them.

Another vivid description by Chevalier de Johnstone in a *Memoir of the Forty-Five*

> They advance with rapidity, discharge their pieces when within musket length of the enemy, and throwing them down, draw their swords, and holding a dirk in their left hand with their target, they dart with fury on the enemy through the smoke of their fire. When within reach of the enemy's bayonets, bending their left knee, they, by their attitude, cover their bodies with their targets that receive their thrusts of the bayonets, which they contrive to parry, while at

the same time they raise their sword arm, and strike their adversary. Having once got within the bayonets, and into the ranks of the enemy, the soldiers have no longer any means of defending themselves, the fate of the battle is decided in an instant, and the carnage follows; the Highlanders bringing down two men at a time, one with the dirk in the left hand, and another with the sword. The reason assigned by the Highlanders for their custom of throwing their muskets on the ground is not without its force. They say they embarrass them in their operations, even when slung behind them, and on gaining a battle they can pick them up along with the arms of their enemies; but if they should be beaten they have no further use for them.

In some accounts, variations of the charge were noted where groups of clansmen made a concerted attack at a single point in order to break through ranks and then wreak havock with their broadswords from the rear — in fact anticipating the devastating tactics of the Wermacht by some 200 years, albeit on a different scale.

Another deviation from the normal charge was witnessed in the Macdonald charge at Prestonpans. Prior to the battle Sir John Cope expressed the hope:

'Don't let us be beat by such a set of banditti.'

The comments by the Young Pretender after the battle: 'They eskaped like rabets'.

The final and conclusive attacks by the Highlanders was vividly related by Lord Drummore.

I could see thro' from Front to Rear, yet to my Astonishment every Front Man covered his Fellowes, there was no Man to be seen in the Open . . . in short though their Motion was very quilk, it was Uniform and Orderly. I confess I was surprised at it.

It was obviously a well ordered and conducted military tactic and perhaps such a first-hand account gives lie to the comment that the charge was just an uncontrolled mass advance.

At Falkirk several months later at the second decisive battle of the '45, the Highlanders of Charles' army took issue with the British forces under General Hawley. Again the charge was used with devastating effect in spite of the advice Hawley gave his troops in his orders of the 12th January 1746:

The manner of the Highlanders way of fighting, which there is nothing so easy to resist if Officers and men are not prepossess'd with the

29

Lyes and Accounts which are told of them. They Commonly form their Front rank of what they call their best men, or True Highlanders, the number of which being allways but few, when they form in Battallions they commonly form four deep, and these Highlanders form the front of the four, the rest being lowlanders and arrant scum.

When these Battallions come within a large Musket shot, or three score yards, this front Rank gives their fire, and Immediately thro' down their firelocks and Come down in a Cluster with their Swords and Targets making a Noise and Endeavouring to pearce the Body, or Battallions before them becoming 12 or 14 deep by the time they come up to the people they attack.

The sure way to demolish them is at 3 deep to fire by ranks diagonaly to the Centre where they come, the rear rank first, and even that rank not to fire till they are within 10 or 12 paces but if the fire is given at a distance you probably will be broke for you never get time to load a second Cartridge, and if you give way you may give your foot for dead, for they being without a firelock or any load, no man with his arms, accoutrements &c. can escape them, and they give no Quarters, but if you will but observe the above directions, they are the most despicable Enimy that are.

Of the actual charge, it was said by O'sullivan (Quarter-master General of the Jacobite army) that Lord George Murray led the Highlanders personally and that it was 'perhaps one of the boldest and finest actions yt any troops of the world cou'd be capable of.' Allowing that O'Sullivan was rather biased in his opinion of this encounter, further confirmation came from Hawley in his short, confused and apologetic letter to the Duke of Cumberland (as his Commander-in-Chief) and which gave credence to the disaster wrought by the clansmen's charge to his forces:

'Sir,
My heart is broke, I can't say We are quite beat today, But our Left is beat and Their Left is beat. We had enough to beat them for we had Two Thousand Men more than They. But suche scandalous Cowardice I never saw before. The whole second line of foot ran away without firing a Shot. Pardon me, Sir, that you have no more this time from The most unhappy, but most faithfull and most dutifull Your RH has,
    H. Hawley.

Undoubtedly, the Highland charge at Falkirk led to completely new thinking on ways to counter its worst effect and the lessons learned were used by British troops to much better effect at Culloden.

For close hand-to-hand encounters and in the absence or loss of the dirk, many clansmen carried a small knife called a sgian h'ochlais which was concealed in the coat sleeve near the armpit. The sgian dubh or stocking knife was not commonly known until the early 1820's where it was only worn for ornamentation.

It is quite evident that the clansman of this period was a veritable walking arsenal with every weapon having a very functional reason for its being carried. To complete this picture of a soldier being completely integrated and self-contained in the manner of arms and swift movement, food was also carried on his person often in a 'small sacken knapsack'. During war-like campaigns he would happily exist on a frugal ration of drammach (oatmeal mixed with water) once or twice a day. Such self-sufficiency in weaponry and food meant that a whole army could move very swiftly from one place to another without having to wait for the necessarily slower support services – almost a perfect example of an army of 'all teeth and no tail'.

As further examples of the mobility of the Highlander, it is reported that in wars with Gustavus Adolphus and in the Anglo-Scottish Civil War the Highlanders were:

> Often mixed with the cavalry, affording to detached squadrons the invaluable advantage of support from infantry, even in their most rapid movements.

And writing of the Scots army in 1664, the author of *Memoirs of a Cavalier* stated:

> I observed that these parties had always some foot with them and yet if the horses galloped or pushed on ever so far forward, the foot were as forward as they, which was an extraordinary advantage. These were those they called Highlanders: they would run on foot with all their arms and all their accoutrements and kept very good order too and kept pace with the horses, let them go what rate they would.

It is not proper to finish an account of Highland arms without mentioning the Highland bagpipe. The Reverend Alexander Hume of Logie (c1600) wrote of the pipe as an 'instrument of war' with the following: 'caus michtalie the weirlie nottis breike on heiland pipes, scottis and hybernicke.'

The Highlander's development of the bagpipe as an inspiring instrument of war came during the 16th Century and the famous piping family, the Mac Crimmons (who were hereditary pipers to MacLeod) evolved with others the ceol mhor (great music) or piobaireachd (anglice pibroch) which is the classical music of the great war-pipe. It was nearly always used as part of the preparation for gathering the clansmen prior to the attack and indeed during action or the charge itself. Its stirring music not only encouraged the Highlanders, but also helped to put fear into the opposition.

It was stated that Cumberland at Culloden when he noted that certain of his Highland troops were carrying bagpipes said:

> 'What are these men doing with such bundles of sticks? I can furnish them with better implements of war.' – an officer rejoined: 'Your Royal Highness cannot do so. These are the bagpipes, the Highlanders music in peace and war. Wanting them, all other implements are of no avail and the Highlanders need not advance another step for they will be of no service.

The piper, unlike other musicians, had essentially a martial role in that they not only inspired the troops but sounded various military movements (e.g. the charge, the recall or the rally). As an example of how the pipes were essential in rallying troops at the battle of Falkirk it was stated by the commander of the Jacobite forces, Lord George Murray: 'Our vast loss was that not a pair or pipes could be gott.'

This was a reference to the fact that the pipers sometimes handed their pipes to their ghillies and charged with the rest. Thus the clan Macdonald and others could not be rallied. Fortunately for the Jacobites, their presence was not required for a different part of the action and other clans completed the rout of Hawley's forces at Falkirk.

Following the '15 and '45 Risings the courts asserted that as a Highland unit never marched without its piper, then the pipes were officially classified as 'a weapon or instrument of war' and that in turn the piper was obviously a fighting soldier. Another reason for pipes being considered in this fashion was their function for passing orders by musical sounds, akin to trumpets and bugles, and other complex signals in actual battle.

Macdonald's *Ancient Martial music of Caledonia* probably should have the last word on this subject:

> In halls of joy and in scenes of mourning it has prevailed; it has animated her warriers in battle and welcomed them back after their

toils; to the homes of their loved (ones) and the hills of their nativity. Its strains were first sounded on the ears of infancy and they are last to be forgotten in the wanderings of age.

Proficiency in arms and the particular way of Highland fighting could only be sustained by the constant use and practice with assorted weapons and by rigourous training methods. Local chiefs were naturally keen to foster this agressive martial spirit within their clanspeople.

Towards this scheme of training they organised extensive deer hunts called tainchels which often lasted many days. At these gatherings, specific Highland games such as shooting, throwing the stone, hill races, wrestling and other exercises were practiced all of which required strength, endurance and skill.

CHAPTER 6
Highland Lawlessness

The braes of the Highlands are fallen very broken — Duke of Argyll, 1666

The Highlands of Scotland, all parts north and west of the Highland line were in a state of constant turmoil during the 17th and first half of the 18th Century. Civil disturbance was rife and was only reasonably contained while major skirmishes and battles were taking place.

Much of the problem was as a result of the Highlander's attitude:

> Their economic creed was to despise labour as slavish and traffic was base. They held the only function, by which a man could live in honour, to be the plunder of the servile dwellers on the plain. — *J.H. Burton, Vol II.*

Obviously such conduct and attitude did not apply to all clans but certain of them in the vicinity of the Highland line and more especially the 'broken men' who belonging to no accredited clan or bearing allegiance to no chief and therefore outlaws, tended to pray upon the Lowland farmers and their moveable property, black cattle.

The 17th and the 18th Centuries were particularly subject to lawlessness in all forms whether by interclan feuding (sorning) blackmail or 'cattle lifting'. Cattle were the principal source of revenue in a mainly pastoral agricultural system and although sheep were almost as numerous as cattle, they were almost always used for home consumption, whether as meat to eat or for the wool which was then woven into crude woolen garments. Sheep therefore did not have the cash value that cattle had, and cash was desperately required to buy the essential lowground cereals for human and animal consumption through the long winter months.

The monarch or the government of the day tried by many means to control lawlessness, which was endemic in the Highlands and the already mentioned Statute of Icolmkill in 1609 was a prime example of the measures brought in to help mitigate the worst excesses. Basically, the chief was held responsible for his own behaviour, that of his immediate kin, his tacksmen and clansmen, but this was only partially successful in most areas.

The majority of the cattle rustling was carried out by cattle-lifters who lived and worked in the borders of the Highland line which meant that the relatively rich grass-growing areas of Perthshire, Angus, Aberdeenshire, Kincardine and Morayshire were prime targets for the rustlers or 'broken men'.

Such thieving was noticeably more prevalent just prior to the '15 and '45 risings, but had been a problem varying in intensity for the previous century. In the hilly and scrubby terrain it was extremely difficult to catch the outlaws and much energy, time and money was spent in a rather fruitless chase over vast tracts of roadless lands. The most favoured way to foil the 'lifters' was to appoint a local watch, but unfortunately in many cases, it comprised of men actually involved in the thieving.

These watch-men employed others who travelled through the country armed day and night, under pretence of enquiring after stolen cattle. By these means they came to know the area well where cattle were being reared and fed – also how these cattle could be removed unknowingly by devious routes.

> And the people thus employed are the very rogues that do these misschiefs, so ane half of them are continued in their former business of stealing that the business of the other half may be necessary in recovering. *Gartmore MSS.*

The payment of 'black meal' or blackmail was rife in that it ensured that cattle stocks were not actually stolen, but at a considerable price or levy to their owners. Other chiefs employed men to try and trace the stolen beasts and offered a reward in secret for information which led to the recovery of the cattle. This latter arrangement was known as 'tascal-money' and although frowned upon by the authorities, was very widely practised.

Shortly after the massacre of Glencoe in 1692 there was a proposal put by Earl Breadalbane to King William that the Highlander could be utilised 'in case of any insurrection at home or invasion from abroad'– Dalrymple's appendix Vol ii: part ii.

This proposal broadly outlined that Highland chiefs should raise some 4,000 clansmen who would be on call to suppress any trouble whether from internal or external forces. The whole to be commanded 'by some principal man in the Highlands', (presumably Breadalbane himself) with Cameron of Lochiel as second-in-command. Also that forty officers should be appointed of 'Highland origin' and that the clan men/soldiers should wear their everyday clothes and carry their normal arms. The suggested numbers and composition of this regulant force was laid out in detail:

Earl of Seaforth	–	200
Viscount of Tarbat	–	50
Lord Lovat	–	150
Earl of Sutherland	–	100
Lord Reay	–	50
The Laird of Ballingoun	–	100
The Laird of Fouls	–	50
The Laird of Strathglass	–	20
The Laird of Glenmoriston	–	30
The Laird of McIntosh	–	100
MacPherson of Clunie	–	50
The Laird of Kilnarock	–	150
The Laird of Grant	–	200
The Laird of Ballindaloch	–	20
Duke of Gordon	–	300
Earl of Mar	–	200
Marquis of Atholl	–	300
Laird of Askintullie	–	30
Laird of Weem	–	50
Laird of Grantully	–	50
Laird of Strowan	–	20
Earl of Perth	–	150
Earl of Murray	–	100
Earl of Monteath (Menteith)	–	100
Marquis of Montrose	–	150
Laird of Luss	–	50
Laird of Macfarlane	–	30
Earl of Argyle	–	500
Earl of Breadalbane	–	250
Laird of Calder	–	100
Laird of McLean	–	100
Laird of Lochiel	–	150
Captain of Clanranald	–	100
Sir Donald McDonald of Sleat	–	100
Laird of McLeod	–	100
Laird of Glengarry	–	100
Laird of McFinzone	–	30

McDonald of Keppoch	–	50
Laird of Appin	–	50
Tutor of Appin	–	30
Laird of Lochbury	–	30
		4000

It is significant that many of the prominent subscribers to this 'lawless list' are landowners with holdings in or near Lowland areas where cattle are often intensively reared. It was obviously very much a charter aimed to eliminate rustlers wherever possible.

While the raising of the 4,000 clansmen suggested by Breadalbane was never taken up by the Government, because to place chiefs at the head of their clans in the legal capacity of military officers would have put at risk the King and Government in the event of Highland loyalty swinging against the house of Hanover. However, it appears some notice must have been taken, in that Independant Companies were subsequently raised to try to contain the cattle-lifting and 'to keep the peace on the Braes'.

To help and authorise legitimate cattle drovers and dealers, General Wade issued licences to such men who belonged to clans which had surrendered their arms and were behaving themselves with regard to neighbouring clans. Arms, however, were forbidden.

> That instead of guns, swords, durks and pistols they now travel to their churches, markets and fairs with only a staff in their hands.

> The imposition commonly called Black meal (blackmail) is now no longer paid by the inhabitants bordering the Highlands: and robberies and depredations, formerly complained of, are less frequently attempted than has been known for many years past, there having been but one single instance where cattle have been stolen, without being recovered and returned to their proper owners. — *Burt's Letters*. Vol II.

While certain clans still indulged in inter-clan feuding the Government took measures, namely commissions of 'fire and sword'. In effect these were merely licences to legalise civil war in that the favoured clan was allowed to burn, waste and slay far and wide within the opposing clan's territory. The fire and sword technique was initially used by James V in 1528 for action against the clan Chattan.

It demanded 'the utter extermination and destruction of the clan leaving none alive but priests, women and bairns.'

The Privy Council who issued these jurisdictions or commissions 'that whatever slaughter, mutilation, blood, fire-raising or other violence' may be carried out by those holding the letters 'shall be held laudable, good and warrantable service to his Majesty and his Government.' It seemed that the powers issued these commissions taking the view that it was a good and necessary thing to have Highland clans feuding one with the other.

The fiery cross was also implemented on a number of occasions during the 17th and 18th Centuries to gather the clans together and it was considered an absolute demand on the services of the clan to muster at a given point. This was symbolised by a wooden cross (crosteric) charred at one end and often dipped in goat's blood on the other.

In a widely dispersed clan area the symbol was carried round by a series of the clanmen and the 'fiery cross' could summon and muster men in a very short space of time generally for war-like pursuits.

In 1724 George I commissioned General Wade to write a report outlining the real problems besetting the Highlands and to suggest ways of bringing the behaviour of his northern peoples more in line with the standard in the rest of Britain. Wade in a lengthy and comprehensive report (see Appendix 1) reported that the fighting power of the Highlands was around 22,000 men – 10,000 loyal to the Hanoverian cause and 12,000 'ready when encouraged to their Superiors of Chiefs of Clans, to create new Troubles and rise in Arms in favour of the Pretender.' He also alleged that blackmailing of

> almost all the Low Country was a feature of Highland life with the main culprits being the Camerons, Mackenzies, the McDonnells of Keppoch, the Broadalbin men and the McGregors on the Borders of Argyllshire.

Blackmail – The polite term for the practice was 'to keep good neighbourhood'. The mighty Marquis of Argyll, for example, paid over 3000 merks to blackmailers in 1640 as he was afraid of constant molestation from 'the Brae Lochaber men'– more than likely from the clan Cameron who were particularly active with 'creachs' at that time.

The report also commented that the majority of Highlanders were disloyal savages living in chaos and anarchy – this attitude towards the clans and clansmen was to mellow over the years as Wade became more aware of the peculiar Highland situation.

Part of the trouble in dealing effectively with the thieves and blackmailers lay in the absence of roads and bridges throughout the north as much of the land area was virtually inaccessible to regular troops and garrisons were relatively far apart. Burt again aptly describes the situation in the early 1720's.

> the old ways consisted chiefly of stony moors, bogs, rugged, rapid fords, declivities of hills, entangling woods and giddy precipices.

Before that time General Monk (under Cromwell) failed to master the Highlands because of the lack of roads for cavalry and/or artillery. Similarly, General Mackay found the same frustrating situation when trying to catch Highlanders in the army of Graham of Claverhouse in 1689. The heavy ammunition boots and breeches of the regular troops were totally unsuitable to catch up with the fleet and lightly clad Highlander with his unencumbered legs and light curans.

The climate too, being generally very much wetter, did not suit English troops, nor even the hardier Lowland Scots; service in Scotland under these conditions was most unpopular with officers and men alike. Their military activity was mostly confined to relatively small areas around the garrisons/fortified houses and outside these areas lawlessness reigned unchecked.

The situation was so serious and so chaotic that it was almost inevitable that steps were taken to levy a local gendarmerie force and as Wade described the position:

> that companies of such Highlanders as are well affected to his Majesty's Government be established under proper regulations and commanded by officers speaking the language of the country, subject to martial law and under the inspection and orders of the Governors of Fort William, Inverness and the officers commanding his Majesty's forces in those parts.

PART II

THE INDEPENDENT HIGHLAND COMPANIES

CHAPTER 7
The Years Before the Union

MacDonnel of Keppoch, when asked the extent of his income, replied 'I can call out and command 500 men'.

Authorities often called upon local chiefs to carry out 'punitive justice and to quell disputes' where there were no official Crown forces.

The King in sanctioning these 'commissions of fire and sword' in many cases caused some of the worst atrocities in the history of the clans.

These local disputes, sometimes between kindred clans, brought about many casualties in savage forays. However, the most common cause of mainland Highland strife was found to be in the plunder of Lowland areas south the Highland Line, but which clans laid territorial claim to from bygone times – these claims were deliberately vague in terms of deeds and legal documents!

These raids or forays were normally successful as they were unexpected; carried out by swift, light-clad but heavily armed men who used familiar glens and passes to strike terror into the Strathmore, Athol, Moray and Deeside areas.

In the more remote western areas, communication was mainly by water – 'the Highland galeyis' were most often used with war-time crews of 3/4 men per 1 oarsman. As these galleys generally were manned by 16 to 24 oars and the smaller 'birlinns' up to 16, this meant an effective fighting force of between 50 to 100 clansmen were carried per ship and caused great havoc in the Hebrides and Western coastal areas. In the West, perhaps the first tentative step to use irregular Crown forces was seen when in 1498 Alistiar MacLeod of Dunvegan was granted a royal charter to undertake the maintenance of 3 galleys: one 26 oared and two 16 oared vessels 'for peaceful forays'. Little is known concerning the success or otherwise of this ploy, but it was obvious that such vessels were essential in these seaboard areas for the maintenance of seagirt castles such as Dunvegan. Other castles, such as Eilean Donan and Strome in Wester Ross were reckoned 'richt necessar for the danting (daunting) of the Isles' when some of the island chiefs rose against James IV in 1503.

Meantime, on the mainland in 1475 James III promoted and initiated the policy of appointing Lieutenants to help oversee law and order, much as was the case in the Borders, where Wardens of the Marches had a somewhat similar function.

The main chiefs at this time were Argyll and Huntly and this of course meant that the Campbell and Gordon followers had a chance to become seasoned and trained troops acting (perhaps only nominally) on the 'King's business.'

So, in the absence of a standard police force or true standing army, it was thought necessary to use clan chiefs who could command sufficient clansmen to help keep the peace in the Highlands. Unfortunately and all too often, these clansmen were used to settle old feuds and debts completely unconnected with the original given orders.

Though it was extremely difficult for royal authority to be restored and warring factions kept apart, it is significant that this underlying authority was indeed sufficiently strong for James IV at an earlier date to be supported by a surprisingly large body of Highlanders at Flodden in 1513 against the English.

Some years later in 1528 James V issued a commission of fire and sword against the Clan Chattan for disdemeanours in Badenoch and in some other Highland areas. Whilst the order was not fully carried out it occasioned some terrible consequences 'the utter extermination and destruction' of the clan and it's supporters leaving alive 'only priests, women and bairns'. Again a few years later James travelled to the West along with friendly supporters bringing back captured Mackay, Mackenzie, Maclean, MacLeod, Macneil and MacDonald chiefs. This most effectively quietened large areas in the Highlands and Islands.

Much of the blame for the continuance of troubles in the Highlands, and especially the Western Isles, was due to the insistance of central Government in trying to impose feudalism which contradicted the older principles of patriarchy. This led to almost constant revolt by clanmen who rejected the new system.

While the West was gradually coming under some semblance of order the central Highlands (especially in the areas around the vast moor of Rannoch) were the havens for the 'broken men' and 'broken clans' who raided for cattle Lowland areas of Loch Tay, Doune, Perth, Stirling and Dumbarton, generally by way of the valleys of Glenorchy, Glenlyon, Glen Ogle and Glendochart.

These outrages were of such a severe economic nature that they exposed the Macgregors and other 'lawless' clans to relentless severity.

While the Macgregors were not acting alone, they were generally to be seen in the main raids and were therefore convenient scapegoats. In 1544 while the Government was heavily involved in a war against English forces, clans loyal to the Government were called out to deal with the Macfarlanes, Stewarts, Campbells of Strachur and –

> 'certain uther grete thevis, lymaris, robaris, qmoun sonaris upoun the liegis, throtcuttaris, murtharis, slaaris of men's wiffis and barnis and yr complices', who invaded the lands of Luss, and there 'crellie slew and murdrest nyne of his pure tennents in yr beddes and hereit his hale cuntrie baith his self and his pure men alswels of all insy gude wt in houss as of nolt and schap and vthir bestiale . . . and ar gaderand to yaim ma thevis and lymmares, tending to hery ye haill cuntre to Glasgow and Striveling and yai be not resisted.'

Immediately prior to the Union of the Crowns in 1603 James VI began to exert possibly the strongest influence ever over the warring and feuding clans and although the Highlands and Islands had not been conquered in any sense by the Scottish Crown, they were being gradually forced to accept rule from Edinburgh.

Feudal chiefs were already responsible for their followers' lawful behaviour, but James decided to increase the pressure on this situation by getting chiefs, chieftains and local lairds to sign bands (bonds) to maintain the peace and to pay heed to royal authority – these yearly bands to be guaranteed by defined penalties. This was new to the Highlands although such bonds were already working successfully in the Border areas. In 1587 these bonds became law, making it legal that offenders had to be handed over to their chief for due justice measures and that reparation had to be paid to the injured party.

Chiefs and captains of all clans were required to find sureties for amounts proportional to their wealth and the number of their clansmen. They were also liable to recompense any injuries committed by their followers and were also liable to be fined as well. Also in the Act was the appointment of 105 landlords and baillies in the Highlands and Islands where 'broken men hes duelt or presentlie duellis' – also are listed 34 clans who lived on the lands of various landlords but who were dependant upon the 'directionis' of their own chiefs, chieftains and lairds although 'oftymes aganis the willis of thair landlordis.'

This Act of 1587 dealt unfairly with clans who were dependant and who lived on the lands of other clans. Most famous (or infamous) of all in this context was the clan Macgregor, whose chief held no superiority. James set out to make an example of 'the wicked and unhappie race of the clan Gregour' and orders were given 'to pursue and prosecute them with all rigour and extremetie'.

The whole clan was proscribed and the name was ordered to be abolished because

> the bair and simple name of McGregoure maid that haill Clane to presume of their power, force and strenthe, and did encourage them to go forward in thair iniquities.

Although members of the clan Gregour were undoubtedly the main lawless culprits, many other clans (or part clans) were included in the black-list of the Act of Parliament in 1594 and initiated by James. The Macgregors were naturally at the head of this list.

> For punishment of theft, reif, oppression, and sorning – Our Soverane Lord and his estaits in Parliament Consider that notwithstanding the sundrie Acts made by his hienes and his most noble progenetorrs for punishment of the authoris of thift, reif, oppression, and sorning, and masteris and sustenaris of theives, yet such has been and partly is the barbarous cruelties and daily hardships of the wicked theives and lymmaris of the Clannis and Surnames following . . . inhabiting the hielands and Isles. Thay ar to say Clangregor; Clan Farlane; Clanlawren; Clandowill; Clandonochie; Clanchattane; Clanchewill; Clanchamron; Clanronald in Lochaber; Clanranald in Knoydert, Modert, and Glengarie; Clanleyid of the lewis; Clanlewid of harriche; Clandonald, south and north; Clangillane; Clanayroun; Clankinnoun; Clankenzie; Clanandries; Clanmorgun; Clangun; Cheilphale; and as many broken men of the Surnames of Stewartis in Atholl, and Lorne, and Balquhidder; Champbellis; Grahames in Menteith; Buchannanis; M'Cawlis; Galbraithis; M'Nabbis; M'nabriches; Meneis; 'fonis', Fergusons; Spadingis; M'intosches in athoill; M'thomas in glensche; ferquharsonis in bra of Mar; M'inphersonis; grantis; rossis; fraseris; monrois; neilsonis; and others inhabiting the sherfdomes of erygle, bute, dumbartane, Striuiling, Perth, Forfar, aberdene, bamf, elgin, forres, narne, Inverness, and cromartie, Stewarties of Stratherne and menteith, etc. etc.
>
> And understanding that his mischief and shamefull disorder increases, and is nurced by the oursight, hounding out, resett, mentainence, and non-punischement of the thieves, limmers, and vagabonds, partly by the landlords, masters, and baillies of the lands

and bounds wher they dewell and resort, and partly through the counsells, directions, ressett, and partaking of the Chiftanis, principallis of the branches, and house-holders of the said surnames and 'Clansis' which beris quarrell and seeiks revenge for the leist hurting or slaughter of any of their unhappie racess, altho it was by the order of justice or in resquie and following of trew mens goods, geir, solten or reft. So that the said Chiftanis, principallis of the branches, and householders, worthilie may be estiemated the very authors, fosterars, and maintainers of the wicked deeds of the 'Vagabundis' of thair Clannis and Surnames. *Acts of Parl. Scot.*, p. 71. Vol iv.

This showed James at his savage worst, but in 1609 followed the more humane and constructive side of his nature in the Statutes of Iona (or Icolmkill) – thcsc statutcs arc dcscribed in detail in Part 1.

A special committee of the Privy Council was set up to secure the agreement of all landlords throughout the Highlands and Islands (and the rest of Scotland) to this new 'General Band', which pledged them to become responsible for the behaviour of their kinfolk and vassals.

As a further curb on the power of the chiefs all were ordered (in 1598) to produce their land titles by the middle of May and to find surities against any non-observance of the law. All rights to chief-ship and land titles could be forfeited if such land titles and sureties were not produced for scrutiny. Little is known of just how effective were these 'General Bands' at the time but certain Highland and Island territories were indeed forfeited.

As examples, the MacLeod territories of Harris and Lewis along with the estate of Dunvegan and Glenelg were declared to be 'at the King's disposal'. Lewis was then deliberately colonised by a group of Lowlanders from Fife, but these new settlers could not establish themselves economically, militarily or socially, and the idea was eventually dropped. Also Alan MacIan Dubh of Lochiel (Chief of the clan Cameron) being one of the rebels in 1598 dared not appear before the Council to exhibit his title deeds – estates were forfeited until Ewen (17th chief) purchased them back in 1665.

James VI was under no illusion concerning his troublesome chiefs and his attitude becomes abundantly clear in Basilicon Doran, published between the years 1599 to 1603:

As for the Hielands, I shortly comprehend them all in two sorts of people: the one, that dwelleth in our main land that are barbarous, and yet mixed with some show of civilitie: the other that dwelleth in the Isles and are all utterlie barbarous, without any sort or show of civilitie. For the first sort, (he advised his son and heir), put straitly in execution the laws made already by me against their overlords and the chiefs of their clans, and it will be no difficulties to danton them. As for the other sort, think no other of them all than of wolves and wild boars; and therefore follow forth the course that I have begun, in planting colonies among them of answerable inlands subjects, that within short time may reform and civilise the best inclined among them, rooting out or transporting the barbarous and stubborn sort, and planting civilitie in their room.

There was a great deal of confusion existing with regard to chiefs being responsible for the actions of clan members, tenants, sub-tenants and others residing on their lands even if only for a short time. This caused considerable hardship and trouble to not only chiefs but chieftains, tacksmen and law-abiding clansmen as it enabled the Highland thieves and 'broken men' to elude capture by simply walking across the border into another chief's land where no one could follow to bring them to justice. The Act of 1587 was almost unworkable and it was nigh impossible to deal with, control or indeed punish the 'broken men' and outlaws. In effect the Act was so frustrating to the chiefs that it even fostered the spirit of rebellion within all the ranks of the clan.

Against this background in seemed inevitable that properly or-ganised policing was the only worthwhile answer to ensure a relatively peaceful Highland area, and from 1603 onwards is to be seen the small beginnings of the raising of the Independent High-land Companies.

CHAPTER 8

The Early Days of the Independent
Highland Companies (1603–1660)

Chosen Highlanders cloathed in their ancient proper Caledo-
nian Dress and armed with Broadswords, Targets, Guns, Side-
Pistols and Durks, alias Daggers. Statement by Lieut-colonel
Duncan Mackenzie in 1724 as Captain of the 3rd Independent
Company.

General Monck told Oliver Cromwell (prior to the Restoration):
I cannot reduce my forces in Scotland untill these broken people
bee disposed of by sending some regiments beyond seas to serve
some Forraigne Princes or States.

Reigning Monarchs/Protectors
1603–25	James VI of Scotland and I of England
1625–49	Charles I
1649–51	Charles II
1651–58	Oliver Cromwell
1658–59	Richard Cromwell

The origins and background of the first Independant Companies are
difficult to discover in view of the scarcity of records. However, they
probably originated in actions taken in 1603 after James I of
England and VI of Scotland had established his particular monarchical style of Government.

The lawless state of Scotland and especially the Highland areas,
required that strong action be taken and this was to be seen in the
many hangings, brandings and transportation which were the
punishments in vogue at this time. Of the lawless clans the most
infamous, as has been stated was the clan Gregor, along with
another active opponent of the Government at this time, the Earl of
Argyll and his kin who 'having schakin of all dew obedience, and
without all feir of God and of their Majesteis as thair wer na law nor
authoritie above thair hedis, wickitlie and crewellie makis per-
schippis, incursionis, and depredationis in the Lawlandis and
utheris adjacent thairto, slayis and murtheris the inhabitantis

48

thairof, rasis fyre and maisterfullie reiffis, and takis away thair cattell and gudis, mynding to lay the saidis cuntries, as far as in theire lyis, waist and desolat' (Reg. P. C. Sc. 1, 388).

Commissions were often issued for the extermination of other clans, or of the population of wider districts. All in all a desperate situation with the Government straining to see that justice was being done fairly. In most situations cases had to be dropped because of the difficulty in getting both parties to be present at the same time – inevitably also the evidence given was almost always very biased and one-sided.

Following the Union of the Crowns in 1603, it was thought essential that firm rule from the centre was the only answer to the state of lawlessness which existed in many parts of the Highlands. At the same time the actions taken had to be seen to be fair while also seeming to be effective in controlling the activities of the numerous caterans, beggars and broken men who were so numerous in the Highlands.

Historians generally take the date of 1624 as the starting point for strong and central Government action, but the formation of the first 'policing' unit as early as 1603, becomes a very strong contender for the time beginning of the Independent Companies.

This action taken by the monarchy was limited in size, but surprisingly large in effect. A small body, called the King's Guard, was raised for purely gendarmerie purposes in 1603 – it consisted of only a few individual (number unknown) mounted troops. In the early years following 1603 it performed a variety of tasks connected with law keeping.

The King's Guard was used with considerable success on two notable occasions. Firstly, it took part in Lord Scone's expedition to the Western Isles in 1605 in order to bring some semblance of order and to bring the local chiefs to heel in terms of tax payment and lax judicial administration in many parts of the Isles.

Lord Scone, a close kinsman of Tulliebardine, was formerly Sir David Murray of Gospetrie, created Lord Scone in 1605. He and his able lieutenant Robert Hepburn and the Guard were successful in obtaining rent arrears, gaining control of various fortified houses as well as obtaining guarantees of future compliance with the law from the local chiefs and chieftains.

The King's Guard was used once again in 1608 after further futile efforts by James to pacify the Highlands. On this occasion it was led by Andrew Stewart, Lord Ochiltree as the appointed King's

Lieutenant and co-commissioner with Andrew Knox, Bishop of the Isles. Again the supporting Lieutenant was Robert Hepburn.

Ochiltree was determined to obtain effective and specific guarantees and, backed by Royal authority, hit upon the plan to ensure the success of the venture. The Island chiefs were enticed aboard the King's ship named the 'Moon' ostensibly to hear a sermon by Bishop Knox – after the sermon the chiefs were refused permission to leave the ship and in fact were carried off to imprisonment at Dumbarton, Stirling and Blackness. Edinburgh castle was not used on this occasion, as it was already full of 'warders' – witness to James's activities in other fields.

The captive chiefs and chieftains included Hector and Lachlan Maclean of Duart, Donald Gorm of Sleat, Clanranald, Alexander Macleod (brother of Rory Macleod of Dunvegan), and Allan Maclean of Ardgour. McNeil of Barra and Rory Macleod of Dunvegan were the only ones to evade capture.

The chiefs were most ashamed and embarrassed that they had fallen into such a simple trap and to save face – even Bishop Knox was unhappy about his part in the deception – they gladly agreed that they had made a voluntary surrender. Later on the authorities were keen to show leniency in this matter, with Lord Ochiltree reporting that the chiefs had 'come all in to him frelie and of thair awne accord, without promeis, band, conditioun or assurance.'

In terms of the subsequent release of the chiefs, the following terms were announced:

> That so this worke, whiche hes bene hithertilles so endles, to oure grite greif and to the grite trouble of oure goode subjectis thair by reasoun of roadis and taxtis for that same effect, and whiche hes bene also a reprotche to that Estate to haif ony parte of the same inhabited with suche monstrous barbaris, may be once finished, to Godis glorie, oure contentment, and for the weale of the whole kingdome.

This occasion was to be followed by a further meeting of the chiefs at Iona under the chairmanship of Bishop Knox. The Statutes of Iona were agreed at this meeting, leading initially to a very much improved reign of law within the Highlands for some time. (See Chapter 14).

Apart from these two notable and important occasions the King's Guard carried out an enormous amount of day-to-day law duties throughout the Highlands by arresting criminals for assorted crimes, gathering unpaid fines, reducing defended properties and generally enforcing the dictates of the Scottish Council. The success of such a small body of men acting on behalf of James, showed the way for future action – just how powerless was central government in the past and yet how simply this lawlessness could be contained. In other words introducing 'religion and civilitie' among them.

So successful was this very limited policing action by this small force, in reducing crime in at least the most accessible parts of the Highlands, and such was the improvement in law affairs generally, that it was decided to disband this mounted company because of economy! However, some wisdom prevailed and it was kept alive for some years after the Statutes of Iona, albeit in a slimmed-down version. As always, no-one wanted to pay taxes for the preservation of order when life became relatively peaceful.

Little actual detail is known of this small force (recorded in Reg. R. C. Sc. VI) but it is assumed that this mainly mounted body would have worn tartan trews, as the full belted plaid was not really suitable or functional for mounted action. It is also supposed that they were armed with broadsword, pistols and dirk in the normal Highland manner although no records have been kept of their weaponry.

It is also doubtful that the musket of this era, heavy and cumbersome, would have been suitable for equestrian use.

No records can be found of the personnel of this mounted company other than its two captains, Lord Scone and Lord Ochiltree, with a shared lieutenancy in the name of Robert Hepburn. At this time, at the beginning of the Union, it was perhaps thought unimportant with this completely novel military force to the individuals, or even their clan loyalty. However, it is reasonable to surmise that as Scone and Ochiltree as Stewarts were kinsmen of the Earls of Atholl – that the centinels and non-commissioned officers were recruited in the Atholl area and were Athollmen. Both Scone and Ochiltree were prominent and wealthy landowners, as is shown where the Earls of Atholl were financially beholden to Ochiltree on at least two occasions.

The King's Guard of 1603 undoubtedly signalled the first time that the Crown had raised a regular force of its own based on clan recruitment. They became the model for later Independent Companies, which were formed from clan sources more often than not Whig clans, and were paid, clothed and equipped by central government. A century and a half later, their like were to become the Highland recruits within the British Army.

A few years later in 1624, the troubles caused by the clan Gregor and assorted 'broken men' required that further and more positive action be taken by the Government to bring law and order especially to those areas adjacent to the Highland line and where most of the 'cattle lifting', kidnapping and general mayhem was taking place. However, on this occasion the Government decided that the local chiefs should become more involved in trying to solve these problems of lawlessness and the initiative was firmly placed under their hand and jurisdiction.

The chiefs decided upon a very mature and forgiving attitude towards the clan Gregor, by not asking for special measures to be taken against this specific clan. Instead they looked ahead to a more general state of law control covering all clans, but it is ironic that the Macgregors' intransigence was the direct cause of setting up this new policing policy.

This was most definitely a sign that the Government was preparing to trust the clan chiefs and asking for their co-operation, rather than the previous high-handed policy of dictating measures. A three day conference was called in Edinburgh in 1624 where 36 landlord chiefs plus 21 members of the Privy Council met together to discuss the total situation, in what might call a strategic fashion. This meeting followed a loose confederation of clans which formed together in 1609 to control 'controversies, quarrels, questions and hosts' this was the confederation of the clan Chattan formed by clans related by blood to the Mackintosh chiefs and was granted Royal authority in 1622 to utilise the military services of:-

'All and sindrie persones of the Clan Chattane quairever they dwell.' Whilst this was not an Independent Company in the true sense it had certain similarities. This only applied to the northern highland areas but again served as an example for the 1624 agreement.

The Edinburgh meeting in 1624 was a great success and very positive proposals arose from the discussion. Indeed one of the participants, the Laird of Keir went as far as declaring himself 'content to remitt unto the Clan Gregor all biganes.'

The outcome of the meeting was to elect two 'Highland Captaincies' or 'His Majesty's Captains' from a number of contenders. The elected men were both Stewarts as were Scone and Ochiltree in the early days of the King's Guard. The first was James Stewart the Steward Depute of Menteith who was commissioned to look after and control Strathearn, Menteith and Lennox. The second was Robert Stewart, the young Laird of Ballechin for the area around Atholl. No record exists on the background of James Stewart, but Robert Stewart of Ballechin is recorded in the Atholl papers as being 'proceeded against' in November 1622 for having 'worn hagbuts, and pistolets and shot wildfowl and venison between 1618–1622.' These minor misdemeanours were obviously forgotten upon his appointment as one of His Majesty's Captains. Robert Stewart's father was Sir James Stewart of Ballechin and one of the Justices of the Peace for the Atholl district: perhaps he had to dispense justice against his own son for the wildfowl and venison episode!

Again, as with the King's Guard, the size of the 1624 forces in relation to the problems was very small and the two Captains commanded only twenty men in each party and they were ordered 'to co-operate when necessary' when trying to police the whole middle Highland area. It was anything but an ambitious scheme but in its way quite a breakthrough in terms of accountability.

The two Captains held permanent commissions from the King and controlled small and professional standing forces serving for fixed pay. Such a venture was very different from the normal haphazard issue of letters of fire and sword, or commissions of lieutenancy which were given (often unfairly) to the enemies of the offending party. In the latter case, the reward of spoils was granted after vengeance had been extracted.

The appointment of paid, professional soldiers was undoubtedly a major change in trying to make law control effective and indeed was a logical extension of the actions taken in 1603 and the formation of the King's Guard. It also very clearly marked the significant change from a state of feudal divergence to a monarchical emergence of Governmental power.

The formation of the two Highland Captaincies and other law giving policies were continued after the death of King James in 1625. The result of the twin captaincies (only controlling those areas in the neighbourhood of the Southern Highland line and mid-Perthshire) has been difficult to quantify. Certain difficulties arose with payment for the troops, a not unusual state of affairs in early Scottish history. Officers and men alike declared that after serving faithfully and diligently they did not receive their entitled pay and they complained that they were 'Drifted, postponit and delayit, upoun allegeance and excuissis that the taxatioun destinit and appointit for thair payment is not yit ambrocht.'

The persons responsible for the collection were asked to make a full account, to show 'quhat is intromettit with, and in auhais handis thair is ony restand.' They failed to do so and were denounced rebels.

But this did not ensure that the 'waged souldiers' received their just dues.

Because of inadequate numbers, the policing action of the small companies had to be reinforced by the old measures of harsh legislation and indeed in 1633 Parliament passed an act confirming and enhancing all the former laws against the clan Gregor and other outlaws. Unfortunately also, many of the chiefs continued with feuding and other disorders, making the task of the two companies almost impossible under such lawless conditions.

While the two small companies of horsemen could not possibly cope with the scale of public disorder, their actions which were effective but limited, did show the way for the future. Thus in a sense they were the forbears of the very much larger military forces under the authority of the crown.

While future Independent Companies were to be based strictly on Highland clan recruitment, it should be noted that in the very early days the King's Guard of 1603 and the Highland Captaincies of 1624 were backed and raised by the Earls of Atholl: They were not strictly clan chiefs, but were essentially feudal lords, who commanded the allegiance of many highland groupings. These were mainly Stewarts and Robertsons but also Murrays, Morays, Ramsays Spaldings, Fergussons and some lesser names. Until 1629 the Earls belonged to various branches of the Stewart family until the male line died out and a daughter married a Murray of Tulliebardine.

So it is likely that both the King's Guard and men of the Highland Captaincies were comprised mainly of Stewarts and Robertsons, with a smaller number coming from some of the clans already mentioned. Although many records of this period are still available in the Chapter room of Blair Atholl Castle, no muster rolls have been found to back up this theoretical mix of names.

During this early period and up until the Restoration of Charles II in 1660, many of the greatest Highland robbers were active in most of the Highland areas bordering the lowground cattle rearing districts. This was the 'age of the great caterans' (ceatharnaich) who roamed almost at will to terrorise the lowland farmers and village folk. Among the most famous were people like Black John (Iain Dubh Cearr) who operated in the north of the Highlands and raided almost exclusively in the counties of Kindardine, Angus, Banff, Aberdeen and Moray.

Also notorious was James Grant of Carron (Seumas An Tuim) who stole cattle and sheep for over a 30 year period (1615–1645), until he received absolution for his crimes by his support of the then Government at the battle of Auldearn against the forces of the Marquis of Montrose.

Donald Macdonald of Bohuntin was another infamous reiver who was very active before 1660 and was nick-named the Halket Stirk (spotted bullock). He was executed in 1691. In another area Coll Macdonald of Barrisdale in Knoydart earned, at the height of his activity, some £500 one year in blackmail 'to help keep good neighbourhood'.

The situation almost everywhere throughout the Highlands indicated a grave state of lawlessness and as a measure of this Argyll paid over 3,000 merks in 1640 'because he was afraid of being constantly molested by the Brae Lochaber men.'

During this period in the early 17th century many Scots served overseas – 'Continental soldiering' from 1618–1648 in the Thirty Years War. The activities of the early Independent Companies were also considered of minor importance when compared with the battles and the extraordinary marching feats of the forces under James Graham, Marquis of Montrose in 1644–5. The amazing 6 victories of Tippermuir, Aberdeen, Inverlochy, Auldearn, Alford and Kilsyth ended with the severe defeat of his troops at Philliphaugh.

During the last few years prior to the Restoration in 1660, the Cromwellian garrisons achieved some local effect in curbing the worst excesses of the caterans. However, even General Monck with all his military might, had to resort to professional and local clan 'watches' in order to try and contain the situation.

Even the Camerons, undoubtedly the most staunch supporters of the Stewart cause within the clan system, formed a quasi-Independent Company in 1659, when they helped General Monck subdue the Macdonalds of Glengarry in their lawless escapades.

Indeed many of the clan chiefs (not actively reiving themselves) formed their own 'watches', notable amongst them were Cluny Macpherson and Mackintosh of Kylachy. Another example of a clan watch is recorded in the Menzies archives:

'The humble supplication of Captane James Stewart of Arditie, and Robert Menzies, my Lovetenant ovir the Erle of Tullibardin's men of

Glenalmond, to the lordis and wthers of the honorabill committee of Estaite. That quher in the moneth of May last, 1645, pleisit the Estaties of this kingdome and my Lord Tulliebardine to appoynt me captane ovir his lordship's landis and men of Glenalmond, and wpone the 30 of Maii we mustart 100 men in North Inch in Perth, and for the spaice of thrie monethis there after I watchit and keipit the cuntrie so that there was nothing stollin nor reft therout of the enemie, and tuik sundrie of the personers.

Apart from the famous individual robbers already mentioned, there existed a clan dimension in that three main clans, Camerons, Macdonalds of Keppoch and the Macdonalds of Glencoe not only sheltered the caterans but were notorious for raiding in their own right. This is well illustrated by the famous letter written by Alan Cameron of Lochiel where he apologised to the Laird of Grant for a robbery on his land by a Cameron party en route for 'Morrayland quhair all men taks thair prey.'

The situation was very aptly summed up by a current poem of the day. Written in the gaelic it translates as:

> Why should we be without cattle
> When the lowlanders have herds?
> We shall get cattle in the Mearns
> And sheep from Caithness.

No great detail is available of the eventual fate of the two initial and tiny policing groups – the early Independent Companies. It seemed as the public chaos grew and increased in both scope and intensity, so these groups, without proper and popular support in either numbers or finance, simply faded away. The successful lessons of 1605, 1608, 1609 and 1624 had simply not been learned.

CHAPTER 9

Between The Restoration and the Glorious Revolution (1600–1688)

The areas bordering the Highlands had 'Never bein in such quyet and security for above 20 yeirs befor' 1684 report from Lieutenant-General Drummond and the Earl of Breadalbane (formerly John Campbell of Glenorchy.)

Reigning Monarchs
1660–1686   Charles II
1685–1688   James VII of Scotland & II of England

Many Highland estates had resorted to private watches. Tenants, under selected tacksmen, formed rosters so that vigilance could be maintained constantly. These private watches were self-financed in the main and were found to be necessary in areas nearest the Highland line, although on occasion forays deep into the Highlands were organised by the caterans. Estates were forced to pay out considerable sums of money to finance this constant guard on their 'drivable goods' — mainly cattle, but often sheep flocks as well.

In this critical situation where theft was rife much illegal blackmail had to be paid and in this area of semi-legality 'tascal-money' was demanded in return for secret information about the caterans. This is turn often descended into 'theft-bate' where talks were actually conducted with the thief in person.

In 1660 when Charles II regained the throne, this heralded the end of military rule under Cromwell and General Monck which had so successfully subdued the clans. The forts and garrisons were 'slighted' or at least partially destroyed, when English forces were withdrawn, so 'that they might not be continued for the Entertainment of new Garrisons of the Natives.' This removal of military might, immediately caused the Highlanders to break into even more violent behaviour, robbing and raiding almost at will, when they found themselves free of restraint.

Many of the more law-abiding chiefs suggested that the garrisons which had been built by the English at Fort William and Inverness should be rebuilt and used as strong bases against disorder. However, it seemed that public opinion was against any semblance of maintaining these symbols of English domination under the Commonwealth. Thus the caterans were left to their own unlawful activities and everywhere in the Highlands 'the law was set at nought with an audacity which seems at times to have filled the Council with despair.'

In 1661 Parliament and the Privy Council appointed special watches, but with little effect as they were too small and too poorly funded. 1662 saw a Parliamentary Act binding parishes to reimburse losses when robberies happened in their area and actively to pursue the caterans. The whole procedure had a very limited effect and hardly affected the problem.

In this desperate situation the Privy Council appeared to be powerless and in the hope of restoring some state of order, they fell back on the policy of James VI and ordered the chiefs to appear. Not many of them obeyed the summons and in the succeeding years the same monotonous and feeble edicts were sent out only to be ignored. There was also a plan in 1664 to establish garrisons at Ruthven, Inverlochy and Braemar. While Ruthven was occupied by a small force, Inverlochy and Braemar came to nothing — indeed another private watch was quickly established to protect the North-East. This was to prove totally inadequate in protecting the vast areas of Moray and the Mearns, where cattle-raising was the standard agricultural practice. Meantime, lowground Perthshire was equally liable to severe raiding.

In the period until 1666 the Government tried various courses, most of them based on garrisons adequately policed by local watches but they were never fully implemented or controlled. So there was a return to the conventional, well-tried but generally useless measure of summoning the chiefs to give bonds for the good behaviour of their clansmen. While some efforts to carry out the Statutes of Iona were tried, there was generally a lack of will to implement their main measures.

Argyll at this time wryly commented that: 'If it were seriously gone about, few need be hanged, though some must.'

This suggestion was not taken up seriously, as he himself was under suspicion of instigating some of the worst raids.

He complained in 1666: 'the cry will be at Glenorchy and so at me: but it concerns no subject more to have them peacable.'

In fact, Argyll was authorised by Charles to form a watch (for one year) of not more than 60 men to defend his own land against robbery and thieves. This being the case with royal authority (and presumably royal funding) to raise men from the clan Campbell, this could be considered as the first Independant Company to be formed in the Restoration period. Little is known or recorded about this company, or how successful it was in this very localised situation.

However, a very much more serious effort was attempted the following year (1667), when under the Great Seal of Atholl, the Earl was commissioned to raise men as 'a constant guard' for securing the peace of the Highlands — thus was created the most important early Independant Company which established the pattern for future companies to be embodied.

So in August 1667 the Council granted the Earl of Atholl this general commission for one and a half years, to cover all the counties from Inverness-shire south to Dumbartonshire. Meantime, Seaforth was also granted a similar commission for north of the Great Glen. The following is taken from the *Chronicles of the Families of Atholl and Tullibardine* (pages 156.7.8.)

> in 1667 the Government determined to raise a permanent force of Highlanders, who were to wear their own dress and be quartered in the Highlands, to preserve the peace, &c. The first commission for this purpose was granted to the Earl of Atholl as follows:
>
> August 3, 1667.– Forsameikle as notwithstanding that there be many good and excellent lawes and acts of Parliament for quyeting the Highlands, and Isles against theift, sorning, depredation, murther, fyre-raising, and such other odious crymes, and for punishing broken, lawlesse, and wicked men, committing the said crymes within the bounds forsaid, and those who doe harbour, resett, or give any supply or countenance to them, and albeit be the lawes and acts of Parliament all barrons, landslordes, and their baylies, Cheiftanes of Clannes, and other persons of power and interest within the Highland Shyres, be liable and obligded to endevour and concurr for the preventing and repressing of the saids disorders, and that the saids lawes may be putt in execution, yet in respect the said trust and deuty doethly upon many persons in generall, and noe person doeth make it his work and is interested and employed in speciall to that effect, the said disorders, the number, insolency, and villany of theives, sorners, and other wicked and lawlesse persons, doe abound and increase daylie within the said shyres, to the great affront of our

authority and oppression of the people. For vindication whereof we, with advyce of the Lords of our Privy Councill, have given and granted and by this our commission give and grant, full power and command to our right trusty and will-beloved cousine and Councillor, John, Earle of Atholl, to raise and keip such a number of men as he shall think fitt, who are to be commanded by him and such persons as he shall employ, and are to be constant guard for securing the peace in the Highlands and to watch upon the braes and in other places where he shall think fitt, and where theives and broken men doe resort within the shyres of Inuernes, Nairn, Murray, Bamff, Aberdein, Mairnes, Angus, Perth, Clackmannan, Monteith, Stirling, and Dumbartoun, with power to the said John, Earl of Atholl, his said company, and those whom he shall employ to command them, to doe exact diligence, to search persons, take and apprehend all theives, sorners, and broken men . . . and being sua apprehendit, with power to him, his said watch, and these whom he shall employ to command them, to secure their persons, and to present them either to the Justice Generall of Shereffes of the Shyres, Stewarts of Stewartries, or baylies of the regalities respective where the crymes were or shall be committed, that Justice may be done upon them according to law.

The strongholds appointed for the incarceration of offenders were as follows:

Inuernes and Nairn . . . The Castle of Ruthven of Bad Enoch
Murray and Bamff . . . Balachastell in Strathspey.
Aberdein, Mairnes and Angus . . . The Castletown of Brae of Marr.
Perthshyre . . . The Blair of Atholl.
Clackmannan, Monteith, Stirling and Dumbarton . . . The toune of Glengey.

The Act of Council proceeds:

And for the said John, Earl of Atholl, his encouragement, and the entertainment of him and his compony, Wee, with advyce forsaide, Doe hereby give, grant, and assign to him the escheits of all persons who shall be convicted and found guilty of theift, recept of theift, or the other crymes forsaide.

The commission was ordained to take effect from September 11, 1667, and to continue in force until the 'feist and terme of Candlemas 1669.

> And to the effect the said Earl of Atholl may be inabled to raise a
> competent number of men for that service, the saide Lords doe
> recommend to the Lords Commissioners of the Theasurie to make
> payment to him presently of the soume of ane hundreth lib sterling.

It is interesting to note that the Earl was allowed to raise as many
men 'as he shall think fitt', surely a sign and a measure of the
concern the Government felt about this standard of lawlessness
throughout the land.

At the same time, Argyll was also offered a company to guard the
West but, due to reasons of his own, refused this request, although
he was to lose a considerable amount of income by this act.

Huntly also promised his support in this entirely novel venture
and on the 27th October, 1667 wrote the following letter to
Atholl:

> Marquis of Huntly to Earl of Atholl
> Mr Lord, — Y^u may be fullie persuaded that I am so veell satisfied
> with the choise His Matie & the Councele have mad of yor Lo/ for
> rendering peacable the haylandes that I estime it as done to my selff,
> as my Uncle Georg can inform y^u, & ashur y^r selff lickvayes that ther
> is non of my mene bot y^u may fullie imploy, & it is my earnest vish &
> order to them that they be both faithfull & dillegent to y^{r}Lo/for non
> shall vish y^u more hapines then, My Lord,
>   Y^{r}Lo/most aff^{at} cussing & humble servant
>   HUNTLY
> I rocomend the berar herof, Robert Grant, to y^{r}Lo/favor.

It is reasonable to surmise that had Atholl's commission been of
a permenant nature and with the backing of Argyll, Seaforth and
Huntly, these four great chiefs would have been quite able to 'render
peacable the Haylandes' for all time. However, such a reasonable
and logical outcome was not to be!

The reality was that his commission was to be of a temporary
nature and in order to appear effective during this relatively short
period, the following conditions were laid down. If the company was
informed within 36 hours of the theft of goods or cattle, they must
regain the stolen property or repay the value. This money, in theory,
was to be raised from the forfeited property of those robbers
previously tried and convicted.

This Independent Company appeared to be highly successful
from the very start and as early as the following February, (1668)

the Council reported that the whole country was free of further robberies and incursions. However, while all appeared serene on the surface, it was suspected that this apparent lull in 'lifting of cattle' and other blackmail ploys came about by rather underhand methods. Indeed in 1669 the Council was warned that:

> last yeere the theefes were only quiet because they were employed to keep the rest from stealing and for that hade great liberties allowd them and besides many thefts were not complained of because they would not offend the person who was answerable for them, being too great for such an imployment.

Argyll, jealous of Atholl's prominence in law-making affairs via the Independant Company and it's many wide-spread powers, hinted to the Council that Atholl was, in devious ways, encouraging the thieves. The Council shared this fear and did not renew his commission at Candlemas in 1669. Atholl's expenses – £100 to pay his company plus a further grant of £200 for expenses were settled and he was later to receive some of the property forfeited by convicted robbers. This amount of money seemed a small price to pay for comparative peace in the Highlands, but the Council seemed to lack conviction in this matter and as always, sought ways to balance the power among the great chiefs.

It is claimed that this particular company raised by Atholl (numbers unknown) often designated as the first important one, heralded the origin of the Black Watch. Certainly it was a true Independant Company, raised by the chief, clad by him in their national dress, but paid and maintained by the government of the day.

The list of officers appointed by the Earl has not been found and the only reference is to William Vic Lachlan Mackintosh, the VIII laird of Kyllachy who was designated 'captain of the Watch from the Lochaber march to the River of Spey' before 1670.

Kyllachy's main exploit in law-keeping concerned the catching of a party of Lochaber men who had stolen a large herd of cattle from Kilravoch. This cateran party was overtaken and slain on the Braes of Strathdearn. This was certainly an example of summary justice.

On 28 January, 1669 the Earl of Atholl ceased to command the Independant Company and the commission, under almost identical conditions, passed to Sir James Campbell of Lawers. This time the commission did not come from the Crown, but from the Privy

Council. His commission was helped by the fact that his previous financial connection with the Covenanting people had left him virtually penniless and also because he was not popular with any of the important landed chiefs: 'He hath no dependance but upon the King's favour and the Counsell's countenancing him, for all the great men of the Highlands hate him, especially his cheef.'

This being so Argyll ('his cheef') tried unsuccessfully to arrest the commission.

Sir James Campbell was the eldest son of Colonel Mungo Campbell of Lawers, who, in turn, was the youngest brother of John, the Earl of Loudon. James was knighted before 1655 and carried out political services as a Justice of the Peace for Perthshire. Prior to this commission, he had a varied military career encompassing service, as a Captain with his father's regiment (Col. Mungo Campbell's Scots Regiment of Foot) at the Battle of Auldearn on 9th May 1645. He succeeded to the command of this corps as colonel on the death of his father at Auldearn.

He was appointed captain of the Independant Company on 28th January 1669. He held this appointment aided by a party of local deputes including:

> Alexander Chisolme, baylie of Dumblaine, at Dumblaine.
> John Stewart, merchand burges of Perth, at Perth.
> Duncan Campble in Ochtertyre, at Straphillan.
> Donald Dow McLean. Vic Conochy, at Castletoun in Brae of Marr.
> Alexander Cuming, nottar, at Ruthven of Badzenoch.

The huge area to be covered by the company included most Highland counties south of Inverness (and what is now the Caledonian Canal or the Great Glen) and as far south as Dumbarton. For this purpose he received £300 to arm and clothe his men, with the £100 per annum for maintenance – this latter figure was increased to £300 and his commission was to be reviewed annually.

Sir James had some notable successes during his captaincy including the capture of some notorious thieves of the clan Cameron. Whilst recovering stolen goods and capturing other robbers it is said that he used 'methods of dubious legality' although he gave his word not to employ common caterans.

The Judiciary Court hanged one of the agents he used to recover stolen items, suspecting him of organising the outrages himself. However, in those times it was not uncommon to use a poacher turned gamekeeper, even if the turning was not exactly a hundred percent.

Such was Lawers' success in mainly capturing thieves, that the Council renewed his commission and did so in 1671, 1672 and 1673. But for no good reason, on 1st January, 1674 they decided upon a change and asked Sir James to resign his commission. So ended another Independant Company which had functioned very effectively in most difficult circumstances.

In 1674 Sir James was replaced by Major George Grant, fourth son of John Grant of *Freuchie.*

His initial commission commenced on 1 March 1674. Little is known of his immediate background but he was considered to be a most trustworthy and diligent captain. As with Sir James Campbell of Lawers, George Grant was given a group of local deputes to aid his commission:

> Campbell of Lochdochart, at Glenfalloch.
> William Given at Drymen, near Buchanan.
> Alexander Stewart, brother to Bellachen, at Blair of Atholl.
> Alexander Ferquherson of Innercald or John Ferquherson of Innerey, at Castletoun of Brae of Mar.
> Mr. Alexander Grant of Ballachastell in Strathspey.
> Lieutenant-colonel Patrick Grant at Ruthven of Badzenoch.
> Donald McIntosh of Kellachy at Stratherne.

The Privy Council decided that 'it was inconvenient' to send prisoners to Edinburgh for trial and the local deputes were empowered to try them within their respective areas. This enabled justice to be administered more swiftly.

Major Grant's commission was further renewed twice until March 1677

The Privy Council although they found no serious fault with Grant or his company, again opted for a change and decided to re-elect Sir James Campbell of Lawers to fill the vacant captaincy. This time, the commission was for one year only – i.e. from 1st March 1677 until 1st March 1678. For this commission no aiding deputes were appointed, while the Council tried to underpin a permanent solution to the peace-keeping of the Highland areas. The committee, within the Council decided that the task of patrolling and controlling such a vast land area was too great for any one person and his company, however vigilant and hard-working they might be. So they decided upon a second support company under the command of Aeneas Lord Macdonnel of Arros, who was known previously as Aeneas Macdonnel of Glengarry. These two commissions, one to Lawers and one to Glengarry, commenced on 1st September 1677 and were scheduled to run concurrently for a period of 12 months.

It was also agreed that the commission could be terminated by either party provided 'that reasonable notice was given.'

The payment given to the captains was £200 for the execution of the commission and each was required to form his company of:

> 'such a competent number of persons as he should find it necessary to employ.'

Thus the numbers of each company was to be the decision of the captains concerned. It was also decided at this stage that deputes would be appointed (14 September 1677.)

The local deputes were:

> Given at Drumen in the Lennox.
> Duncan McNab at Strathphillan in Perthshyr.
> Alexander Stewart at Blair of Atholl.
> George Lumsden, messenger, at Perth.
> Duncan McKenzie, forester, at Castletoun of Braemarr.
> James Innes of Drumgask at Aboyne.
> David Cumine at Ruthven.
> Donald McDonald at Inergary.
> The Governor of the garrison of Inverlochy.
> Duncan Campbell at Killin.

Following the appointment of the deputes, on 14th October one hundred firelocks were on issue to Lawers and Glengarry.

The proposal was that the garrison at Inverlochy should be set up when repairs were complete along with a justiciary court where Argyll, Moray, Glenorchy, Caithness and Aboyne would judge the captured robbers.

Many of the proposed plans for a firm justiciary were shelved when gentry in the south-west declined to accept the bond which would make them liable for their tenants' religious misdeeds. The famous (or infamous) Highland Host formed of 5,000 gaelic-speaking Highlanders plus 3,000 regular troops, occupied an area around and south of Glasgow in Ayrshire. Meantime, Lawers and

Glengarry remained in the Highlands 'to keep watch on the Braes.'

In the opinion of the Privy Council affairs in the Highlands were not entirely to their satisfaction. In September 1678 King Charles II proposed yet another scheme. This was to increase and fix the number of men in each company at 150. Argyll and Caithness were asked to raise two Independant Foot Companies with Sir James Campbell in command of one and Colonel James Menzies of Culdares in charge of the other. In addition a company of Foot Guards was 'to march to the Highlands to joyn with these two Companies of Highland men.'

The Foot Guards (later the Scots Guards) were to be placed in garrison at Inverlochy and the Council authorised 9,000 merks to refurbish the garrison.

Meantime, Argyll intended using the companies against the Macleans of Mull, in order to end his long-standing feud with this clan. In the history of the clan Maclean a description was given of the action taken by the two companies, plus a 'commanded company' of the Earl of Linlithgow's regiment (i.e. the Scots Guards). After some random fighting in Mull, the Macleans were forced to surrender.

Lawers was not at all happy at this turn of events in that he was taken away from his prime task. He said that guarding of the braes 'was despysed and neglected.' It was a very difficult situation for Lawers when he had to argue his case against his chief, Argyll. There was no doubt that the Independant companies had been used for completely unlawful purposes, but such was the complexity of the situation that the Council turned a blind eye to the misuse of Government forces for private ends. However, a little later the Council decided to take a firmer line and wrote to the Earl of Argyll, then engaged with the Earl of Caithness in the Western Highlands crushing a rebellion of the Macdonalds and Macleans, commanding him 'to desentagle himself from the expedition for which he was commissionated against the rebellious people in the Highlands.'

The commission to Sir James Campbell was recalled and a new one issued to the Earl of Caithness to be captain of the company. So on the 27th September 1678 Sir James was demoted and became 1st Lieutenant under Caithness, but Colonel James Menzies retained the captaincy of his company.

The following taken from *A Military History of Perthshire* outlines the new establishments:

Rank	Name	Commission Dated
Captain	The Earl of Caithness	5 Sept. 1678
1st Lieut.	Sir James Campbell of Lawers	27 Sept. 1678
2nd Lieut.	Alexander Campbell of —	27 Sept. 1678
Ensign	Alexander Mackartor	27 Sept. 1678
Captain	Col. James Menzies of Culdares	5 Sept. 1678
1st Lieut.	Archibald Campbell of Inveraw	27 Sept. 1678
2nd Lieut.	John Campbell of Airdes	27 Sept. 1678
Ensign	— Campbell of —	27 Sept. 1678

The first company of the Watch remained on its former establish-ment and pay. The pay of the second and third companies was — for a captain 8s stg. per diem, for a lieutenant 4s., and for an ensign 3s. The sergeants, (of whom there were three in a company) received 18s. scots per diem each; the corporals (four in a company) and drummers (two in a company) 12s. scots per diem each, and a foot-soldier 5s. scots per diem A chirurgeon at 3s. stg. per diem, with £15 to furnish a medicine chest, was added to the strength, and the 'accompt of necessaries' to be furnished to the second and third companies, in addition to 300 firelocks, consisted of the following:

Item for 300 baggonets for the 300 fyrelocks at 2s stg. per peice	£360 00 00
For two pair of Collours to them	100 00 00
For four drums at 24 1i. per peice	96 00 00
For fifteen hundred flint stones	20 00 00
For four pair calmes for casting of bullets, each pair casting 12 bullets at once, at 71i.4s the pair, and for two pair calmes for casting bullets to the blunderbusses at half-a-crown the pair, and for a pair of shiseris for cutting the bullets after they are cast, 81i., inde, in all	<u>39 16 00</u>
	<u>£615 16 00</u>

In addition, eight firelocks, four blunderbusses, and three hun-dred stands of bandoliers were provided. The list of necessaries to be furnished by Lawers, and Culdares for the use of the garrison at Inverlochy included 'forty axes, twenty mattocks, brewing loomes for thrie bolls at a tyme, two iron potts, fifty payr of bedplayds, 150 wooden playtts, 300 horn spoones, fourscore two pynt stoopes, ten duzon of timber trencheours, four score tupp horns for drinking.'

At the same time a warrant was issued for building a 'fitt lodging' for the troops at Inverlochy, and while the barracks were in course of erection, the garrison was stationed at the castle of Dunolly.

It seems highly probable that it was during this period that the now famous epithet of 'The Black Watch' or 'Am Freiceadan Dubh' was first applied to the Highland companies, the name being bestowed to distinguish them from the Guardsmen, who were called the 'Saighdearan Dearg' or 'Red Soldiers.'

From February to October 1679 John Campbell of Succoth drew the warrants for the pay of the Breadalbane company although apparently no commission as such was granted to him. The pay rates for each company of Foot in the Scots Army (1661–88) were:

	Per Diem £ s. d.
Captain	0 8 0
Lieutenant	0 4 0
Ensign	0 3 0
2 Sergeants, each 1s. 6d.	0 3 0
3 Corporals, each 1s.	0 3 0
2 Drummers, each 1s.	0 2 0
Clerk	0 2 0
100 Soldiers, each 6d.	2 10 0
	3 75 0

This is a strange business as the company captained by the Earl of Caithness and with Lawers as 1st Lieutenant was commonly known as 'Breadalbane's'. One possible explanation is that John Campbell yr. of Succoth became an appointed quartermaster to the company and did not feature in the normal command structure. He was also an advocate and deputy sherrif of Dunbartonshire.

In April 1679 there was a warrant to the keeper of the magazine of Edinburgh Castle to supply six hundredweight of gun powder and ball for use of the Highland companies and at about the same date Robert Campbell is paid for conveyance of provision and ammunition to the garrison at Inverlochy.

In April 1680 Argyll sent Colonel Menzies to Tiree with 200 men of the Highland companies ostensibly to relieve the garrison. However, this expedition (leaving Lawers alone to guard the Highlands) was spent almost entirely in treasure-seeking in Tobermory. Again another example of Argyll (and occasionally Caithness) using the companies almost exclusively for their own ends.

In 1680 Caithness was ordered by Charles to maintain order in the North and the company on 13th April advanced towards a band of lawless people led by the clan Sinclair. They charged and the Sinclairs fled in confusion. Caithness tried to restrain his men but in their fury they killed over 100 clansmen, captured another 100 losing only two of their own men in the exchange. Caithness reoccupied Thurso, built a garrison and started rent-collection. The Government appeared to back this harsh action and ordered both he and Menzies 'to quarter their companies for arrears' in Lochaber, Badenoch and the Isles.

From 1679–81 Colonel James Menzies of Culdares drew the pay of his company from the date of his commission in September 1678 until June 1681, when the last payment was made two months after disbandment. Similarly, the Earl of Caithness drew company pay from October 1679 until June 1681.

Colonel James Menzies' background history is not well known according to the Clan Menzies Society. The Culdares Menzies were a collateral branch of the main line of the Menzies of Weem arising from the descendants of James, second son of the second marriage of Alexander Menzies of Menzies (1504–63). The Clan Society is at the present time negotiating the purchase of an oil painting of Colonel James and his wife Susannah, but no detail is known of his family history as many of the Menzies records have been irretrievably lost.

In March 1681 there was a reported suggestion that James got the Privy Council to agree to raise two Highland companies, but that the sentinels had to come from Lowland Scotland so that 'such neutrall and disinterested persons would receave more universal obedience from and be more terrible to all of them [the clans] than any natives can be.'

This new concept was also to be linked with a request that the chiefs should be summoned to Edinburgh. These twin orders proved to be ineffectual in practice and never actioned.

Charles II informed the treasury that he could no longer afford to maintain the cost of two companies, as well as regular troops and militia, so he decided again to disband the Highland companies. So on the 15th April 1681 the two companies were added to the Earl of Mar's regiment (21st Foot, later Royal Scots Fusiliers) which was to be permanently stationed in the Highlands.

These two companies (under the aegis of Mar's regiment) was captained by Kenneth Mackenzie of Suddie, the other by Captain Alexander Cairnes.* The roll of captain Mackenzies's company and captain Cairnes's company are shown at Appendices 3 and 4.

These two companies had the task of maintaining peace and order in the Highlands, but they proved quite unequal to the task. Later in 1681 the Council ordered that a garrison should be established at Inverlochy but in early 1682 Cameron of Locheil captured the whole garrison and 'drove out the soldiers with contemptuous ease.'

In August 1682, to support this lawless situation, the Crown issued a commission of 70 nobles and chiefs of clans who were to be held responsible for the behaviour of their clansmen. The Highlands were divided into 4 districts (each with its own commissioners) who were directed to meet every 6 months at the following centres:

> a. Caithness and Sutherland at Lochnaver.
> b. Ross, Inverness, Cromartie, Nairn and Elgin at Lochness.
> c. Banff, Aberdeen, Kincardine and Coupar at Kincardine of Neill.
> d. Perth, Stirling, Dumbarton and Argyll at the Kirk of Balquhidder.

These commissioners in turn were empowered to appoint officers in every Highland parish, who were to be responsible to the Commissioners for the Peace of their districts-the jurisdictions of sheriffs, stewarts, and bailies of regalities being always preserved.

At the same time the company of the Watch at Inverlochy was reorganised. The entire force there was in future to carry fire-arms. It was to consist of 100 men with a captain, lieutenant, four sergeants, and four corporals, the force being divided as follows: —

Suddies Independent Company

Captain	Kenneth Mackenzie of Suddie	(Comm. dated 7.4.1681)
Lieutenant	William Sharp	(Comm. dated 7.4.1681)
(successively)	John Dalziel	(Comm. dated 7.6.1688)
Ensign	Christopher McDougall	(Comm. dated 7.4.1681 pay ceased Aug. 1685)
(successively)	James Buchan	(Comm. dated 7.11.1685)

Cairnes Company

Captain	Alexander Cairnes	(Comm. dated 7.4.1681)
Lieutenant	John Levingston	(Comm. dated 7.4.1681)
Ensign	— Wood	(Comm. dated 7.4.1681)

three parties-each consisting of a Sergeant, a corporal, and 23 men-were to be stationed at the head of Loch Ness, the castle of Braemar, and Aberchalader respectively, and a lieutenant, a sergeant, a corporal, and the remainder of the men at Inverlochy. These parties were stented upon the different counties concerned. The Commissioners of Excise of Inverness were to provide meat and drink for the Loch Ness party, those of Aberdeen for the party at Braemar, and those of Perth and Dumbarton for the party at Aberchalader.

It was further claimed that the major part of the reason for the failure of the two companies to maintain peace adequately was due to the single fact that the captains kept too few men in arms, in order that they could pocket the excess pay.

James, acting on behalf of his brother Charles II, then suggested that the money spent on the support of the companies should be used instead to pay the four great chiefs/nobles in the Highlands, Huntly, Argyll, Seaforth and Atholl. This would mean some £700 each per annum and in return, they would undertake to make themselves responsible for all misdemeanours in their areas of power. Payment would only be made if the great chiefs carried out their duties with due effect and zeal. It was also thought that this could also ensure their total dependancy on the Crown. However, this novel plan was never fully acted upon and indecision reigned once again.

The garrison at Inverlochy was so distant from any other part of the UK and communication was generally by sea, as the road system in the Highlands was virtually non-existent at this time. The food was generally inadequate, the quarters were cold and damp and the safe area around the barracks was extremely limited. In the surrounding Highlands clan feuds and general mayhem were the order of the day. While the Independant Companies, could perhaps deal with straightforward cattle and sheep lifting, inter-clan feuds were a different and more difficult matter altogether.

On 15 October, 1685 Captain Kenneth Mackenzie of Suddie received instructions from the Privy Council to step-up more aggressive and punitive action against the caterans and 'broken-men.' He was so successful in this task of preserving peace in the northern Highlands that it was recommended to set up another Highland company to keep peace in the south, specifically the Braes of Strathearn and the Ochill Hills. To house this company it was proposed to build a fort near Stirling (called James' fort) although

71

this was later cancelled due to lack of funds. The new company (commanded by George Barclay and with 1st Lieutenant Patrick Ronnald and ensign Henry Maxwell) was then formed into no. 11 company of the Foot Guards:

INDEPENDENT COMPANY, FORMERLY UNDER THE COMMAND OF
CAPT. GEORGE BARCLAY, ADDED TO THE REGT. OF FOOT GUARDS.
Commissions dated at Whitehall, 20th Nov., 1685.

CAPT.	LIEUT.	ENSIGN
Major Robert Middleton	Patrick Ronald	Henry Maxwell.

Barclay (or Berkeley) was subsequently appointed major of Sir Edward Hales' Regiment of Foot, 28th November 1685. Lieut.-Colonel of the said corps in October 1686. Later he became joint commander of Sir Donald Macdonald of Sleat's regiment at Killiecrankie. He fell into an unsuccessful plot to assassinate King William III in 1695.

Meantime, Captain Kenneth Mackenzie was called upon to help the Mackintoshes and their followers the Mac Gillivrays who were given a commission of fire and sword by the Privy Council against Macdonnell of Keppoch. This commission allowed:

> 'That whatever slaughter, mutilation, blood, fire-raising or other violence' may be done by the persons holding the letters, shall be held 'laudable, good and warrantable service to his Majesty and Government.'

This was to be the last great clan battle, at Mulroy on 4th August 1688, where the Macdonnells were victorious and where Suddie and many of his men were killed in action. Suddie and his men had been outnumbered by Keppoch and two of his neighbouring clans, the Camerons of Glen Nevis and the Macmartins of Letterfinlay.

They launched a fierce Highland charge with swords and Lochaber axes – Suddie was mortally wounded in the affray.*

A soldier in Suddie's company, Donald McBane subsequently wrote:

> 'The Macdonalds (Macdonells) came down the hill upon us, without either shoe, stocking or bonnet on their heads: they gave a shout and

*Kenneth Mackenzie of Suddie was a descendant of Kenneth of the Battle (blar-na-pairc) and had served in Dumbarton's regiment in France and was described as having 'the character of a fine gentleman and brave officer.' He was a professional soldier of the highest calibre.

then the fire began on both sides and continued a hot dispute for an
hour. Then they broke in upon is with sword and target, and Lochaber
axes which obliged us to give way.'

This was a very matter-of-fact description of what must have been
a particularly bloody encounter. In the same vein, Keppoch later
described the battle of Mulroy 'the unhappie accident I had with
McKintoshe at Millroy'. Since various political and military events
were taking place at this time, called the 'Glorious Revolution',
regular troops were increasingly withdrawn from Scotland and
mostly during the month of October 1688. King James' aides made
a hurried but wise decision to secure peace throughout the Highlands and the Lowlands as well. The main chiefs were asked to
supply a certain number of soldiers in order to amass a force of
some 500 men. These troops, according to the Privy Council were
to remain in the central area around *Stirling during the months of
November* and December 1688. The composition of the troops was
organised as follows:

	soldiers	lieuts	ensigns	sergts	pyperis
The marquess of Atholl's men	200	4	4	8	4
The Earl of Perth's men	50	1	1	2	1
The Laird of Weim	50	1	1	2	1
The Laird of Gairntullie	50	1	1	1	1
The Earl of Breadalbane	100	2	2	4	2
Strowane Robertson and McFarlane	48	1	1	2	1
The Marquess of Montrose	20	1	—	1	—
The Earl of Monteith	50	—	1	1	1
The Lairds of Luss, Keir, and Lenie	50	1	1	2	1
The Earl of Murray	25	—	1	—	—
The Earl of Mar	100	1	1	2	1
The Duke of Gordon(unstated)	—	—	—	—	—
Colonell Patricke Grahame (unstated)	—	—	—	—	—

The rates of pay were: for a lieutenant 30s scots per diem, an ensign
20s., a sergeant 14s., a piper 10s., and each soldier 3s. 'with a peck
of meal ilk seavin dayes to ilk souldier.' In addition each officer and
man received a pair of shoes and 'ane elne of plyding' for stockings.
Among the papers preserved is a receipt by Mr. Leonard Robertsone
of Straloch for 220 flints for the use of the Marquess of Atholl's men,

a fact which seems to show that the Marquess proved the victor in his struggle with the Privy Council for flintlocks instead of matchlocks.

The force was not present all at one time, and its numbers were continually varying. The Menzies detachment was first on duty — entering on pay and rations on the 12th of October — but the greater part of the force did not arrive until early in November. It was ordered to disperse by warrant from the Privy Council of the 28th of November 1688, but it continued under arms by relays until the 3rd of December, when, the funds appropriated for its pay having come to an end, what remained of the force returned home.

This force was unlike any previous and single Independant Company in that it was made up of a number of clans but as it was organised, authorised and paid for by the Government, it fell within the category of at least a quasi-Independant Highland Company.

The period from the Restoration to the Glorious Revolution (1660–1688) was amongst the most unruly and unlawful ever witnessed in the Highlands. The previous 25 years had seriously upset the settled clan society with a very marked increase in the number of 'broken men' available to create trouble and general mayhem. Many clansmen had lost the land they had previously farmed and had become almost addicted to a life of violence and robbery. These 'broken men' if they could not find the shelter of a clan willing to accept them were virtually forced into a life of crime. So much of the trouble caused in the 28 years between 1660 and 1688 had origins in the violent upset and warring which occurred between 1637 and 1660.

Another factor of great economic importance was the increase in number of cattle bred in the Highlands and surrounding Lowland areas, to satisfy an ever-increasing English market for Scottish lamb and beef.

The large number of stock travelling to southern markets were easy prey for the caterans and led to attempts to licence the drovers so as to avoid competition between the two. The fact that the English military rule, so firm under Cromwell, had virtually disappeared following 1660, also added to the general state of lawlessness.

There was no doubt that the Independant Companies helped to maintain some semblance of order but unfortunately they were never fully nor completely backed by the Privy Council.

The Council tended to vacillate between the use of the Companies and reliance upon the main chiefs to bring their clansmen to heel.

The Companies were not numerous enough nor did they employ enough men per individual Company. Some captains did not engage their full complement and kept the financial excess for their own private use. Fierce inter-clan rivalry and jockeying for possession of land could not be dealt with such small forces, but at least a start was made in establishing paid permanent troops, clad in local dress, speaking the same language as the native clansmen and capable, when fully accoutred and well led, in maintaining peace of a kind.

CHAPTER 10
Killicrankie, Cromdale and Glencoe
(1688–1700)

*Coming down 'like a living flood' and almost before the bayonets
of the soldiers could be brought from the 'present' to the 'charge'
the swordsmen would be among them 'stooping below the
charged bayonets they tossed them upwards by the target
(targe), dirking the front rank man with the left hand, while
stabbing or hewing down the rear rank man with the right: thus
as usual in all highland onsets the whole body of soldiers was
broken, trod underfoot and dispersed in a moment'. The Highland
Charge at Killiecrankie.*

Reigning Monarchs
1689–1702   William and Mary

Scotland followed England in dethroning James VII in favour of the
protestant William III of Orange, whose wife Mary was a Stuart
princess. James went to France hurriedly and it was assumed that
he had forfeited his crown. This change in kingship re-established
the presbyterian form of church government, but episcopacy was
still very popular especially in the gaelic Highlands. James still
retained a block of support in the country and leading figures in
this situation were General John Graham of Claverhouse, Viscount
Dundee and his fellow Jacobite, George, Fourth Duke of Gordon.

The kinsman of Dundee, the great Marquis of Montrose had
virtually devastated Scotland in the 1640's backed by a mainly
catholic army from Ulster. The Scottish government recognising the
danger from Dundee and his backing from the cavalry soldiers of
King James insisted that he recognise the legitimate government of
the country. However, in April 1689 Viscount Dundee raised King
James' standard on Dundee Law. This was the start of the Jacobite
story which was to last until it's disastrous end 57 years later on
Culloden Moor in April 1746.

Dundee found little support in the Lowlands and even from his
own area, the town of Dundee. In view of this he was forced to look
to the Highlands for support, and even there only Cameron of

Lochiel was the sole Highland chief of any note actively to espouse his cause. However, somehow or other Dundee managed to scrape together an army of some 1,000 men, comprised of mainly people from the lesser clans and their adherents. The MacGregors, who had regained their clan name some 30 years earlier, the Macdonalds of Keppoch, Glencoe, Sleat and Clanranald, the Macleans of Duart and the MacNeills of Barra. By this time, Dundee's army now numbered 2,500.

Facing this motley mix of clans, were the forces of the government led by General Hugh Mackay of Scourie, himself a Highlander and gaelic speaker, who had gained his considerable military experience on the continent with the Scots Brigade in the Dutch service. His force consisted of some 4,000 men — one battalion from each of the three regiments of the Dutch Brigade, Hasting's Leven's (later 25th Foot, King's own Scottish Borderers) and Kenmuir's.

In addition he had some small cannon and two troops of Scottish Horse, Annandale's and Belhaven's. In addition to the Dutch and English troops Mackay had the support of an Independent Highland Company of the clan Menzies (from Weem in central Perthshire) and led by the young chief, Captain Robert Menzies.

The following taken from the *Red and White Book of Menzies*, tells how this company came into being and about it's actions fighting on behalf of William:

> After the flight of King James II of Great Britain, the royal standard of the exiled King was raised by the chivalrous Viscount Dundee, who on leaving Edinburgh to send the firey (sic) cross round the Highland clans, said to a friend in answer to the question, Where was he going? 'Wherever Wherever the spirit of Montrose shall direct.' Dundee soon found himself at the head of a considerable army, with which after many marches, sometimes pursuing, sometimes retreating against General Mackay, the first stage of the war was concluded without a decisive battle. Immediately after Dundee's call to the royal clans to arm and come out, he was joined by the Aberdeenshire Menzies', under Chieftain Menzies of Pitfodels, and also by Chieftain Major Duncan Menzies, each with a body of followers. These Menzies stuck to the last to Dundee and the royal cause. On the other hand, the Chief Sir Alexander Menzies and his son, Junior Chief Captain Robert Menzies, took the side of General Mackay and the Protestants.

On the 26th of July 1689 General Mackay left Perth at the head of an army of 4,500 veteran soldiers and a fair force of cavalry. With this force he proceeded to renew the war, and just before starting he despatched a messenger to Chief Sir Alexander the Menzies, and specially to his son Captain Robert Menzies, asking him to procure scouts for him. Here is General Mackay's letter:

> St Johnstone, 26 July 1689. General Hugh Mackay for the Laird of Weems, Younger. I received yours of last night at ten the cloak. I doe not beleeve that Dundie is neare, though I wish he were, let his forces be what they will. I forgot to speak to you to send out men of inteligence, which I pray you to doe. I would take on 9 or 10 persons in pay during this expedition at such a rate as they may be content, for guides and inteligence, which I pray you to look out for, and that they be men who know the country perfectly well; but faile not upon recepte hereof to send towards the enemy for sure inteligence and where they are. The persons I shall pay as you shall juge raisonable. I shall dispatch my march as much as possible.
>
> I am Sir, your most humble servant
>   H. MACKAY.

Initially, Mackay only asked Clan Menzies to supply 9 or 10 men for 'guides and intelligence', but Robert Menzies brought out his total fighting force of 100 men to aid the General's cause.

Following the battle on 27 July, 1689 and the disastrous result for the forces of William, the following account, found in the Charter Room, Castle Menzies (no. 138) succinctly outlines what happened:

> Mackay pushed on to Dunkeld, where at midnight he received notice of the approach of Dundee from Sir Alexander. Next morning, 27th July 1689, at daybreak, he proceeded in the direction of the Pass of Killiecrankie.
>   During his march Mackay was joined by the young chief, Captain Robert Menzies, at the head of over 100 Highlanders of the Clan Menzies. The old chief, Sir Alexander the Menzies was too old to take the field, and therefore remained at Castle Menzies to make preparations in case the doings of Montrose should be repeated by Dundee. His sons, Captain Robert and Captain James Menzies of Comrie, with the clan, fought at the battle of Killiecrankie, where General Mackay's English and Dutch army was totally defeated. But Mackay with a few of his men saved themselves in the descending darkness, by flight over the mountain bye-paths to Castle Menzies, where they knew the old chief, Sir Alexander the Menzies, would do all in his power to save them from being cut off.

No hard facts have come to light on how the Menzies company

performed at Killiecrankie, but it is believed that they fought Dundee's Highlanders along with a part of Leven's regiment. From contemporary accounts this was the one part of Mackay's forces which withstood the shock of the Highland charge and 'they apparently acquitted themselves well on the day'.

Mackay in his memoirs states: 'There is no regiment or troop with me but behaved like the vilest cowards in nature, except Hasting's and my Lord Leven's'

No record of losses are available in the Menzies archives, but it appeared that most of Mackay's losses occured when his men were fleeing from the pursuing Highlanders. Those who stood their ground, preserved ranks and beat an orderly retreat fared better in terms of losses.

Mackay, after the battle summarised very precisely the effects of the dreaded Highland charge:

> The Highlands are of such quick motion that if a Battalion kept up it's fire until they be near to make sure of them, they are upon it before our men can come to the second defence, which is the bayonet in the musle of the musket.

As in the battle of Mulroy when Captain Kenneth Mackenzie of Suddie was killed and his company routed by the Highlanders of Mackintosh and the Macdonalds of Keppoch, the famous pipe tune 'Macdonald took the Brae on them' highlighted the advantage the already swift Highlanders had, by initiating the attack from the high ground.

From the Life of Lieut-General Mackay comes this account concerning the Menzies company:

> The young Chief Captain Robert Menzies acted with great bravery at the battle of Killiecrankie, where he won the admiration of General Hugh Mackay, with whom he was ever afterwards a firm friend.

General Mackay himself says of his retreat, after the battle of Killiecrankie:

> Marching them off, as he had concluded, he met in the obscurity, about two miles off the field of battle, with Colonel Ramsay, who had kept up the matter of 150 runaways altogether almost without arms, and knew not in the world how he should best get them off, whom the General having joyn'd into his party, continued his way up a little

79

river, which fell into that which he had crossed before, till he came to some little houses where he saw a light, and having got the man of the house, enquired of him concerning the ground and the way to Strath Tay and the Laird of Weem's lands (the chief of the Menzies' and the Menzies country), who was our friend, his eldest son having been in the action with a company of 100 Highlanders, which he levied for their Majesties' service. The countryman, having sufficiently informed him of all his demands, and guessing himself at the situation of the country by the map so far that he could not carry him far out of the way, he crossed the second river, and passed ill ground over hills and bogs 'to Weem.'

In fact, the Menzies force did not actually become an accredited Independent Company until after the battle. The Duke of Hamilton sent an official commission to the young chief Robert Menzies to be a captain of an Independent Company of a hundred Highlanders of clan Menzies, which he had raised and had fought at Killiecrankie. They conducted themselves so much to the satisfaction of General Mackay that, on his informing his Majesty William III of the undaunted coolness and bravery of the young chief, he ordered a commission to be sent to him (dated 23rd August) some 26 days after the battle.

It became the first royal commission to be so granted and it established the first action by an Independent Company in a major battle.

Shortly after Killiecrankie, where Dundee was tragically shot by a stray musket ball, the Highlanders attacked Dunkeld under General Cannon, who was Dundee's sucessor.

In this case, the Highlanders were driven off by stalwart defensive action by a force of regular soldiers, the Cameronian regiment (later 26th Foot). Thereafter the rebellion faded.

General Mackay then selected Castle Menzies to be one of a number of garrisons to help keep the Highlanders in check. Others were Finlarig, Drummond Castle, Cambusmore, Meggernie, Landross and Drumnakill. This completed a chain of communication from the remotest part of Perthshire to the town of Inverness.

In the following years Robert Menzies headed the Menzies contingent at Weem and at Meggernie in Glen Lyon.

The young chief had his governorship of Castle Menzies granted on the same day. This was on the recommendation of General mackay, who saw he was well qualified in military tactics. The governor's commission is as follows:

'Commission by Major-General Hugh Mackay in favour of Captain Robert Menzies, younger, to be governor of the garrison in the Castle of Weem. Perth, 30th September 1689.' Charter Room, Castle Menzies, No. 221.

Following this, he received the additional appointment to be commander of the old Menzies' stronghold, Meggernie Castle in Glenlyon, belonging to the Culdares' branch of Clan Menzies. The substance of the commission reads as follows:

Perth, 7th October 1689. General Mackay to the Laird of Weem, younger, Captain of an independent company, and Commander of the Castle of Weem. Desires him to establish a sufficient garrison in the house of Miggernie in Glenlyon, should the said house be capable to secure it, for the better protection of the country against the rebels — *Charter Room, Castle Menzies,* No. 141.

In July 1690 Captain Menzies had extra duties thrust upon him when General Mackay was instructed by the government to appoint him as second-in-command of the garrison and fort of Inverlochy. But before this could be implemented, the government forces (under Livingstone) surprised the Highlanders at the Haughs of Cromdale. Having beaten them at this skirmish, this decided the government to go ahead with the building at Inverlochy the garrison of 'Fort William'.

General Mackay on 18th June 1690 marched north with a force of 3,000 men (horse and foot). On his way north he was joined by Captain Robert Menzies and his company. On arriving at Inverlochy, they commenced work on 5th July and completed the outer wall by the 16th. On this day, the young chief was officially declared Lieutenant-Governor and received the following commission:

Fort William or Inverlochie, 16 July 1690. From General Mackay — The commission of Robert Menzies of Weem to be Lieutenant-Governor of Fort William not having yet come down from His Majesty, and the service requiring that he be presently put in exercise of his said office: Therefor Mackay appoints him Lieutenant-Governor of the fort and garrison of Fort William, formerly called the Fort of Inverlochie. Charter Room, Castle Menzies, No. 151

While Captain Menzies and his company were stationed in Fort William, a body of Highlanders further south began to give trouble. Accordingly Mackay ordered Menzies and his men to join him in

Perth. But having reached Perth, they had to travel north again to counter lawless Highlanders under General Buchan and the Earl of Seaforth. Mackay, plus the Menzies contingent quickly dispersed the Highland forces and Seaforth was taken captive. So ended the troubles in the northern counties for the time being.

Captain Menzies also had a political role vis-a-vis the other northern chiefs. The chiefs in Lochaber trusted Robert Menzies in that he, like them, was a Highlander. In sympathy with the Highland chiefs he asked for and was given permission to mediate in their cause and General Mackay gave him the allowance to carry on this task:

> The Camp at Ruthven of Badenoch, 30 June 1690. General Mackay grants liberty to the Laird of Weem to answer any letters received by him from the men of Lochaber, and to meet and converse with them until further orders. — Charter Room. Castle Menzies No. 150

Menzies scored a major success in his talks with the chiefs around Fort William — so much so that the whole area became extremely peaceful. He continued with his useful work in parleying with the chiefs and helping to maintain the morale and training of all the troops at Fort William, but especially his own company and those of Balnagown and Mackay — the latter two joined after their muster in 1689.

Robert died unexpectedly in April 1692 at the tender age of 32, having achieved a great deal in his short life. He did much to maintain peace in the Highlands at a critical time and showed just how successful an Independent Company could become, when used in it's primary role of peace-keeping and in the suppression of robbery.

It is fitting to end his career with a heading taken from the '*Red and White' Book of Menzies*:

> Junior Chief Captain Robert 'Menzies,' Knight, 55th in Descent as Heir of 'Fiar,' 18th Baron of Menzies.
>
> Lieutenant-Governor of Inverlochy Castle and Fort William; Commander of the Garrisons of Castle Menzies and Castle Meggernie;
>
> Captain of the First Independent Company of Highlanders; and Founder of the Black Watch.
>
> Born 1660. Died 1692.

It is interesting to speculate that had Robert Menzies lived and retained his position as Lieutenant-Governor of Fort William, then perhaps the massacre of Glencoe need not have occured.

The infamous plot was first hatched by Sir John Dalrymple, Master of Stair who was the Secretary of State for Scotland. He colluded with Breadalbane in this matter, who wanted to make his particular branch of clan Campbell the most important and power-ful in the land. The plan was willingly (or not knowingly) approved by King William — thereafter the whole sorry business ran it's course.

Had Robert Menzies been ordered to carry out the plan it is reasonable to assume that he, as son and heir to a noble Highland chief, would not have complied with this dark deed or perhaps would have taken the necessary steps to give the clan Macdonald prior warning.

King James had been defeated at the battle of the Boyne on 1st July 1690 and this defeat in Ireland meant that he lost all hope of victory in that country. James then retired to France and allowed his chiefs in Scotland 'to do what may be most for their own and your safety'. Most of them, by the first of January, had taken the oath to King William following the royal proclamation stating that 'the utmost extremity of the law' would be used against those who did not meet the deadline. One of the major chiefs who was late in confirming his allegiance was the leader of the Macdonalds of Glencoe — this inevitably led to the massacre.

As it happened the new deputy-governor, being a purely military appointment and a Campbell as well, meant that the orders were willingly carried out to the letter. Certainly Sir John Hill, the governor was not in favour of the action against the Glencoe Macdonalds and it was left to Major Robert Duncanson of the Argyle regiment and Lieutenant-Colonel James Hamilton, who was the new deputy-governor of Fort William, to arrange the massacre.

Major Duncanson, also a Campbell although he did not assume the chief's patronymic, then superior to Captain Robert Campbell of Glenlyon, directly ordered the massacre on the 12th February 1692.

Fortunately, the Independent Companies, although they were stationed at Fort William at this time, were not asked to carry out this act of treachery. It was left to Robert Campbell of Glenlyon and his Argyll regiment to carry out this deed. Having had hospitality for himself and his men from the Macdonalds for the period 1st to 12th February, in the dead of night rose and massacred most of

83

their hosts. This tragedy inevitably led to further Jacobite activities and the Highlands remained uncowed by this action by King William.

A large number of Independent Companies had been raised just prior to the battle of Killiecrankie in 1689. Only four of these were true Highland Companies.

1. *The Laird of Greenock's Company.* Captained by John Shaw yr. of Greenock. The company was raised at Greenock but no record remains concerning it's deployment or activities. Date of commission 25th April 1689.

2. *The Laird of Macfarlane's Company.* Captained by John Macfarlane yr. of that Ilk. The Laird financed the company from his own pocket, the Treasury only being liable for one Lieutenant, two Sergeants and a Piper. His only condition was that he be appointed Colonel with authority to name his own officers. Initially his offer was to was to raise a regiment of six companies of 50 men each drawn from his own clan, followers and friends. In fact, he only mustered 50 men to guard the passes between the Highlands and Dunbartonshire, which were so frequently used by the caterans. The company does not feature in any exploits which have been recorded and appeared to act solely in a containment role against cattle lifting.

3. *The Laird of Weem's Company.* Officially commissioned on 23rd August 1689 although it had already been in action with General Mackay at Killiecrankie. Captained by Robert Menzies yr. of Weem His exploits have been previously recorded. The other officers were Lieutenant Duncan Campbell: ensign Thomas Fleming plus NCOs and 100 private men.

4. *The Laird of Balnagown's Company.* The captain was David Ross of Balnagown. This company was raised in 1689 and it is thought that it saw action along with the Menzies company and associated with Leven's regiment. However, no definitive record exists of their presence on the day of the battle, although they did feature with the Laird of Weem's company in garrison duty in early July 1690 at Fort William.

All four Highland companies raised in 1689 were disbanded in 1690 by virtue of Treasury economics. The exception is the Laird of Weem's company which was incorporated with Colonel Sir John Hill's regiment on 16th July 1690.

It is difficult to understand the claim in the official Menzies records, where they state that this Independent Company remained viable under the captaincy of Robert Menzies's younger brother, Captain James Menzies of Comrie. It is also recorded that, in turn, his son John Menzies of Comrie took over command. To quote:-

> 'This kept the command of the first Independent Company of High-landers in the line of Menzies until the regiment was commissioned.'

The suggested explanation is that this company remained as a separate entity within the overall scope of Sir John Hill's regiment.

In July 1690 it was reported that some 10 Independent Companies were on the strength of Colonel Hill's regiment at Fort William, comprising mainly of clan Grant and clan Menzies sentinels. The Grants were under the command of Major John Forbes of Culloden (brother to the 3rd Laird), with the Menzies contingent under Captain Robert Menzies.

There are no recorded muster-rolls to back up this report and it is extremely doubtful if such a large number of Independent Companies ever existed. The actual total strength of Highlanders under Hill was known to be extremely variable at this time, bearing in mind the high rate of defection in these garrison situations.

It is also very unlikely that Major Forbes and Captain Menzies would have had more than the normal 100–120 sentinels under their separate command at any one time and it is difficult to believe that the government, normally tight-fisted in the extreme, would have willingly financed such a large group of soldiers committed mainly to garrison duties.

While Hill was trying to use the labour of the Highlanders physically to repair and refurbish the fort, he objected very strongly to the 'brutish' Grants, many of whom absconded when they were not allowed to pillage the local area. The Menzies men were scarcely better and equally did not take kindly to physical work, which they considered was below their dignity as fighting men.

It is worth retreating our footsteps to view what other chief and Independent Highland Company commanders were doing.

Prior to the massacre of Glencoe, the government was very divided in it's attitude towards the payment and training of Highland clansmen. On the one hand they could be used effectively to curb the worst excesses in terms of overall lawlessness: on the other hand there was the danger that soldiers being trained at the expense of King William, could be put at the disposal of King James if the occasion arose.

The Earl of Breadalbane, the second greatest Campbell chief and noted for his cunning and sagacity, suggested that perhaps the best way of solving this problem was that the government should fund a capital sum and that the chiefs should share in the interest derived from this sum as payment. This would ensure the continuity of their source of reward, but with the knowledge that the money could be withheld if their allegiance to William became suspect.

Breadalbane's territory lay centrally in the Highlands and was surrounded by a host of formidable Jacobite chiefs. Except for the Macdonalds (the arch enemy) Breadalbane seems to have been acceptable to the chiefs, as he apparently sympathised with their political fears and hopes. He was well known and trusted by most of the chiefs although a contemporary said of him:

> He is as cunning as a fox; wise as a serpent; but as slippery as an eel. No government can trust him but where his own private interest is in view.

The new government in Scotland was reluctant to commit this capital sum, although the notion that one of their chiefs could distribute such monetary bribes was appealing and if successful, would by-pass the need to arm and train soldiers who could in certain circumstances, be possibly used against the crown.

The authority for Breadalbane to conduct this negotiation with the other chiefs is dated 24th April 1690. The people approached were Macleans, Clanranald, Lochiel, Glengarry, the Mackenzies and Sir Donald Macdonald (Sleat). Their allegiance was either to be bought by money or by a promise of an earldom. To make the bribe more certain in it's result, the chiefs were further required to swear an oath of allegiance to William by the first of January 1692.

Those who failed to give this oath were threatened with the due consequences of being labelled treasonous and themselves liable to military attack and control.

The concerned chiefs, led by Lochiel, condescendingly agreed to make peace but only after being permitted to do so by their exiled King James.

It is not recorded whether the bribery money was ever circulated among the chiefs. According to Breadalbane, when queried on the subject, he said: 'The money is spent, the Highlands are quiet and this is the only way of accounting between friends.'

Furthermore, he afterwards said that along with the government money entrusted to him he had in addition 'spent another £2,000 in pacification.' and as this was his own money, he demanded repayment.

Another report from Colonel Hill, governor of Fort William dated 26th June 1660 stated:

> Breadalbane is the manager and hath met with Maclean, Lochiel and some others; but I find he hath done nothing with them. They (especially his cousin Lochiel) will not trust him. He tells them that the money for them is locked up in a chest in London; but they believe (if he say true in that) he will find way to keep a good part of it for himself.

With regard to the oath of allegiance most of the chiefs postponed their oath until the very last moment (January 1692) and even by February both Cameron of Lochiel and Glengarry had not submitted. However it was considered that the prime person to be made an example of was Macdonald of Glencoe, although the chief made strenuous efforts to comply with the dictat by William the Massacre went ahead.

The massacre destroyed any possible trust in King William's government and centred their trust in the return of the Stuarts.

1691 saw yet another reversal in government policy towards the subject of 'policing and containment' in the Highlands. So once more the Independent Companies were reinstated in 1691, following their earlier disbandment in 1690.

This ran contrary to another suggestion by Breadalbane that a 'Highland Militia' would be a more appropriate way of securing peace. But the old policy of recruiting Independent Companies linked with an efficient system of 'garrisons and strong Houses' throughout the land, was seen as the only reasonable answer to general disorder.

As a measure of efficiency of the Independent Companies a report in May 1691 by Lord Tarbet stated:

> The people hereabouts have robbed none all this winter but have been very peaceable and civil and later Wee are at present as peaceable hereabouts as ever, and all are quiet, except broken men and thieves.

There was another good reason for re-employing the services of the Independent Companies in various garrisons throughout the Highlands. English and Lowland Scottish troops did not take kindly to the conditions in the Highlands, where the rainfall was high,

87

where the weather was generally colder and where local food supplies were not suited to the bread and biscuit eating soldiery of the south.

All in all, garrison duty in the Highlands was the least sought after posting by both officers and men. While Colonel Hill did not favour the use of Highlanders at Fort William, General Mackay was far-seeing enough to recognise that local soldiers under their own Highland and gaelic-speaking officers, we better suited to the harder and more rigorous life in the northern garrisons.

Again Mackay summed up the situation succinctly from a safety point of view on behalf of the English and Lowland forces:

> When wee place south countreymen and strengers in those Highland countreys among the hills, they dare not stur a foot from their garison, by raison they cannot trust to the guidance of the country-men who are about all our garisons, and ennemis in their heart to our Kings service.

So in the view of the general unpopularity of serving in the Highlands it was found necessary and expedient to enlist the aid of the well-trained and well-proven Independent Companies in such a situation.

In 1691 the government acted by mustering five companies and they appeared on the Scottish establishment over a 20 month period from February 1691.

The first of these was commanded by Major George Munro and was mustered initially in February, March, April of 1691 at Finlayrige (Finlarig) and thereafter a year later in 1692. The company consisted of two officers, lieutenant Robert Taylor and ensign John Mitchell plus 6 non-commissioned officers, two drummers and 100 sentinels. Major George Monro (Munro) was thought to be Sir George Monro of Culcairn who had estates at Newmore in Easter Ross and who died in either 1693 or 1694. The company seemed to be mostly stationed at Finlarig, at the West end of Loch Tay, but occasionally at Fort William.

Then came the company captained by Major George Wishart, son of the Rev. William Wishart, who afterwards became a Lieutenant-Colonel in Hyndford's Dragoons.

Major Wishart's lieutenant was Alexander Ross and his ensign, James Murray. In common with other companies there were three sergeants, three corporals, 2 drummers and 100 sentinels. Mustering commenced in August, September, October 1691 with the first completed muster rolls dated 5th November 1691. The company was stationed at Abergeldie and receipts for pay started from 1st February 1691. Major Wishart and his company alternated between Abergeldie and Inverness, by sending a force of 50 men to the other garrison.

This company was soon followed by the formation of the third under the command of Lieutenant-Colonel Robert Lumsdaine of Invergelly. Musterings initially at Perth during May, June, July of 1691 and later at the Blair of Athole (Blair Atholl) until April of 1692. Muster strength again was 100 men in addition to lieutenant James Lumsden and ensign William Teisdale. Teisdale was replaced by John Heigham in August 1692. Colonel Lumsdaine was also to send 50 of his men on detachment to Fort William in December 1691.

May, June, July of 1691 saw also the formation of Captain Hugh Mackaye's company at Ruthven of Badenuch (Badenoch). The company was the same size as the others and was utilised on detachment between Ruthven and Inverness.

Lastly in this mustering series came the emergence of Captain Archibald Murray's company. Captain Murray was the son of Sir Archibald Murray of Blackbarony. The company was first mustered in August, September and October of 1691 at Ballandalloch (Ballindalloch). The company lieutenant was William Munro, with ensign Alexander Cuming and normal complement of non-commissioned officers and sentinels. Their force split half and half-alternated between Ballindalloch and Inverness. See Appendix 5.

Looking broadly at the five companies raised in 1691 and 1692, they formed a very effective line of garrisons throughout the central, northern and western Highlands. Had such a situation continued with some 500 men under arms, the Highlands would have remained reasonably peaceful. But, as ever, the upkeep cost of such an effective and well-situated force was thought to be too high and from 1693 onwards began a period of cutting back on a fairly large scale.

Firstly, the five were carried on the strength of various regiments within the regular army and latterly (9 February 1693) put on the pay list of two regiments about to be levied, those of Colonel Robert Mackay and Colonel George Hamilton. Then followed a constant series of changes as regiments were sent abroad or disbanded. The companies were then attached to other units and by April 1694 they appeared on the strength of Moncreiff's regiment, in a much diluted state in terms of numbers and Highland personnel. So ends a chapter in what might have remained as a positive force for peace in the Highlands.

In 1691 and 1692 there was almost universal peace throughout the Highlands with the Independent Companies occupying Finlarig, Blair Atholl, Aberfeldie, Ruthven and Ballindalloch. So much so that Colonel Hill reported 'Lochaber was as quiet as the streets of London or Edinburgh.'

So, on the absorption of the companies into forces raised for action in Ireland, Hill's regiment of regular troops, now on it's own, was forced to carry out all the garrison duties including those previously manned by the companies plus the additional locations of Duart, Cairnburgh and Eilean Donan. Fortunately it was a period of comparative peace which, in the early 18th Century, was doomed to break into open rebellion against the forces of the crown.

CHAPTER 11

The Act Of Union, Sheriffmuir and the Risings of 1708 and 1715 (1700–1717)

Not at all military but like the cloathing of the natives there, that they may the better discover any designs or machinations against the Government of the country. — Part of a War Office report in 1709 on the Independent Companies.

Wha the deil hae we got en for a King,
But a wee, wee German lairdie.
— *Jacobite Relics of Scotland*, James Hogg. (1770–1835)

Reigning Monarchs
William III (1689–1702)
Anne   (1702–1714)
George I   (1714–1727)

At the turn of the century two main forces still held sway in the Highlands.

The first was the split in the loyalties within the clan system, those clans who had Jacobite tendencies and those who favouring Whig principles, supported the governmental institutions.

In general terms, the Jacobites in the main came from the north east and from the Catholic and episcopalean coastal counties and the Outer Isles; the Macdonalds, Mackenzies, Camerons, Macintoshes, Macleans, Macphersons and other lesser clans. The Whig sympathisers were the Campbells, Mackays, Rosses, Munros, Grants, Forbes and those who came from north of the Great Glen and in the south west.

The second was the continuing belief that there was no great distinction between dealing and stealing – many clans felt it quite righteous 'to drive a spraigh'. Indeed many chiefs fostered the spirit of adventure to be found in reiving and saw it as excellent training for more war-like activities. It also offered some excitement for clansmen who lived a life of enforced idleness and with often a great deal of poverty.

In the years just before the turn of the century, there was a succession of poor harvests in the Highlands, the worst being in 1698 when the incessant rain virtually wiped out all crops. This in turn, stepped up the incidence of cattle stealing and robbery in general. Sometimes crime went beyond the normal cattle-rustling and on occasions cattle drovers were killed for their money, people of substance were kidnapped and attacks made against large houses.

In 1701, against the background of a very unstable situation pretty well everywhere in the mountains, two Independent Companies were brought back to help keep order along with units of the regular army.

Captain Alexander Campbell of Fonab on 24th June 1701 was commissioned as 'captain of a company added to Colonel James Ferguson's Regiment of Foot . . . for the security of the Highlands and adjacent counties' The strength of the company was less than those mustered in 1691/2 and reduced in 1693/4 and totalled only 3 sergeants, 2 corporals, 2 drummers, 1 piper and 60 sentinels.

The supporting officers were Colin Fairfoull as 1st Lieutenant and Campbell of Glendorowell as 2nd Lieutenant. First mustering was in August and September 1701 at Crief — thereafter at Killin and Kinachlachar in 1702 and 1703. Alexander Campbell of Fonab (variously spelled Finab, Finah, Finart), eldest son of Robert Campbell of Fonab, had an extremely interesting and diverse military career. Initially commissioned as a captain in the Earl of Argyll's Highland Regiment of Foot in 1693 and later in 1694–97 as captain in Lord Lornes's Regiment of Foot. In 1699 he was sent to join the African and Indian Company in Scotland and featured as the 'Hero of the Darien Expedition'. His military activities in Central America were the only bright spots in an otherwise disastrous Scottish financial venture. His force of 200 colonists and 40 Indians routed a very much larger force of nearly 1000 Spanish troops.

On his return to Scotland in June 1701, his Independent Company was attached to Colonel Ferguson's regiment (the Cameronians) and he was appointed a Brevet Lieutenant-Colonel. He also served for the Government against the Jacobites in the '15 Rising and took an active part in the fighting and prevented the western chiefs from joining the Earl of Mar, by his activities in Argyllshire when he was also responsible (via the deputy lieutenants) in raising the militia. He was also active in trying the persuade Lochiel, Sir Duncan Campbell of Lochnell and Stuart of Appin to remain out of the fray and indeed to join with him against the Earl of Mar. Unfortunately, Lochiel and Appin were not persuaded, and they 'went into the Rebellion'. After the battle of Sheriffmuir in 1715, he actively chased after the remnants of the Highland army in the north-east.

He remained in charge of his Independent Company until it was disbanded in 1717.

Again on 24th June 1701 Captain William Grant was commissioned and his company mustered at Lochness on October, November and December of that year. His 1st Lieutenant was Robert Urquhart of Burrisyards, and 2nd Lieutenant, Alexander Rose. Again only 60 sentinels were mustered initially at Lochness and later (in 1702/3) at Lochend of Ness and Killiwhinnen. Captain William Grant of Ballindalloch, 2nd son of James Grant, third of Rothiemurchus, raised the first Grant Company. He married in 1711; his date of death is unknown. The Ballindalloch family were the chief's principal supporters or Clan Captains and as such wore the single feather – Wm. Grant was 'a one-feather man'.

Both companies (Fonab's and Ballindalloch's) were split across two areas. Grant's company to look after the northern district and Campbell's to guard and patrol the southern district. Both companies were commissioned to be assistant to the courts of justice in preventing thefts and apprehending guilty persons.

In a further letter on 18 November 1701 King William divested that the two companies:

> must be always in motion from place to place, and in different conditions of service from our other regiments and companies, our Privie Councill have recommended them to you for full pay . . . and that the captains must provide cloaths and other necessaries both now and hereafter to their companies, who by reason of their special service will need the same more frequently.

Later in 1703 muster rolls showed a slight variation in commissioned officers listed and that, in the case of Fonab's company, the men were split into five groups with parties as Achalader, Poble, Glentarbert and Kilnabug with the main group at Kinchlachar. Ballindalloch's company, on the 14th July, was split into three with the main party at Killichiumen and the smaller bodies in Kintail and Badenoch.

While these two companies showed flexibility and some measure of control over large areas, they were not numerous enough in terms of men or patrols to be really effective in monitoring or controlling the widespread troubles. Indeed, the Earl of Tullibardine in February 1703, seeing that the Independent Companies were not coping with the situation, offered to raise a regiment of 800 of his own men to serve instead. His offer unfortunately contained the condition that no Campbell be allowed to serve in this regiment, as this would lead to fisticuffs among his followers. Needless to say his offer was not taken up!

In view of the small number of sentinels in each company a decision was made to add yet another company to look after 'by north and west Lochness', an area not effectively patrolled previously. This new commission was granted to Lieutenant-Colonel Duncan Mackenzie. While this was apparently a sound move to improve numbers some of the men mustered were taken from the existing two companies – 10 men, one sergeant and 1 piper from each; two men from each company within the Earl of Mar's and Lord Strathnaver's regiments; one man from each company of the Marquess of Lothian's and the Earl of Hyndford's dragoons. The muster roll is dated 1st June 1704:

> Captain – Lieut-Colonel Duncan Mackenzie
> Lieutenants John Mackenzie,
> Hugh Fraser of Dumballoch
> Two sergeants, 2 corporals, piper Duncan Bayne and 50 sentinels.

Duncan Mackenzie was the second son of Colin Mackenzie, second of Kincraig. Captain and brevet Lieut-Colonel Scots Guards 1704. Transferred as captain to this new Independent Company on 12 April 1704.

From 1705–07 the three companies are regularly recorded on the army strength. As the accounts of the Scottish Treasury cease with the Union of 1707, the last accounts of pay for the three companies are said to be in December of that year.

The Union itself seems to have had little effect on the formation or payment of the companies and as always, they formed some sort of defence against lawlessness and in many cases proved to be a deterrent against clans fully involving themselves in the Jacobite cause.

While the Independent Companies were carrying out fairly mundane duties and trying vainly 'to keep the peace on the Braes', the political situation was developing along lines which were to bring irrevocable changes between England and Scotland.

King William died in 1702 and left the crown of both countries in the hands of his sister-in-law, Anne. The situation with regard to the succession of the throne had already been agreed by Parliament some 12 months before William died. The crown was to pass to the Electress Sophia of Hanover, who was the grand-daughter of James VI. No discussion was held with Scotland over this matter and the Estates declared that it would make its own decision over this question and hinted that it would favour the young son James Francis Edward Stewart currently living at the royal court of St. Germain just outside Paris.

Before William died, he had anticipated the trouble over succession and had persuaded the English Parliament that they should opt for political union. While negotiations started in the first year of Anne's reign, they foundered when England would not grant Scotland the equal trading rights which were demanded by the Scots as their price for allowing the Electress to rule.

England then retaliated by outlawing the import of coal, linen and cattle from Scotland and further declared that Scots would become aliens if they did not agree to political union. The need to regain trading rights was undoubtedly the most important factor in the issue of union, especially as the Darien Venture had proved such a disastrously financial exercise for Scotland. England then agreed to pay Scotland £400,000 to liquidate their debts along with some repayment of the capital stock lost in the venture. The financial and political pressure was intense especially on the Scottish aristocracy. Two Scots, the Duke of Queensbury and the Earl of Mar along with the impoverished Duke of Hamilton led the Scots into the Union and in 1707 the Act of Union was a fait accompli.

Scotland was in an uproar over this most unpopular union and the Jacobites were heartened that this move would very much strengthen their cause in the country. The new Jacobite claimant to the throne declared that the time was now ripe for action. Many Scots noblemen and influential persons asked Louis XIV to back an expedition on behalf of James stating: 'the moment the King lands, the whole nation will rise and dissolve the present Government.'

Louis responded (March 1708) by arranging a small French naval force to carry the 19 year old James and some French troops to Scotland. The idea being that if he was accepted in Scotland this would force England to negotiate—England at this time was already locked in a crippling war with France. However, just before leaving Dunkirk the Pretender, James Edward Stewart caught measles and the whole effort was delayed. After James' recovery, the little flotilla set sail and anchored in the Firth of Forth, with a plan to land and to capture Stirling as their first objective. Meantime Jacobite leaders were in arms and ready to support them. However, Admiral Byng arrived with the British naval task force and the French fleet commander Admiral Forbin, deciding that discretion was the better part of valour, the French left without landing any troops or the Pretender. Scotland at this time was almost devoid of government troops and supported by only two weak Independent Companies. Had the French landed supported by the Jacobites, the outcome could have been successful for James and the Jacobite cause. This was perhaps the best opportunity for success in comparison with the succeeding Jacobite enterprises up to and including Culloden.

Meantime in the Highlands, the companies were kept busy in daily work trying to stop cattle lifting on a large scale. Lord Lovat claimed that by 1708 the companies had managed to control most of the serious robbery, but it is difficult to know just how accurate was his assessment of the situation. It was foremost in his mind that he would have liked the command of a company and wanted no other jurisdiction which might clash with his own regality.

The government's recipe for keeping order and policing the Highlands was based on the new Inverlochy garrison and surrounding fortified castles or houses: for the first time since the Restoration it assumed effective direct control over the Highlands. The warring and robbing chiefs were beginning to realise that their territories were no longer safe strongholds for rebellion and major crime.

In 1707 before the expected landing of James in Scotland, Colonel Grant's company was asked to keep a watch on the north-east coast which was the expected invasion spot. But as no-one could be expected to know when the landing could possibly take place and as the coastal area was so extensive, it was an almost impossible task for such a small group of men. Indeed there were also very strong counter rumours that the west coast would offer a safer landing place, although it was thought that such a venue would not encourage the considerable Lowland Jacobite support.

However, as the proposed landing did not in fact take place, due mainly to faint-heartedness on the part of Admiral Forbin, by late 1708 it was considered that as the invasion threat had so diminished it was fitting that the Independent Companies could return to their traditional duties of law-keeping in the Highland areas.

Little detail of the joint activities of the three companies between 1708 and 1715 has been recorded. In the year 1709 there were only 50 private men (sentinels) in each company, but in 1710 an exception was made in the case of the Grant company when up to 80 private soldiers were mustered — it is assumed that the reason for the extra men in this particular unit was due to the increased incidence of cattle lifting in the northern district. However, by 1715 numbers were again level in all companies with a total of only 49 in each including N.C.O.'s and officers. In the succeeding years of 1715, 1716 and 1717, the numbers were again raised to 70 private men in each. The names of the commanders at this time were recorded as Colonels Campbell, Grant and Munro. This latter name meant that in this 1715–17 period Colonel Munro must have replaced Colonel Duncan Mackenzie.

The three companies also played an active part before and after the battle of Sheriffmuir in 1715. Already mentioned was the fact that Campbell of Forab was active in the west and north trying to dissuade the clans (mainly Camerons, Stewarts of Appin and Campbell of Lochness), from joining the Earl of Mar. He was only partially successful in this venture. After the battle he 'harried the Rebells' in the north east. Colonel Munro also after the battle was active, along with a detachment of Sutherlands, Mackays and Rosses, in trying to disperse the Highlanders who had fought under the Earl of Mar.

Munro was also governor of Inverness for a time and along with some regular troops, forced the rebel Mackenzies to give up their arms at Brahan, where they made Lord Seaforth's home 'a garrison for his Majesty King George.' He also along with parties of Grants, Rosses, Mackays, forced the surrender of the Earl of Seaforth at the Moor of Gilliechriest. Colonel Grant played a lesser part in containing the rebels following Sheriffmuir, but helped in establishing a garrison at Brahan. He also took possession of Castle Gordon and maintained it until they were relieved by regular troops.

In the number 1 company, led by Campbell of Fonab, the 1st Lieutenant was Colin Fairfull with 2nd Lieutenant Colin Campbell.

With the No. 2 company, commanded by colonel William Grant the 1st Lieutenants were, successively:

Allan Cameron 1712
James Macpherson 1714
Colin Campbell of Skipnish 1715

2nd Lieutenants were, successively:

> James Gordon of Barnes 1706
> Daniel MacNeil 1715

The strength of this company between 1707 and 1717 remained at around 50 sentinels in addition to NCO's and commissioned ranks.

For a period following 1707 a cut back in pay was introduced and the two lieutenants had to accept ensign's pay. This was yet another example of the penny-pinching way the Independent Companies were treated. When all was well and quiet within the countryside there was a tendency to hold back on remuneration.

The third company, initially led by Colonel Duncan Mackenzie, had successively Colin Campbell in July 1714, Robert Munro in August 1714 and Simon, Lord Lovat in June 1716 as Captains. The 1st Lieutenant in March 1711 was Roderick Bayne and John Campbell of Carrick in August 1714. The 2nd Lieutenant in August 1714 was Alexander Fraser of Culduthell.

During the period prior to the 1715 rising and following the accession of George I in 1714, the Jacobites were again convinced that they had a more than fair chance of restoring the Stewart monarchy by rebellion. The Union was bitterly resented in Scotland, an English spy reported, 'I never saw a nation so universally wild.' England seemed determined that Scottish industry would not have advantages that the Union should have brought about. The staple industry, the manufacture of linen, had a heavy export tax imposed upon it and English merchants persuaded the government to subsidise the Irish linen trade instead. American wood was imported in preference to Scottish timber. Many other unfair practices were imposed upon Scotland at this time and the maxim 'have we not bought the Scots and a right to tax them?' summed up a most unfair situation.

The Earl of Mar, known as 'Bobbin' John because of his lack of consistency — raised the Jacobite standard on the Braes of Mar in September 1715. His movement was committed to replacing the much hated Act of Union and in the this he got the backing of many of the Scottish chiefs and nobles.

George Keith, Earl Marischal of Scotland joined Mar along with the Earl of Airlie and the Earl of Southesk. Those who 'came out' for James VIII included the Earl of Seaforth, the Marquis of Huntly, the first Duke of Atholl, the Macgregors, the Macdonells of Glengarry and Keppoch, the Camerons, Clan Mackintosh and even the Earl of Braedalbane. The Jacobites occupied Perth and Inverness. The Battle of Sheriffmuir near Dunblane, was the only real battle in the Rising, and even with a 2 to 1 numerical superiority Mar contrived to bring about a very dubious and negative result. Again, as in the 1708 Rising, the chance was lost and this time undoubtedly through indecisive leadership.

Had Mar swept aside the Hanoverian forces, led by Argyll, at Sherrifmuir and linked up with Jacobites from the North of England, it is doubtful if the Hanoverian cause could have survived. With all the support he had from the main Highland chiefs and nobles, it was almost inconceivable that he should have lost the cause. An observer after the battle wryly exclaimed — 'it required real talent for Mar to lose the game.'

It is difficult to establish exactly how the Independent Companies featured in the '15 Rising, but some unsubstantiated reports indicate that a portion of the companies (partly Grant and partly Munro) actually fought at Sherriffmuir against their Jacobite cousins under the generalship of Argyll. It has been definitely established that their main activities were to be seen in pre-battle action in dissuading clansmen from joining Mar and in escorting arms from Glasgow to Inveraray for the use of militia forces.

As already recorded, after-battle actions consisted of harrying some of Mar's defeated clansmen and occupying castles and fortified houses until the regular troops arrived. Their role in convincing clans not to join in the Rising is difficult to quantify and while they enjoyed a partial success in this matter with Duncan Campbell of Lochness, both Cameron of Lochiel and Stewart of Appin joined the Jacobites. The companies also had valuable help from the predominant Whig clans (Sutherlands, Mackays, Rosses and Munros) and they, simply under their clan banner, exerted influence in trying stop Seaforth joining in the fray. In the background also was Forbes of Culloden, who along with Ross of Killravock, Lord Lovat and some Grants managed to head off Macdonell of Keppoch ('Coll of the Cows') from joining with the Mackenzies at Inverness. In these complex and often confusing exercises, the three company captains (Munro, Campbell and Grant) co-ordinated and took command of the unregimented Whig clans in denying the Earl of Mar any more reinforcements. An another example of the actions of the Whig clans, (mainly Sutherlands, but aided by Mackays, Rosses and

Munros) was seen when Seaforth was drawn to Alnes for a period up to October 15th and so missed the battle at Sheriffmuir on the 13th.

Later on, these very Whig clans were to feature very largely in the formation of the 18 Independent Companies which were to be raised in 1745/6 by the stout efforts of Duncan Forbes of Culloden.

After the '15 Rising had fizzled out, the Independent Companies were widely used in disarming the rebel Highlanders. Colonel Munro of Foulis, aided by his brother Munro of Culcairn, accepted the arms given up at Blair Atholl while the Grant Company disarmed the clansmen at Ruthven in Badenoch and also at Fort William. Certain resistance to handing over weapons surfaced at Brahan and a compromise was reached when regular troops, with companies in the background, actually carried out the disarming exercise. This defused a difficult situation and saved a great deal of Highland pride. However, in defiance of the spirit if not the letter of the Disarming Act, the Highlanders, more often than not, hid their best and treasured weapons and handed in useless and damaged ones. However, this seemed to satisfy the authorities.

By 1717, the government passed an Act of Grace which in effect pardoned all the rebel clans — again with one exception the infamous clan Gregor.

In Scotland, most people were very cautions about using the word Rebellion or Rising and were often heard to use the phrase the Affair or the Scrape of 1715.

Now that an uneasy peace had descended yet again in the land, the economic situation improved and in 1717 an excuse was found 'to reduce the Companies'.

General Wade, who was to play such a prominent part in the future of the Companies, in a letter to King George I, was reported to have commented about the 1717 disbandments in this manner:

> They were composed of the natives of the country, injured to the fatigue of travelling the mountains, lying on the hills, wore the same habit and spoke the same language; but for want of being put under proper regulations corruptions were introduced, and some who commanded them instead of bringing criminals to justice (as I am informed) often compounded for the theft, and for a sum of money set them at liberty. They are said also to have defrauded the government by keeping not above half their numbers in constant pay, which (as I humbly conceive) might be the reason your Majesty caused them to be disbanded.

CHAPTER 12
General Wade to the Rescue
(1717–1739)

Where did the name Black Watch come from?

An equally plausible theory is that the 'Black' stands not for the colour of the kilt, but for the black Hanoverian hearts of the wearers of the kilt. Black as the pit, black as the forest of Rannoch, blacklegs, they must have seemed to the rebellious Jacobite clans. After all, non-Campbells in Scotland still talk cheerfully and automatically about 'black Campbells'. Or how about 'Black' for the Blackmail which the Highland Watch was in business to suppress? Philip Howard in his book *The Black Watch*.

Reigning Monarchs:
George I   (1719–1727)
George II   (1727–1760)

After 1717 and the reduction of the Independent Companies, there followed a period when the security of the Highlands was left in the hands of regular troops based on the four main garrisons — Inverlochy (Fort William), Killichiuman (Fort Augustus), Bernera in Glenelg and Ruthven in Badenoch. To back up the regular troops and to act as guides and interpreters in an area virtually devoid of roads and where Gaelic was the common language of the day., some thirty Highlanders were posted in each garrison along with their Highland officers. The main function of this regular army/Highland Company mixture in each garrison was to maintain peace, to cut down on robbery and general mayhem but also to ensure that the Highlanders did not rise in arms yet again.

The Highland soldiers in their companies did not form Independent Companies in any sense. Their members were not necessarily of an accredited clan, nor were they raised by the backing and efforts of the clan chief.

These sentinels and officers were drawn from a wide variety of

101

sources, often men from 'broken' clans and at best could be described as temporary or interim Highland Companies. So from a period from 1717 to 1724 the true Independent Companies ceased to exist as such and it is correct to say that this very interim organisation of Highlanders was a failure.

One of their officers (Robert Gordon of Haughes) was commissioned to apprehend:

> All thieves, robbers, and trafficking priests within the sheriffdoms of Dumbarton, Stirling, Perth, Argyll, Angus, Kincardine, Aberdeen, Banff, Elgin, Nairn, Inverness, Cromarty, Ross, Sutherland, and Caithness.

It was patently obvious that this limited force could do very little against a very disturbed situation across virtually the whole of Scotland north of the Highland line.

Meanwhile some four years after the 'Fifteen', James Stuart found an unlikely ally in Spain to support his Jacobite cause. Initially the Spanish force was 5,000 strong and bringing with it arms for a further 30,000 to dispense among the Jacobite clans. However, when this force sailed from Corunna it was struck by a gale which raged for almost two days. The invasion fleet was scattered, stores and guns were lost along with many of the soldiers. — Shades of the Spanish Armada some 130 years previously.

Eventually, only some 330 regular Spanish soldiers made it to Scotland, there to be joined by Lochiel's Camerons, MacGregors under Rob Roy, Mackenzies and a few Atholl men.

Against them were the Government forces led by Major-General Wightman, who had also fought at Sheriffmuir. He had under his command 850 regular infantry, 120 dragoons and some hastily mustered Independent Company men from the Grant and Munro clans, 130 in all.

The Spanish force, very much reduced in numbers, landed on the shores of Loch Alsh and marched inland as far as Glen Shiel and placed their stores and ammunition in that rugged stronghold castle Eilean Donan. But on the 10th of May 1719 Captain Boyle, in command of three British warships, battered the castle and it's 45 Spanish guards into submission. Meantime, the main Spanish party and the assorted Jacobite clansmen chose the narrow Glenshiel for the encounter. The Hanoverian forces and the Jacobites had roughly equal numbers — about 1,000 each.

The Munros were a very staunch Whig clan and their Independent Company, most ably led by Captain George Munro of Culcairn (younger brother of Sir Robert Munro of Foulis), guided the Government forces through the mountains and led the way up the slopes of Glenshiel, following a most accurate a mortar barrage. For some 3 hours the battle raged but the superior power of the Hanoverian grenadiers along with the aggressive forays of the Munros won the day for the Hanoverians.

The Jacobite leaders decided that there was no hope in further guerrilla tactics and the clansmen simply disappeared back to their glens. In view of this, the remaining Spaniards, with no support and now no ammunition, surrendered to Wightman. This '19 Rising was initially well conceived but ill-luck dogged the main invasion force of 5,000 who were due to land and establish a bridgehead in the West of England — the storm saw to that. The failure of the '19 Highland affair was also due to the lack of support from the Jacobite clans. Lochiel only supplied 150 men, Seaforth did better with 500 Mackenzies and Lord George Murray could only muster a handful of men from Perthshire.

The Independent Company of Munros evidently played a major role in the battle and proved yet again how important it was to know the land, and to recognise how to fight effectively against their own countrymen.

Captain George Munro of Culcairn did not wait for permission from the Government to raise an Independant Company from among the Munro clan. The Company was primarily mustered from his father's clan and George Munro paid all expenses (in wages and arms) from his own pocket. It is said that he expressed a hope concerning repayment by the government, but the government, always tight-fisted once the trouble had been settled, conveniently forgot to settle up.

To add insult to injury, or rather injury to insult, Culcairn was badly wounded in the thigh during the battle.

The senior Jacobite General the Earl Marischal, James Keith, having seen his plans dashed by the 'ruffle at Glenshiel' when trying to capture Inverness, now fled to the Western Isles with Seaforth and Tullibardine. Before leaving for France the Earl Marischal is reported to have said to his Jacobite forces 'make your way wherever you please' — a rather sad and inept phrase to end an enterprise of some magnitude.

The years between the '19 and the '45 Risings were particularly difficult for all Scottish people — chiefs, nobles and clansmen alike.

103

In order to punish those who had rebelled against the government, a legal system was introduced whereby landed property could be transferred 'from the rebels to the well — affected'. However, when the government tried too hard to invoke legal powers, it ran into a reluctance by both the judges and the juries to bring about convictions. The whole judicial system, from the Edinburgh lawyers to the judges, was seen to be extremely conservative in attitude and in general shied away from any commitment to forfeit heritable estates.

The 'Commissioners Appointed to Enquire of the Estates of certain Traitors in that Part of Britain called Scotland' ran into a great deal of trouble when most of the Scottish judges adjudicated against them whenever possible. The main obstructions came from the legal ploys, where the estates under duress were ordered to pay off relatively small fines and were therefore immune from forfeiture, while these unimportant legal wrangles were being addressed. The payment of legitimate debts had to be recognised as a prime factor by the Government, even if the estate was overdue for forfeiture. In this way, certain important Jacobite chiefs and landowners were allowed to go Scot-free because of these minor legal niceties and errors in the form of indictments.

Meantime in the Highlands attempts were made via a Disarming Act to control any future risings or outbursts of violence. All clans, including those who supported the Government, were asked to surrender their weapons. The loyal Whig clans conformed to the letter but the Jacobite followers either chose to ignore the order, or handed in weaponry which was obsolete, broken or of very little further use.

The Disarming Act was very badly regulated and under the Act, payment was to be given for arms delivered up. Even the obsolete and broken arms were valued at above their actual price and there was a brisk trade with Holland at this time for such useless weapons, so that they could be exchanged for cash. The net effect of this exercise was that the Jacobite Highlanders were better off financially while still retaining their main arms. The Act, in total, cost the Government some £13,000. They were not to make the same mistake when a further Disarming Act was invoked in 1725.

Scotland appeared to be a land bowed down with failure and calamity, the unpopular Union with England; no increase in trade; interference with the Scottish legal system; the abolition of the Scottish Privy Council, the imposition of a Malt tax where the duty

on malt was three times as high as in England; the failure of the
'08, '15, '19 Risings; the disastrous Disarming Act of 1716, where
the loyal clans gave up their weapons leaving them to the mercy of
the disloyal clans and therefore a return to a more lawless state.

It was time for change and part of that change came about from
a most unlikely source — Lord Lovat, chief of clan Fraser and an
arch-schemer of great reknown. Much of what he wrote to George I
in 1724 was obviously meant for his own financial, social and
political benefit but he showed a great sense of understanding of
what had become an almost impossible situation in the Highlands.
He made suggestions which, if one removes his unique and personal
ambition, made a great deal of sense in an age where the rule of law
was, more often that not, the rule of the claymore.

He started off in his famous Memorial by stating:

> That the people of the Highlands are entirely different from those of
> the Lowlands in language and dress, and 'do remain to this day much
> less civilized.' They are 'very ignorant, illiterate, and in constant use
> of wearing arms, which are well suited to their method of using them,
> and very expeditious in marching from place to place.'

He then talks of the 'quarrels and jealousies among the chiefs', and
continues:

> the use of arms in the Highlands will hardly ever be laid aside, till,
> by degrees, they begin to find they have nothing to do with them. And
> it is no wonder, that the laws establishing the succession of the crown,
> should be too little regarded by those who have not hitherto been used
> to a due compliance with any law whatsoever . . . One of the evils
> which furnishes the most matter of complaint at present is the
> continual robberies and depredations in the Highlands, and the
> country adjacent. The great difficulty in this matter arises from the
> mountainous situation of these parts, and remoteness from towns,
> and part thereof consisting of islands, dispersed up and down the
> western seas, the criminals cannot be found by any methods now
> practised, much less seized and brought to justice, being able to
> outrun these they cannot resist . . . The bad consequences of those
> robberies are not the only oppression which the people suffer in the
> loss of their cattle and other goods — but by the habitual practices
> of violence and illegal extractions. The Highlanders disuse all their
> country business, they grow averse to all notions of peace and
> tranquility, they constantly practise their use of arms, they . . .
> increase their numbers, by drawing many into their gang who would

105

otherwise be good subjects, and they remain ready and proper materials for disturbing the government upon the first occasion.

Lovat then dismisses how ineffective the law has become and how people were forced to pay protection money. This was called 'Black Meall'.

In turn he discusses the raising of Independent Highland Companies during King William's reign and just how successful they had been in policing the Highlands.

> 'But after the late unnatural rebellion, the Highlanders, who had been in arms against the government, fell into their old unsettled way of living, laying aside any little industry they had formerly followed, and returned to their usual violence and robberies.'

Lovat then describes at some length just how disastrous was the Disarming Act of 1716 and how it left the clans loyal to the Government virtually defenceless against subsequent pillage and robbery. Also, that the disbandment of the Independent Companies in 1717 encouraged the lawless situation to run riot:

> Thus, then, violences are now more notorious and universal than ever, in so much, that a great part of the country has, by necessity, been brought under the scandalous contributions before mentioned (i.e. Black meall).

He then went on to reinforce the need for the reinstatement of the Independent Companies in preference to regular lowland and English troops:

> After the disarming Act was passed, and those companies were broke, there were some other measures laid down for preserving the peace of the Highlands. Barracks were built at a very great expense, and detachments were made from the regiments in the neighbourhood to garrison them, and to take post in those places which were thought most proper for the repressing these disorders; but all this had no effect. The regular troops were never used to such marches, with their usual arms and accutrements; were not able to pursue the Highlanders; their very dress was a signal to the robbers to avoid them; and the troops, who were strangers to the language and often relieved by others, could never get any useful intelligence, nor even be sufficiently acquainted with the situation of the several parts of the country, so as to take the necessary measure for pursuing the robbers when any violence was committed.

106

This was then followed by a plea to re-establish a proper and effective legal background which was so necessary for overall peace in the countryside:

> The officers of the law, for the peace, are the Sheriffs and Justices of the Peace; and, in time of commotions, the Lieutenants and their deputies; which office, long disused, was revived and re-established at the time of the late rebellion . . . It would seem to be highly necessary to the government, that the Sheriffs and Lord Lieutenants should be persons having credit and interest in the shyre they are to govern.

This Memorial was shrewdly written and argued and while it clearly announced that Lovat was the man to bring about 'the ideal situation' in the Highlands, George I and his advisers were not taken in by his pleas. This is not to deny the very precise and cogent points which Lord Lovat, as a major and powerful chief brought forward as answer to most of the pressing problems in the Highlands.

So George I decided to ask the opinion of a person who had less to gain from such radical suggestions — this person was General George Wade, an Irishman, who was to feature largely in the future of Scotland and the British army over the immediate 22 years and the subsequent 250 years.

George Wade was a Protestant soldier, born in Ireland, who had seen much actual service in Flanders, Portugal and Spain in the Wars of the Spanish Succession. He was extremely able and conscientious and was a man with considerable reputation as an administrator and security specialist.

Following George's command, on the 3rd July 1724 General Wade was sent to the Highlands to report (in Wade's own words):

> . . . how far the Memorial delivered to Your Majesty by Simon Lord Lovat and his Remarks thereupon are founded on Facts, and the present Practices of those People; and whether the Remedies mentioned therein may properly be applied for preventing the Several Grievances, Abuses, and Violences complained of in the said Memorial.

General Wade's subsequent report was submitted to the King on the 10th December of the same year. In many ways it echoed the sentiments and the facts which were contained in Simon Lovat's Memorial.

He confirmed that the Disarming Act had been both ineffective and counter-productive, that blackmailing of almost all the Low Country was a feature of Highland life, the principal offenders being the Camerons, Mackenzies and the McDonnell's of Keppoch, the Broadalbin Men, and the McGregors on the Borders of Argyleshire.

To Wade, as his report confirmed, the majority of Highlanders were disloyal savages living in chaos and anarchy: however, he was later to renounce this sentiment as he came to understand the Highlanders better. He also reported that Justices of the Peace were very few in number and indeed that three of the deputy Sheriffs in Inverness-shire were Jacobite supporters during the '15 Rising.

Wade stated that there were 22,000 clansmen in the Highlands available as fighting men 'and capable of bearing arms'. However

> only 10,000 of those were well-affected towards the Government, the remainder have been engaged in Rebellion against your Majesty, and are ready, whenever encouraged by their Superiors or Chiefs of Clans, to create new Troubles and rise in Arms in favour of the Pretender.

There came a discussion on how clans were organised, the method of fighting and the Black-Meal. In turn he pointed the finger at those clans who were at the root of the troubles.

Described in detail is the method employed by the reivers:

> Those who are robbed of their Cattle (or Persons employed by them) follow them by the Tract and often recover them from the Robbers by Compounding for a certain sum of Money agreed on, but if the Pursuers are Armed and in Numbers Superior to the Thieves and happen to seize any of them, they are seldom or never prosecuted, the poorer sort being unable to support the charge of Prosecution . . .
> They are likewise under the Apprehension of becoming the Object of their Revenge, by having their Houses and Stacks burnt, their Cattle stolen or hockt, and their lives at the Mercy of the Tribe or Clan to whom the Banditti belong. The Richer sort (to keep, as they call it, good Neighbourhood) generally compound with the Chieftain of the tribe or Clan, for double Restitution, which he willingly pays to save one of his Clan from Prosecution, and this is repaid by a Contribution from the Thieves of his Clan, who never refuse the payment of their proportion to save one of their own fraternity. This Composition is seldom paid in Money, but in Cattle stolen from the opposite side of the Country to make reparation to the Person injured . . . The Chiefs of some of these Tribes never fail to give Countenance and protection to those of their own clan; and tho' they are taken and committed to Prison, by the Plantiff, [who is] better satisfied than if the Criminal

was Executed, since he must [be] at the Charge and Trouble of a tedious dilatory and expensive Prosecution and I was assured by one who annually attended the Assizes at Inverness for four Years past, that there had been but one person Executed there by the Lords of Justiciary and that (as I remember) for Murder, tho' that Place is the Judicature, in Criminal Cases, for the greatest part of the Highlands.

Wade then outlines yet another twist to the cattle-lifting story:

There is another Practice used in the Highlands, by which the Cattle stolen are often recovered, which is, by sending Persons to that part of the Country most-suspected, and making an offer of a Reward (which the Highlanders call Tascal-Money) to any who will discover the Cattle and the Persons who stole them . . . By the temptation of the Reward and promise of Secrecy, discoveries were often made and Restitution obtained. But to put a Stop to a practice they thought an injury to the Tribe, the whole Clan of the Camerons (and others since by their example) bound themselves by Oath never to take Tascal-Money, nor to inform one against the other. This they take upon a Drawn Dirk or Dagger, which they kiss in a solemn manner, and the Penalty declared to be due to the said Oath is to be stabbed with the same Dagger. This manner of Swearing is much in practice on all other occasions, to bind themselves one to another that they may with more security exercise their Villany, which they imagine less Sinful than the Breach of that Oath, since they commit all sorts of Crimes with impunity, and are so severely punished if forsworn. An instance of this happened in December 1723, when one of the Clan of the Camerons, suspected to have taken Tascal-Money, was in the Night-time called out of his Hut from his Wife and Children and hanged up near his own Door. Another of that Tribe was, for the same Crime (as they call it), kept a month in the Stocks and afterwards privately made away with.

Then followed an outline of the saga of the Independent Companies to date and how they had failed in their previous form. Also that the reason for disbanding (in 1717) was one which reflected the King's mistrust in their method of payment and their misuse of public moneys:

The Independent Companies raised by King William not long after the Revolution reduced the Highlanders into better order than at any time they had been in since the Restauration. They were composed of the Natives of the Country, inured to the fatigue of Travelling the Mountaines, lying on the Hills, wore the same Habit and spoke the

109

same Language; but for want of being put under proper Regulations, Corruptions were introduced, and some who Commanded them, instead of bringing Criminals to Justice (as I am informed) often compounded for the Theft and for a Sum of Money set them at Liberty. They are said also to have defrauded the Government by keeping not above half their Numbers in constant pay: which, as I humbly conceive, might be the reason Your Majesty caused them to be disbanded.

At the end of the report he then mentions the need for good communication within the Highland area:

> Before I conclude this Report, I presume to observe to your Maty, the great Disadvantages Regular Troops are under when they engage with those who Inhabit Mountainous Situations. The Sevennes in France, and Catalans in Spain, have in all times been Instances of this Truth. The Highlands of Scotland are still more impracticable, from the want of Roads and Bridges, and from excessive Rains that almost continually fall in those parts, which by Nature and constant use become habitual to the Natives, but very difficultly supported by the Regular Troops.

The summary of his initial report seemed to go right to the heart of the matter and shows considerable insight in one who only had a few months to study the most complex situation in the Highlands and to come up with solutions to troubles which almost seemed insoluble a few years previously.

In three short months after the report Wade had produced specific and positive recommendations.

Firstly and most importantly, he wanted to revive the Independent Companies. His suggestion was three companies, commanded by captains, to have between 60 to 70 private men with another three Companies, this time led by lieutenants, with only half that complement of sentinels. This meant a total force of 6 companies and 300 men in all. In Wade's own words:

> That Companies of such Highlanders as are well affected to his Majesty's Government be Established, under proper Regulations and Commanded by Officers speaking the Language of the Country . . . That the said Companies be employed in Disarming the Highlanders, preventing Depredations, bringing Criminals to Justice, and hinder Rebells and Attainted Persons from inhabiting that part of the Kingdom.

110

While Wade was counselling that Independent Companies should be brought back, many local and private 'watches' were being organised by landowners or localities to protect their interests. Robert Campbell, alias Macgregor, the notorious Rob Roy, levied 'watch-money' and was followed by his nephew MacGregor of Glengyle in the Lennox area: shortly before the '45 Macdonald of Barisdale had a watch in Ross-shire and Strathglass; Macdonald of Lochgarry in Strath Errick and probably the biggest and most far-reaching of all, Cluny MacPherson who operated in the huge area between Loch Ness and Dundee.

The idea behind Wade's suggestion was to replace these unofficial private and quasi-watches, so open to roguery, by a regulated force of Independent Companies controlled and under strict military discipline.

Wade also proposed that a barracks be erected at Inverness to prevent Highlanders attacking the fertile lowland areas of the north-east and to prevent rebellious gatherings. Also the barracks at Killihuimen (the present Fort Augustus) which was built in 1716 was to be strengthened and altered by building a reboubt by the lochside plus a connection to the barracks.

To complete the communication between the barracks at Inverness and Fort Augustus he advised:

> That a small Vessel with Oars and Sails be built on the Lake Ness, sufficient to carry a Party of 60 or 80 Soldiers and Provisions for the Garrison, which will be a Means to keep the Communication open between that place and Inverness, and be a safe and ready way of sending Parties to the Country bordering on the said Lake, which is Navigable for the largest Vessels.

General Wade envisaged that the line of three garrisons along the Great Glen would enable Government troops to sally forth and crush any potential gathering or even rebellion. He saw Fort Augustus as 'the most Centrical part of the Highlands,' equal distance from Fort William and Inverness where perhaps up to 1,000 men could be utilised from these garrisons/forts at very short notice. There was also an assumption that the barracks at Bernera (in Glenelg) would hold a small number of troops equal to any military task in Skye and the neighbouring islands.

Equally, that Ruthven in Badenoch could cope with troubles south of the Great Glen.

The legal position in the Highlands was proposed to be made

111

more efficient . . . (i.e. 'proper Persons') to be nominated Sheriffs and Deputy Sheriffs. Also that Justices of the Peace peace and Constables be established for seizing and sending criminals to prison.

Quarter sessions to be held regularly at Killihuimen, Ruthven, Fort William and if necessary at Bennera in Glenelg. Also proposed was an Act of Parliament to punish Highlanders who carried or concealed arms contrary to the law. Because fines could not be readily collected, the punishment for illegal possession of arms could be transportation, even for a first offence.

Lastly, and something which was to be a lasting memorial to this far-seeing Irish soldier, was his effort in establishing communication in the Highlands. The table and map following show the extent of his road and bridge building.

The estimated distances are taken from King's Warrant Books and Treasury Papers, and the map shows the extent of his work visually.

Fort William – Fort Augustus	1725	30 miles
Fort William – Inverness	1726	31 miles
Inverness – Dunkeld	1727–29	102½ miles
Crieff – Dalnacardoch	1730–31	43¼ miles
Dalwhinnie – Fort Augustus	1732	28 miles
Catcleugh – Ruthven	?	8 miles
		242¾ miles

Of great importance also was his development in the building and re-building of Highland forts and garrisons — mainly at Fort Augustus; Fort George (Inverness); Fort William; Ruthven in Badenoch and Bernera in Glenelg. Wade, in addition, had garrisons in smaller yet key places — e.g. Dumbarton Castle, Blackness Castle and Inversnaid on Loch Lomond.

However far-seeing his road and garrison building might have been, it was his effect on the re-organisation of the regular army and most importantly, the Independent Companies, which led to the formation of the first Highland regiment and thence subsequently to other Highland regiments long after his death.

Wade was a very great friend of Duncan Forbes of Culloden, Lord President of the Court of Session and they drank many 'bumpers,' together while they planned to bring Scotland to a peaceful way of life. These two men, singly and jointly were to have the most profound effect on the history of Scotland in the years to come.

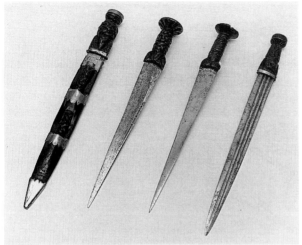

Highland Dirks, showing the evolution from the long knife of the 17th century to the Officer's dress weapon of Victorian times. *National Museums of Scotland.*

Claymore, or more correctly, basket-hilted sword, with an imported Andria Ferara blade. Hilt by John Allan, Stirling, dated 1716. Decorated with chased work and inlaid with silver. *National Museums of Scotland.*

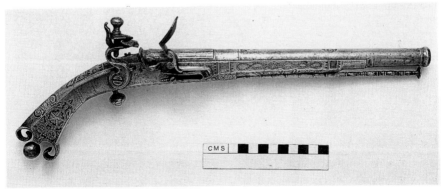

Pistol, flintlock all-steel, with a scroll of 'ramshorn' butt. Made in Doune by Thomas Caddell around 1700. *National Museums of Scotland.*

Plug and socket bayonets, for use with matchlock musket.
Top: 16th century claymore or 'Twa-handit' sword.
Bottom: Basket-hilted broadsword of the time of Jacobite risings.

an example of both plug and socket bayonets

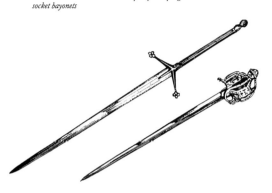

a 16th-century claymore and the basket-hilted broadsword of the Jacobite risings

Officer and Private Man. After a rare engraving of Highland Soldiers of *circa* 1745, supposed to have been executed by one of the brothers Van der Gucht (it is signed 'V.G. del.'), who were engravers in London at that time. This plate was subsequently copied, with slight alterations, and published by Bowles in 1746, and by Grose for his *Military Antiquities*, in 1788. Both figures and uniform details are better drawn than in most other engravings of Highlanders of that period.

TARTAN LENGTH

MIDDLE SECTION ROUGHLY PLEATED WITH A BELT UNDERNEATH. THE MAN LIES DOWN WITH THE BOTTOM LEVEL JUST ABOVE HIS KNEES. HE WRAPS EACH SIDE OVER HIM AND DOES UP THE BELT, AND THEN STANDS UP.

AS HE STANDS UP THE LARGE LOOSE AREA FALLS DOWN LOOKING MOST UNSIGHTLY.

THE LOOSE PART IS TWISTED AND PULLED OVER THE SHOULDER AND TUCKED OR TIED UNDERNEATH THE WAIST BELT THE SIDE FLAPS ARE TUCKED INTO THEMSELVES TO MAKE POCKETS.

THE LATER BELTED-PLAID DIFFERS ONLY IN THE ATTACHMENT TO THE SHOULDER WITH A BROOCH.

How a belted-plaid was worn. Abstract from *Scottish Military Dress*, Peter Cochrane.

In folchem Habit Gehen die 800 In Stettin angekommen Irrländer oder Irren.

Es ift ein Starckes dauerhafftigs Volck behilff fich mit geringer fpeiß hatt es nicht brodt fo Effen fie Würtzeln, Wans auch die Notturfft erfordert Können fie des Tages Uber die 20 Teütfcher meilweges lauffen, haben neben Mufqueden Ihre Bogen vnd Köcher vnd lange Meffer.

German broadsheet of 1631, showing Highlanders, often mistakenly described as 'Irelander oder Irren.' Possibly Mackay's regiment under Gustavus Adolphus. *The British Library.*

Captain Robert Menzies (1660–1692), fought at Killicrankie under General Mackay against forces of Viscount Dundee. Commander of Menzies Independent Company of 100 men. *Clan Menzies Society.*

King James VIII of Scotland and III of England (The Old Pretender),
landing at Peterhead in January 1716. By this time the rising was over. *Scottish
National Portrait Gallery.*

Eilean Donan Castle on Loch Duich. The Spanish garrison surrendered to the Royal Navy
during the 1719 rising and after heavy bombardment. *Royal Commission on the Ancient and
Historical Monuments of Scotland.*

General (later Field-Marshal) George Wade, working a military road-building party in the background, working on a Highland road (unknown artist). *Scottish National Portrait Gallery.*

The Tay Bridge, Aberfeldy. Built by Wade and designed by William Adam. Finished in 1734. *Royal Commission on the Ancient and Historical Monuments of Scotland.*

Private, 43rd Highlanders (later renumbered 42nd). The first known illustration of a Highlander in the uniform of a regular British regiment, 1742. *Scottish United Services Museum.*

Malcolm Mcpherson, Corporal in the Highland Regiment who was shot in the Tower on 18 July, 1743, for desertion. *Scottish United Services Museum.*

Farquhar Shaw. *Scottish National Portrait Gallery.*

Simon Fraser, Lord Lovat, by Hogarth: 'As always, counting his options'. *Scottish National Portrait Gallery.*

Glenfinnan, at the head of Loch Shiel. There, on 19 August 1745, James III was proclaimed King, with Prince Charles as Regent. The Royal Standard was unfurled by the Duke of Atholl. *National Trust for Scotland.*

Prince Charles Edward Stuart, with Donald Cameron of Lochiel on his right and Alexander Forbes, 4th Baron Pitsligo. (Artist: John Pettie, 1834–93). *Her Majesty The Queen.*

Prince Charles handing a letter to Antoine Walsh who was leaving for France. This letter to James III was praising his efforts on behalf of the Prince (Artist unknown). *Scottish National Portrait Gallery.*

Sir Alexander Macdonald, 7th Baronet of Sleat. He and Norman Macleod of Macleod reneged on their promise to support the Jacobite cause and Prince Charles (Artist unknown). *Godfrey, Lord Macdonald.*

Left: Norman Macleod of Macleod, 22nd Chief of Macleod. Named 'The Red Man' or 'The Wicket Man' (*An Droch Dhuine*). (Artist: Allan Ramsay, 1748; painted when the wearing of Highland dress was still proscribed). (*John Macleod of Macleod*). *Right:* Lord George Murray (1700–1760). Joint Lieut-General with the Duke of Perth under Princes Charles's command. The white cockades of the Jacobites are clearly shown (Artist unknown). *His Grace the Duke of Atholl.*

Left: Duncan Forbes of Culloden. Lord President of the Court of Session and 'Saviour of the Hanoverian Succession'. Portrait attributed to Jeremiah Davison. *Right:* The Earl of Loudon from a portrait by Allan Ramsay. *Scottish National Portrait Gallery.*

Colin Campbell of Skipness commanded an independent company during the 1745/46 rising. *The Hon. Hepburne-Scott, Lilliesleaf.*

William Augustus, Duke of Cumberland ('Butcher' Cumberland), third son of George II (Artist: David Morier, 1705?–1770). *Her Majesty The Queen.*

An incident in the Rebellion of '45. The clansmen and the redcoats at Culloden, 16 April 1746. This was the last civil war battle to be fought on British soil (Artist – David Morier, 1705?–1770). *Her Majesty The Queen.*

Flora Macdonald. Daughter of the deceased Macdonald of Milton and step-daughter of Hugh Macdonald of Armadale, Saviour of Prince Charles (Artist – Richard Wilson). *Scottish National Portrait Gallery.*

Lochaber No More. Prince Charles leaving his faithful Highlanders at Loch nan Uamh, near Arisaig, 19 September 1746, (Artist – J.B. Macdonald, RSA). *City of Dundee: Art Galleries and Museums.*

Sergeant James Campbell of the 42nd. He slew nine Frenchmen at Fontenoy in 1745 and lost his arm trying to kill a tenth. *Scottish National Portrait Gallery.*

Left: The Black Watch Memorial (1887), Aberfeldy, Perthshire. Erected on the ancient land of the Menzies clan. The figure is that of Farquhar Shaw of the 42nd who was earlier shot as a mutineer on 18 July 1743. *Right:* Detail from the Black Watch Memorial, illustrating the origins of the regiment from the Independent Companies. *Major and Mrs D.G. Simpson, Meikleour, Perthshire.*

Private John Paterson of the 2nd Battalion The Black Watch (RHR), 1947. A soldier of the Second World War. *The Black Watch Museum, Perth.*

A PRIVATE MAN IN HIS REGIMENTALS,
HIGHLAND INDEPENDENT COMPANIES OF 1745-7,
(From a water-colour drawing specially executed for this account by Captain E. A. Campbell,
based upon contemporary sources of information.)

A private man in his regimentals. *Scottish United Services Museum.*

Wade's attitude and that of Forbes, was that Scotland should eventually map out its' own destiny and that it should be policed by its' own people for its' own good.

For this report and other services General Wade was appointed Commander of the Forces in North Britain. He left London for Scotland in June 1725, having got the go-ahead to implement his suggestions and on 15th May full instructions were sent to Major Duroune to activate the re-establishment of the Independent Highland Companies.

These instructions were based on the edict by King George I that Six Independents Companies to be raised forthwith. . . . in the Highlands of North Britain. The six commissions were all back-dated to the 24th April 1725.

The first three were commanded by Col. William Grant of Ballindalloch, Simon, Lord Lovat and Sir Duncan Campbell of Lochnell. Each of these companies consisted of 114 men. The latter three companies, commanded by lieutenants but carrying commissions as captain — lieutenants, only had 71 men each on complement — they were led by Colin Campbell of Skipness, John Campbell of Carrick and Colonel George Munro of Culcairn.

This meant that the six companies mustered 555 sentinels (soldiers) in all apart from officers and non-commissioned officers. This total was in excess of that Wade originally bargained upon. (see pp. 196–206 for full details of officers, personnel plus commission dates from 1725–1739).

Colonel William Grant of Ballindalloch (already described earlier) was first commissioned in 1701 and captained a company (when allowed) until 1733. He was obviously the senior captain and the most experienced of the six captains.

Simon, Lord Lovat, although a major Highland chief, was extremely proud and keen to have this captaincy. Quite apart from the regular revenue it brought to himself and his clan, it brought much kudos to the area around Inverness. He was assessed as 'the shiftiest rogue of all the captains' and it was amazing that he managed to maintain command until he was stripped of his company in 1739.

The third main captain, Sir Duncan Campbell of Lochnell, VII of Lochnell, also carried his commission through to 1739. Thereafter on half-pay until he captained an Independent Company during the battle of Culloden in 1746. Family records state that he attended Culloden but military records do not agree with this fact.

113

With regard to the three captain-lieutenants. Firstly, Colin Campbell of Skipness (son of Angus Campbell of Skipness) was initially 1st lieutenant to Col. William Grant's company in 1715. The company was then disbanded in 1717 and Skipness was put on half-pay.

Recommissioned on 24th April 1725 as captain-lieutenant of one of the smaller companies. He was later to gain a full captaincy when the Independent Companies were embodied with the 43rd of Foot (later the 42nd). He also served with his company at Culloden. He died in April 1756 and was remembered for his harsh treatment of Jacobite clansmen following the battle.

John Campbell of Carrick, son of Sir John Campbell of Carrick, became 1st Lieutenant in Lovat's company in 1714 which was then disbanded in 1717. His appointment as 'Lieutenant to command' on 24/5/1725. He also captained one of the newly embodied companies of the 43rd of Foot in 1739. He was later killed at Fontenoy on 11th May 1745. See also Appendix 7.

From Clan Munro records, Col. Munro of Culcairn fought with General Wightman at Glenshiel in 1719 and later was given a captaincy along with his brother Sir Roland Munro of Foulis in the 43rd of Foot.

General Wade was not entirely happy with the Independent Company commanders at this time. He recorded that, almost without exception they 'were incompetent and corrupt, embezzling their men's pay and stealing their clothing allowances.'

When this state of affairs was reported to the King be became extremely angry and demanded that the worst offenders be replaced. It was obvious that a smart turn-out at an annual inspection was not sufficient to keep a commanders commission safe and sure.

Wade wisely used this adverse report to tighten up the discipline and training of the Companies, instituted more regular inspections and warned the captains that any breach in financial dealings on the accurate number of sentinels mustered and/or mismanagement of clothing issue, would be very severely dealt with (*see* Appendix 8).

One of the last acts Wade was to make before his work finished in Scotland was to review his companies and which he carried out in August and September of 1738 at Taybridge (Aberfeldy), Fort Augustus and Ruthven. The parade state outlines the disproportion of N.C.O.'s and men in various companies:

Companies	SERJEANTS	DRUMMERS	RANK & FILE	SICK	ON PARTY	EFFECTIVE WITH CORPORALS	WANTING TO COMPLETE
Lord Lovat's	4	2	84	–	–	84	–
Capt. Grant's	4	2	77	2	2	81	3
Sir Duncan Campbell's	4	2	83	1	–	84	–
Capt. Lieut. John Campbell's	3	2	47	1	3	51	–
Capt. Lieut. Colin Campbell's	3	2	50	1	–	51	–
Capt. Lieut. Munro's	3	2	51	–	–	51	–
Totals	21	12	392	5	5	402	3

In addition the 'castle companies' comprising some 300 men were also reviewed in August at Edinburgh, Stirling, Dumbarton and Blackness Castle.

By this time, the six companies were officially known by the name An Freiceadan Dubh or Black Watch. It is suggested that the name came from their sombre dress and was applied to them as distinct to the lowland dress and English regular forces with the Seidaran Dearag (Red Soldiers). The Black Watch wore a tartan mainly of black, green and blue colours while the regular troops had coats, breeches and waistcoats of scarlet cloth.

It is not known exactly when the companies first got the name 'the Watch, the Highland Watch or *Freiceadan Dubh*' but in 1735 Major Lewis Grant (brother of Captain George Grant of the Grant company), in writing refers to 'our Northern troops alias Blak Watch'.

While there is some dubiety about all companies having a tartan which 'consisted so much of the black, green and blue', as the Grant Fraser and Munro tartans were very much more colourful with a great deal of red. General Wade, in almost his very first orders, directed that the company captains:

> take care to provide a Plaid Cloathing and Bonnets in the Highland Dress for the Non Commission Officers and Soldiers belonging to their

Companies the Plaid of each Company to be as near as they can of the same Sort and Colour.

However, in 1727 Lord Lovat wrote to the other company captains announcing that a large quantity of tartan was available for those companies who required it and that the whole tartan was for 'Ye sex companies at 10 pence per yard' – this indicates that there was a move at this time towards a more uniform, standard tartan material. However, it seems certain that by the time the companies were regimented in October 1739, their Colonel, Lord Crawford, being a Lowlander and with no clan affiliation assumed a new pattern of tartan which has ever since been known as the Black Watch or Government tartan.

Letters of service (dated 25th October 1739) were sent to John 20th Earl of Crawford (Crauford) appointing him to command the new regiment formed from the Independent Companies and in May 1740 the 43rd Regiment of Foot was embodied into the line – it consisted of 1,000 men and was later (1749) renumbered the 42nd (*see* Appendix 9).

With the exception of the Colonel, all the officers were Highland and for the most part were bi-lingual in Gaelic and English. Mainly the officers were drawn from old and landed families, others were relatives of sons of Highland Lairds or cadets of houses of good standing.

To each company, large and small, was attached the same number of subalterns – i.e. two lieutenants and one ensign.

Many of the sentinels were of a higher order than those normally found in the Army. Often they were cadets of superior families; sons of large gentlemen farmers; tacksmen related to the chief or chieftain or men who had soldiered in foreign parts. General Stewart of Garth commented 'In addition to the advantages derived from their superior rank in life, they possessed, in an Eminent degree, that of a commanding external deportment, special care being taken to select men of full height, well proportioned and of handsome appearance.'

In Scotland where there was little alternative occupation for young men other than arms, it was not difficult to raise the required number of men of good calibre and where they could carry arms and practice weaponry without any annoyance from the Government. Stewart continues:

'Young men, therefore, gladly availed themselves of the privilege of

116

engaging in a profession which relieved them from the sense of degradation and dishonour attached to the idea of being disarmed.'

When the companies were first raised and even after they were 'embodied in the line', it was quite common for private soldiers to ride to the exercising ground followed by servants carrying their weapons and uniforms. This fact was corroborated by Captain Edward Burt (an engineer in Wade's command) who reported:

'I cannot forbear to tell you, before I conclude, that many of these private-gentlemen soldiers have gillys or servants to attend them in quarters, and upon a march to carry their provisions, baggage and firelocks.'

It was noticeable that these companies were officered from loyal Whig clans (generally Campbells, Frasers, Rosses, Munros and Grants), so that their duties of enforcing the Disarming Act, to gain information of potential rebellious gathering, to restrict cattle lifting and generally control unlawful behaviour, was dutifully and conscientiously carried out.

Because of their intimate knowledge of the countryside and language the companies were well suited to carry out tasks which were sometimes at variance when having to enforce laws against their own countrymen or even friends. To make them even more efficient in policing crime or rebellion it was decided to locate the companies in their own areas.

Culcairn and the Munroes were stationed in Sutherland and Ross-Shire: the Grants (under Ballindalloch) in Badenoch and Strathspey: Campbell of Lochnell and Carrick in Atholl and Breadalbane: Lord Lovat and his Frasers in Fort Augustus and Inverness-Shire. The other Campbell company (Skipness) in parts of Argyleshire, Lochaber and among the disaffected Camerons and Stewarts of Appin.

These companies remained in this situation of local gendarmerie with slight local alterations until the year 1739 when it was decided to embody them and add four other companies to their strength. The initial six companies raised in April 1725 have been detailed earlier in this chapter: the 10 embodied companies can be seen in Appendix 5.

CHAPTER 13

The Great Raising of the Companies and the Road to Culloden (1740–1746)

'Not one single soldier but would have been against such a ffeeld had their advice been askt . . . a plain moor where regular troups had . . . full use of their Cannon so as to annoy the Highlanders prodigiously before they could possibly make an attack.' — Lord George Murray following the Battle of Culloden, April 1746.

Reigning Monarchs
George II   1727–1760

General Wade relinquished his command in Scotland in 1740 and was succeeded by Lieutenant-General Jasper Clayton. His work was well done and it was left to others to carry on the Government's task of keeping the Highlanders contained.

In the early 1740s recruiting for the new regiment continued and it was specifically understood that they were only to serve in Scotland 'to keep the Peace on the Braes'. However, at this time Britain was drifting into confrontation with Spain and it was very tempting to regard the regimented Independent Companies as a reservoir for active service overseas. By 1742, the government had decoyed the regiment south to London ostensibly for the King personally to review the Highlanders. However, the review was taken by General Wade and not by royalty – it was obvious that the intention was to ship the men to Flanders.

Rumour was rife, however, that the intended part of the world was the fever-ridden West Indies and with that rumour, the regiment mutinied. However, this mutiny was quickly crushed by pursuing English regular forces and there followed several executions to reinforce discipline. Another part of the punishment was to send 200 of the deserters to serve with different corps abroad; 50 to Gibralter and Minorca; 40 to the Leeward Islands; 30 each to Jamaica and Georgia. Farquhar Shaw was the most famous of those executed. When the Black watch memorial was raised in Aberfeldy in later times, it was he who was in spirit commemorated.

Farquhar Shaw

There is some dubiety about the family and origins of Farquhar Shaw. Initially he was reported as a cattle drover from Rothiemurchus and only able to converse in the gaelic tongue – one description was that he 'was rough-hewn and lower born than his comrades in the Black Watch'.

Such a description is very much at odds with an early historian who claimed that he was the son of a Strathspey laird and that he 'was a perfect swordsman and a deadly shot alike with the musket and pistol and was known to twist a horseshoe with his bare hands and to drive his dirk into a pine log'.

Shot as a mutineer on 18 July 1743 it is ironic that an 18th century engraving of Shaw was used as a model for this Highlander to represent the regiment on the Black Watch memorial of 1887.

The statue, showing a single feather in the bonnet, certainly denotes that Shaw was the son of a chief and it is unlikely that such an essential and elementary error would have been made when the engraving was commissioned and created by the Victorian sculptor.

The remainder of the regiment was sent to Flanders at the end of May where it joined the army under the command of Field-Marshal, the Earl of Stair. They were too late to be involved in the battle of Dettingen and served on the continent in various quarters during 1743 and 1744. At this time, they were not engaged in active service but continued with standard military training in an effort to regulate the Highlanders natural mode of fighting and to replace it with the more conventional military tactics employed by English and Lowland Scottish regular troops.

By this time their new Colonel Lord Sempill had been replaced by Lord John Murray, son of the Duke of Atholl – their field commander was Lieut-Colonel Sir Robert Munro of Foulis.

The Black Watch were mainly responsible for covering the retreat from Fontenoy and in spite of their vigorous conventional army training, reverted to their normal Highland method of fighting – i.e. discharging their muskets, dropping to the ground when the enemy returned their fire, then rising and charging the enemy with broadsword, targe and dirk before the enemy could reload.

Their Colonel Sir Robert Munro, because of his vast girth, had some trouble in adopting the supine position that his men did. He would get down readily enough, but getting to his feet was a different matter altogether. He was so loved by his men (as he shared their every danger) that they hoisted him up and lowered him down at the appropriate times!

So successful was the Highland charge on the continental battlefield, that the French were driven back time and again and a very successful retreating action of joint British, Hanoverian, Dutch and Austrian forces was achieved. The old strategem described *by furies rushing in upon them, with more violence that ever did a sea driven by a tempest* exemplified the Highland charge and its success on the Flanders plain as well as in the Scottish hills.

The Highlanders lost Captain John Campbell of Carrick, Ensign Lachlane Campbell of Craignish and 30 sentinels: Captain Robert Campbell of Fonab, Ensign Ronald Campbell and James Campbell of Glenfalloch two sergeants and 86 sentinels were wounded. These losses were surprisingly low considering the amount of sustained action by the he Black Watch and their repeated charges. As Stewart of Garth wisely sums up:

> 'It can be accounted for only by the mode of advancing against the enemy, a circumstance well worthy of the notice of all soldiers, as it shows, that if a body of men push forward firmly and expeditious to an attack, the loss will be smaller'.

Meantime, back in Scotland, home security was left under the command of Lieut-General Joshua Guest (over 90 at this time), with only a handful of regular troops to police the Highlands and with no Independent Companies. In fact, the Highlands were governing themselves quite adequately and in the absence of protective troops to control the reviers and vagabonds, chiefs set up a series of 'watches' to guard the ever-expanding cattle trade. In October 1744 at Keppoch an understanding was reached between Alexander MacDonell of Keppoch, John MacDonell of Glengarry and Donald Cameron of Lochiel that they should band together for their mutual protection.

In a document lodged with Sir Alexander Macdonald of Macdonald, these important chiefs appointed senior members of their clans to act as deputies in defined districts, i.e. Alexander MacDonell of Keppoch appointed Ranald MacDonell of Aberarder for Badenoch: his brother Donald for Lochaber along with Donald MacDonell of Tirnadris, Donald MacDonell of Cranachan and Alexander MacDonell of Tulloch.

Other chiefs also joined in with private watches to cover their own clan territories and those of others 'for a due fee'. The most active chief in this matter was Ewen Macpherson, Younger of Cluny who organised a whole series of watches covering all the Grampians from Inverness to Dundee.

Surprisingly, these local quasi-watches were as effective, if not more effective, than the he previous efforts of the Independent Companies. Doubtless the monetary rewards from the increased and more profitable cattle trade were sufficient to fund such an able deterrent.

The War of the Austrian succession began in 1742 after the death of Emperor Charles VI. The British had won a famous victory at Dettingen against the French, but this was reversed at Fontenoy, where 6,000 allied troops were killed and where the Black Watch fought a tremendous rear-guard action. There followed more defeats at the hands of Count Saxe the brilliant Marshal-General of France when he was victorious in capturing Tournai, Ghent and Ostend. The Duke of Cumberland, who had foolishly been given command of the allied forces on the Continent at the very inexperienced age of 24 was forced to retire to Antwerp.

It was painfully obvious that by regimenting the Independent Companies to form another fighting battalion to be sent 'to the blood-bath of Flanders' had no effect on the outcome of that particular war, but by depleting the Great Glen forces of vital local scouting, intelligence and fighting men it undoubtedly allowed the rising in Scotland to take place in 1745.

When the rising did occur in early August, the British government were very unprepared. Cumberland was still in Flanders with the bulk of the British army, the King was in Hanover and both Scotland and England had only a very small number of resident troops.

The uneven effectiveness of the Disarming Acts of 1716 and 1726 will be recalled – the loyal Whig clans were virually disarmed while the Jacobite clans had managed to retain the bulk of their weapons. Into this most unstable situation came the landing of Prince Charles Edward Stuart in the Highlands on the 23rd July 1745. He landed with only the 'Seven men of Moidart', with none of the promised French forces and the only help he could possibly get was from the Jacobite clans, who were ready to fight against the Government, especially when that fighting could be identified as against the clan Campbell.

The initial plan was that 3,000 French troops led by the Earl Marishal would be landed in the Highlands where they would join with the main Jacobite clans. At the same time a larger force of

121

12,000 men under the famous Marshall Saxe and the Prince was to be landed within easy marching distance of London. This grand plan, a two-pronged attack, did not come about for a variety of reasons and the whole burden of fighting the British Government was laid upon the shoulders of the Jacobite clans loyal to the Stewart cause.

To this cause rallied Cameron of Lochiel, the Macdonalds of Keppoch, Glengarry and Glencoe. Macdonald of Boisdale (a half-brother to the chief of Clanranald) was very much against his clan being drawn into the Rising. He also confirmed to the Prince not to expect help from the Macdonalds and Macleods of Skye, even although their aid had been promised previously.

Charles was taken aback by the lack of hoped for support from the Skye chiefs, but refused to accept that his mission was going to fail. So, on the 19th August he raised his standard at Glenfinnan – the white and red silk standard of King James – amid 'loud huzzas and schiming of bonnetts up into the air'. Watching this historic scene were two companies of raw recruits of the Royal Scots who, en route for Fort William, had been captured by the Highlanders.

At this stage the Highland army numbered some 1,300 men with only Keppoch having had any serious military experience. However, the war on the continent had stripped the country of resident troops and only the regiments of Guise's (6th), 5 companies of Lee's (55th), Murray's (57th) and Lascalles's (58th) were available to the Government.

Along with the regular forces was the newly formed Highland regiment under the command of Lord Loudon, which had no military experience or background. In addition to the infantry were two ill-disciplined dragoon regiments. These made up the total troops now under the command of Lieut-General John Cope who was directed to keep 'a strict Eye' on the Highlands by the Secretary of State, Lord Tweedale.

Under Tweedale's authority in Edinburgh was Lord President of the Court of Session, Duncan Forbes of Culloden, who was to play a vital part in the outcome of the rising. Forbes, as a Highlander, had a great knowledge and understanding of the clans, their ways and their politics and who had great sympathy with their aspirations, while remaining a most staunch Whig and loyal government supporter. He had already (in July) told John Cope of the rumoured landing of the Prince in the West with the aim of 'raising an insurrection'. Forbes had also been active in the '15 and '19 Risings on behalf of the government and as early as 1739 suggested that Highlanders could be formed into forces for the government and in a letter to Lord Milton of the Court of Session brought out this far-seeing idea:

> A war with Spain seems near at hand, which it is probable, will soon be followed by a war with France and there will be occasion for more troops than the present standing army. In that event, I propose that government should raise four or five regiments of Highlanders, appointing an English or Scotch officer of undoubted loyalty to be colonel of each regiment; and naming the lieutenant-colonels, majors, captains, and subalterns from this list in my hand, which comprehends all the chiefs and chieftains of the disaffected clans, who are the very persons whom France and Spain will call upon, in case of a war, to take arms for the Pretender . . . If government pre-engages the Highlanders in the manner I propose, they will not only serve well against the enemy abroad, but will be hostages for the good behaviour of their relations at home; and I am persuaded that it will be absolutely impossible to raise a rebellion in the Highlands. I have come here to show you this plan and to entreat, if you approve it, that you will recommend it to your friend Lord Islay, who I am told is to be here to-day or tomorrow on his way to London.

This idea, although well accepted by Lord Milton, Lord Islay and even Sir Robert Walpole was outvoted on this matter in cabinet despite Walpole's support. Cabinet ministers seemed to take the view that to draft so many of the clans into the British army 'would have meant embodying a force for the use of the exiled house.'

The country was to pay dearly for not acting upon Forbes's plan.

Between 1742 and 1745 Duncan Forbes kept pressing home the point of preventive arrangements, to protect the Highlanders from being led into trouble and insurrection. However the policy of the government at this time was wholly retributive and not preventive, so no progress was made on this fundamental common-sense approach.

Forbes was undoubtedly too far-seeing for his rather staid and ordinary contemporaries and was later aptly described as one of those characters which are sometimes to be found in the corners of History but which deserve to be blazoned at large on it's broadest page.

It is not too much to claim that his actions alone ensured the continuity of the Hanoverian dynasty – this will become self-evident as the story of the '45 Rising unfolds.

When news of Prince Charles' movements were known, some alarm was shown by the government, but the Black Watch was not brought back from the continent till November (1745) and even then was stationed in Kent as part of a division in case the threatened invasion by Marshal Saxe and his 12,000 men would actually take place. This meant that the Black Watch soldiers were exempted from taking part in the opposition to the Rising and from having perhaps to fight against friends and/or relatives. It is estimated that roughly 300 of the private soldiers of the Black Watch had close relatives taking part in the Jacobite Rising and it seemed only sensible to keep them well away from the struggle to come.

Three new Black Watch companies had been formed with head-quarters in Crieff early in 1745 to supplement the regular battalion. These men came mainly from Braemar, Atholl and Breadalbane. The commanders were the Laird of Mackintosh, Sir Patrick Murray of Ochtentyre and Campbell of Inveraw. Lieutenants were James Farquharson, Younger of Invercauld, John Campbell, Younger of Glenlyon and Dugald Campbell.

Ensigns were Allan Grant, son of Glenmoriston, John Campbell son of Glenfalloch and Allan Campbell, son of Ballardine. General Stewart of Garth observes:

> 'That their privates, although of the best calibre, did not occupy that social position to which so many men of the old Independent Companies were entitled.'

General Cope decided not to fight to inclement terrain in the Highlands and raced south to catch up with Charles. Battle was eventually joined just south of Edinburgh at Prestonpans, near Haddington on September 21st. The three Black Watch companies kept in reserve in Scotland were divided — one was left in reserve and the other two were sent to join General Cope just before the battle. However, one of the two companies simply 'mouldered away' when the men went home to their glens and only one effectively joined Cope's army. All of its officers, Sir Patrick Murray, Lieutenant Farquharson and ensign Allan Campbell and all of the men were either killed, woulded or taken prisoner by the Jacobites and again the Highland charge was seen to be effective against very demoralised English troops and recently enrolled raw recruits of the Black Watch (*see* Appendix 10).

The Jacobite army at Prestonpans, now grown to some 3,000 strong, made use again of the famous charge, against which Cope's regulars had no answer. The Royal Army was virtually destroyed in a few short minutes. After the battle, Charles returned to Edinburgh where he stayed for a period of nearly six weeks during which time it was hoped to build up the strength of the Jacobite army. The remaining men of the Black Watch were entreated to join the Jacobite forces, but they refused to do so and paid the harsh penalty for their loyalty to the Hanoverian cause.

As time was obviously important, urgent appeals were made for additional troops to join the Jacobite cause. Lord Lovat was still toying with the idea of bringing out the Frasers on the side of Charles but, by this time, the Skye chiefs Sir Alexander Macdonald and Macleod of Macleod had definitely decided to support the Hanoverian cause. The Mackenzies, Gordons, Grants and Mackintoshes had divided loyalties, but the northern clans, the Mackays, Rosses, Munros and Sutherlands, were still staunchly against the Stuarts. However, in spite of many clans abstentions the Jacobite army grew steadily in size. Mackinnon of Mackinnon brought over a hundred men from Skye; Lord Ogilvy 300 men from his Angus estates; Macpherson of Cluny, notwithstanding the fact that he held a commission in Lord Loudon's regiment, brought 300 followers; John Gordon of Glenbucket also led 300 men for Charles; Lord Lewis Gordon, the Duke of Gordon's younger brother also raised 'a goodly force of Gordon men'. Meantime the existing clan regiments were being built up by fresh recruits joining daily. The cavalry section although small, was enhanced by Lord Elcho commanding a troop of Life Guards.

> 'Compleated it all of gentlemen of familly and fortune . . . their uniform blew and reed, and all extremely well mounted.'

Lord Pitsligo also joined with a newly-raised cavalry unit plus Murray of Broughton's Hussars and the Lowland noble Lord Kilmarnock with a small mounted troop.

During the month of October, Charles received arms from French ships docking at Montrose and Stonehaven: they included small arms and a few field guns. Unfortunately, no men accompanied the weapons.

On November 1st the Prince set out with his now enlarged army of 5,000 men to enter England and Carlisle surrendered to the Jacobites on November 15th. The march south continued as far as Derby where Charles was persuaded that it was hopeless to continue their march to London. Very few English Jacobites had joined their cause and it was suggested that the best plan was to return to Scotland to rejoin their reinforcements who were mainly stationed at Perth and Montrose. Charles was still against the move back north 'rather than go back, I would wish to be 20 feet underground.'

But all his commanders were against him and so on December 6th the Highlanders turned north for home. The journey north through Carlisle, Dumfries and Glasgow ended with his army re-occupying Stirling.

Lord President Forbes had not been idle in the meantime. Lord Tweedale had sent him an express letter (dated 4th September) enclosing a number of blank commissions for raising twenty Independent Highland Companies 'from well-affected clans'. See Appendix II.

Forbes was to spend the next months writing letters and cajoling chiefs to support the government to raise their clansmen to fight for the King. He used the offer of a company as a bait to bring waverers to the Hanoverian side. His efforts were tireless and whilst not always successful (e.g. Lovat and Cromarty) for the most part, 'intirely putt a Stop to most of these Gentlemens balancing, as a Great Many that the Prince counted on accepted them.'

In short, he managed to persuade most of the foremost chiefs to remain steadfast on the side of King George. In a letter to his friend Sir Andrew Mitchell he very clearly states how difficult the situation was and yet how much effort he put behind his exertions to stop mass support for Charles in the north:

> Though I was not just treading in the path of a chief justice, the prospect was very flattering, and the errand I came on had no appearance of difficulty. But the Rebells' successes at Edinburgh and Preston Pans soon changed the scene. All Jacobites, how prudent soever, became mad, all doubtful people became Jacobites, and all bankrupts became heroes, and talked nothing but hereditary rights and victory; and what was more grievous to men of gallantry, and if you will believe me, much more mischievous to the public, all the fine ladies, if you will except one or two, became passionately fond of the young adventurer, and used all their arts and industry for him in the most intermperate manner. Under the circumstances, I found myself almost alone, without troops, without arms, without money or credit; provided with no means to prevent extreme folly, except pen and ink, a tongue, and some reputation; and, if you will except Macleod, whom

I sent for from the Isle of Skye, supported by nobody of common sense or courage. Had arms and money come when they were first called for, before these unexpected successes blew up folly to madness, I could have answered it with my head, that no man from the north should have joined the original flock of rebels that passed the Forth; and even as it has happened, it is no small consolation to me, that, except Macpherson of Clunie, whose force does not exceed 300, none from the north have reached them in time to march alongst with them southwards from Edinburgh, that no more than 200 of the clan Chattan have marched, who had got, as last Saturday, no further than Perth, and that notwithstanding the restless endeavours of the Earl of Cromartie, the Master of Lovat and others, no more than 150 or 100 of the Mackenzies have been debauched, and that even those have not as yet passed the Corryaric; no more than the Frasers, who to the number of 5 or 600 have flocked to arms, and who possibly may think better, if the weather permit the force, which we hourly expect from the Isle of Sky, to join us quickly, before they leave the country exposed.

So in spite of all difficulties and the acute shortage of money, Duncan Forbes achieved the task of raising 18 out of the 20 companies from 23rd October 1745 through to 2nd February 1746.

The following, taken from the Culloden papers, shows the names of the Captains and lesser officers along with their dates of completing the raising of the companies.:

List of Officers of the Independent Companies raised in the North: specifying the dates of delivering to them their Commissions, their Companies being then complete

Captains	Lieutenants	Ensigns	Dates of Completeing the Companys
George Monro Esq	Adam Gordon	Hugh Monro	1745 Oct 23
Alexander Gun Esq	John Gordon	Keneth Sutherland	1745 Oct 25
Patrick Grant Esq	William Grant	James Grant	1745 Nov 3
George Mackay Esq	John Mackay	James Mackay	1745 Nov 4
Peter Sutherland Esq	William Mackay	John Mackay	1745 Nov 8
John Mac Leod Esq	Alexander Mac Leod	John Mac Askill	1745 Nov 15
Normand Mac Leod of Waterstein Esq	Donald McLeod	John MacLeod	1745 Nov 15
Normand Mac Leod of Bernera Esq	John Campbell	John Mac Leod	1745 Nov 15
Donald Mac Donald Esq	William Mac Leod	Donald Mac Leod	1745 Nov 15

127

William Macintosh Esq	Keneth Mathisom	William Baillie	1745 Nov 18
Hugh Mac Leod Esq	George Monro	Roderick Mac Leod	1745 Nov 28
Alexander Mackenzie Esq	John Mathison	Simon Morchison	1745 Dec 10
Colin Mackenzie of Hiltown Esq	Alexander Campbell	John Mackcrae	1745 Dec 10
James Mac Donald Esq	Allan Mac Donald	James Mac Donald	1745 Dec 31
John Mac Donald Esq	Allan Mac Donald	Donald Mac Donald	1745 Dec 31
Hugh Mackay Esq	John Mackay	Angus Mackay	1746 Jan 6
William Ross Esq	Charles Ross	David Ross	1746 Jan 8
Colin Mackenzie Esq	Donald Mackattlay	Kenneth Mackenzie	1746 Feb 2

Inverness 12th May 1746.

> I hereby certify, that, pursuant to the trust reposed in me by His Majesty, Commissions were by me delivered to the Officers of the Independent Companys above mentioned, on the days also mentioned; and that these Commissions were not delivered until their respective Companys were compleat.
>
> [signed] *Dun. Forbes*

Culloden and State Papers

It will be noticed, that in some of the companies, the officers are not of the clan name of their company. The 4th MacLeod is commanded by a MacDonald; Campbells are found as lieutenants in both a MacLeod and a Mackenzie Company; the chief of the Gunns commands a Sutherland Company, one of its subalterns being a Gordon, the other company of that name having two Mackays as subalterns; five out of the six subalterns in the three Mackenzie's Companies are not of that clan's name; while a Gordon is to be found in the Munro Company, and a Munro (Monro) in the MacLeod of Assynt Company. The larger clans, however, were not made up of one surname only, but included others, some being of lesser clans subordinate to them (such as MacRaes, MacAulays, Mathesons and Murchisons who followed Seaforth, Chief of the Mackenzies; and MacAskills who were dependents, or a sept of the MacLeods). Others, again were of incomers to the country of another clan (e.g. the above MacDonald, Monro, and the two Campbells and Gordons), or who had through transfer of territory come under another chief, such as the two Mackays, whose lands were now held from the Earl of Sutherland, and not from Lord Reay (the Mackay chief). The small clan of the Gunns held their lands of and followed the Earls of Sutherland. In the eighteenth century, the Gaelic prefix 'Mac' ('son of') was often spelt in English 'Mack,' hence we still have 'Mackintosh,' 'Mackay,' 'Mackenzie,' etc.; but, nowadays (and not as in list above), 'MacAulay,' 'MacRae,' etc.

See appendix 12 for detail on company captains (family and military history where available.)

The following extract of a letter from Patrick Sutherland to Captain Gun dated 8 April 1746 (Original in author's possession) is of interest:

> I received yours with letters included. I have been all night and this morning gathering the men of the Strath together and we will with all expedition march them to the parish of Kildonan, as to your last orders I sent your different captains last night none of you needs be surprised at them as I only defined (?) their marching this way in case they were sure of your enemy marching to this country and now I think Breakachy is your most proper place of rendezvous please acquaint your captains that this is my opinion, or at least that they should be within a few hours march of one another, for it will not do to attack to march by — — to attack an enemy and above all things I would have you take care that they be not surprised by your enemy. Acquaint me that the men are collected and I shall instantly march to you and leave your men of your Strath to be brought up by your officers here, after bringing with myself as many as I can.

Further details of records concerning the Independent Companies can be found in the Public Record Office, KEW:

Independent Companies of Foot

Disbandments in Scotland	1717	W.O.26/14	276.277 KEW
Formation of six Companies in Highlands	1725	S.P.44/179	41,49,53,88,90 CHANCERY LANE
Disbandment of eighteen Companies raised in Highlands	1746	W.O.26/21	71,86 KEW
Formation of six Highland Companies	1760	W.O.4/62	231–236 KEW

By any standards the raising of the Independent Companies was a gigantic task, especially when slowness of correspondence and other considerations were taken into account. Duncan Forbes undoubtedly had persuasive powers in plenty, when the buoyant feeling in the Highlands for insurrection was heightened by the Jacobite successes at Prestonpans and Falkirk.

During this time, Forbes was under considerable pressure and indeed found himself in great danger when his home Culloden House was under attack by the Jacobites in October 1745. Fortunately the attack was driven off, but later he had to flee to the security of Skye to escape the pursuing Jacobites. Naturally, he was hated by the followers of Charles as he became successful in raising almost all the Independent Companies: He has rendered himself a scandal to all Scotsmen, and a nuisance to all society, was Lochiel's angry comment.

The eighteen Independent Companies were allocated as follows:

Macleods (Skye and Harris)	4
Mackenzies (Earl of Seaforth)	3
Macdonalds (Sleat)	2
Sutherlands	2
Mackays (Lord Reay)	2
Grants	1
Macleods (Assynt)	1
Munros	1
Rosses	1
Town of inverness	1

The latter was the only company not raised by a Highland clan nor by the edict of the clan chief. It was raised solely by the people of Inverness and captained by a town magistrate, William MacIntosh.

While Independent Companies 'were plums in Highland politics' Forbes had some difficulty in apportioning the numbers of companies to individual clan chiefs because of inter-clan pride and jealousy.

This task was made doubly difficult by the recommendation of the Secretary of War that three of the companies should be granted to the Munro clan, because of their previous loyalty and their promptness in offering help.

Forbes ignored this dictat and allocated only one to the Munro clan. Claims of other clans were recognised when three of the total were given to the Mackenzies and four to the Macleods of Skye. While both the Mackenzies and Macleods had been mainly Jacobite in the '15 and '19 Risings, they now showed firm allegiance to the Hanoverians. Also, the Macdonalds of Sleat were given substantial influence through their two companies as were the Mackays and Sutherlands. The remaining five clans were allocated one each.

The many difficulties Forbes had to face over the lack of money (much of which had to be found by Forbes himself) was also increased by the lack of weaponry for the sentinels. When Edinburgh on September 17th was captured by the Jacobites the store of 6,000 arms was seized and other arms (mainly muskets and bayonets) had to be shipped north by sea. Also the Disarming Acts had taken away many of the broadswords even from clans loyal to the Government. Pistols and targets were reckoned to be in plentiful supply, along with dirks which were always regarded as a personal possession and essential for defence and domestic purposes.

While the Independent Companies were being raised in the north, Charles and his army on 17th January 1746 were forced into battle with Government forces at Falkirk. The Government army commander was General Hawley, a brutal and insensitive leader, who made the mistake, yet again, of underestimating the Highlanders and their fighting ability. On the evening of the 16th Hawley was joined by part of Lord John Murray's regiment the Black Watch and they took part in the violent battle the next day.

Again the forces of Charles won the day in a violent rain storm. Hawley claimed that the Highlanders had no answer to attack by cavalry, but initially the very accurate musket fire of the Jacobites halted the charge of his very effective dragoons. Then came the much vaunted Highland charge from mainly the Macdonalds of Keppoch, Glengarry and Clanranald using their scything claymores and terrible war cries to great effect. No record has been kept of the activities of the Black Watch company on that day, but it seems that they must have been swept away along with many of Hawley's seasoned regular troops. The two regiments of dragoons who had run away ('the Coltrigg Canter') when Edinburgh was first occupied by the Jacobites bolted again and the left of Hawley's battle line was destroyed. However, some of the forces on the right (Legoniers, Barrel's and Price's) who were the most seasoned of his troops stood firm and this was seen as a bad omen for future encounters.

Among the Hanoverian forces killed at Falkirk was Sir Robert Munro of Foulis, who had so valiantly led the Black Watch at the battle of Fontenoy. It is claimed that the members of the Black Watch company who 'ran like sheep before the Rebells' were not Highlanders, and certainly the calibre of new recruits did not stand comparison with the original companies formed in 1725 and 1739.

The battle of Falkirk only lasted some 20 minutes and while clearly a Jacobite victory, darkness and rain prevented a complete rout. A good proportion of Hawley's army regrouped and retreated in orderly fashion.

After the battle of Falkirk Charles retired north having split his army in two with the main body heading for Inverness.

In early December of 1745, the Independent Companies were to receive their first taste of active service. Lord Loudon, with 600 men of the Grant, two Sutherland, Munro and Mackay companies liberated Fort Augustus from the Fraser clan after a small skirmish.

The next occasion was when the companies were put against the Jacobites under Lord Lewis Gordon in both Banff and Aberdeenshire. The companies on this occasion were four Macleod companies of Skye led by Macleod of Macleod, along with the one Assynt Macleod company under Captain Hugh Macleod of Geanies. They arrived in Elgin on the 12th December and seized all the boats on the Spey to stop the Jacobites making use of them. At this stage reinforcements arrived in the shape of a Munro and Sutherland company captained jointly by Captain Munro of Culcairn.

The Jacobites met them at Inverurie where battle commenced. Lord Lewis Gordon, having numerically superior forces defeated the Independent Companies under Macleod and inflicted considerable casualties.

In the words of a report to President Forbes:

> 'McKlaudes Resolute Behaviour in running to the Enemy with so few of his men about him and the stand they made with not one half of their little army against 900 till they were over-powered by numbers is much to his honour'. This note says that 60 Jacobites were killed and 20 wounded (*More Culloden Papers*, IV, p.180.)

MacLeod of Macleod and Culcairn retired across the Spey into Elgin and Forres where they remained till the Prince had moved south from Stirling when they rejoined Loudoun.

Amongst the prisoners taken was the famous piper Donald MacCrimmon and all the pipers in the Jacobite army refused ever to play again until MacCrimmon, 'pre-eminent in the musical art of piping', was set free.

At around the same time Lord Loudon with two Sutherland, two Mackenzie companies, Mackays, Grants, and Munros — some 800 men in all — went in search of Lord Lovat (who had recently allowed his son to go off with a band of Frasers to join Prince Charles) to try to bring him back to Inverness where he would be 'a hostage for the Peaceable behaviour of his Clan.'

However, Lovat, having initially agreed to this move, suddenly escaped from his home, Castle Downie and evaded capture. This action was to stop any more of the Fraser clan joining his son (the Master of Lovat) and the 300 men who had already defected to the Jacobites. Lovat made the feeble excuse 'that he could not govern his son and some of the young men of his name.' It was disappointing that this considerable force of Independent Company men had not managed to stop the Fraser reinforcements but 'at least the haemorrage was Quelled.'

At this stage (mid-December) all the 18 companies had been raised although only 13 of them had actually reached their focal point. The two Macdonald, one of the Mackay and the Ross company were expected to arrive in the very near future while the Mackenzie of Lewis company was kept in Lewis in order to dissuade any islanders joining the Prince.

So by early February, Loudon in Inverness had nearly 2000 troops under his command, mostly men from the Independent Companies although 150 of his own regiment were in that number. There they waited in Inverness for the Prince to arrive. But Forbes countermanded this decision and ordered Loudon and his men to quit Inverness in view of the superior size of the Jacobite troops. The Independent Companies and Loudon's regiment were then transported (safely and without loss) over the Cromarty and then the Dornoch Firth into Sutherland. The approaching Jacobite army occupied Inverness and accepted the surrender of the two Independent Companies who were guarding Inverness Castle — the companies were the Grant and Ross companies and they gave up their charge without a fight. After Culloden they were reformed and carried out useful service for the government in the aftermath of the battle.

Just prior to their occupation of Inverness and while the Independent Companies were still in the Inverness area on the 16th February, Charles reached Moy Hall, a few miles short of the city. Loudon with 1700 men under his control decided to try to capture the Prince, as he was only attended by a few men at Moy Hall, with his main force several miles away.

The Prince's host was Lady Mackintosh of Moy, an ardent Jacobite supporter, in spite of the fact that her husband, Aeneas Mackintosh of Mackintosh was a captain of a company in Loudons regiment. Loudon attacked at night with 1500 men (including at least 10 of the companies) but fortunately that most fearless and resourceful woman Lady Mackintosh (nick-named 'Colonel Anne') got wind of the attack and the Prince escaped from the house.

133

Colonel Anne ordered the local blacksmith, Donald Fraser, and four of her estate workers to create noise with muskets and drums and shouted orders apparently to Charles' clansmen. These 5 bold men created such a diversion that the Independent Companies feared that they were facing a Jacobite force of some strength. In the confusion and darkness, Loudon and his 1500 men panicked and retreated from Moy Hall in great confusion.

This rather laughable incident, known forever as the Rout of Moy, reflected badly on the Independent Companies and their rather inept commander, Lord Loudon—this was certainly not their finest moment and the redoubtable 'Colonel Anne' had not only saved the Prince from capture, but had humiliated 1500 soldiers with a handful of her servants.

Some time later her husband was captured by the Jacobites and was ignominiously sent home — a report stated:

> Among the prisoners taken at what was called the Battle of Embo, fought on 20 March, was the Laird of Mackintosh. The Prince sent him back to his wife at Moy, telling him that he could not receive safer or more honourable treatment anywhere else.

On being greeted by his wife, she said 'Your Servant, Captain' it is reported that he replied 'Your Servant, Colonel'.

When Loudon and his men left Inverness they made their headquarters, safely they thought, in Dornoch and guarded against any attack from across the Dornoch Firth by seizing all the boats which could be used to ferry troops across. He also defended specific ferries and all likely landing places.

But by the 20th February and helped by a thick mist, the Jacobites obtaining some boats from further down the coast, made a surprise attack across the Dornoch Firth at Tain. At the same time, a force of 600 Highlanders took over fishing boats at Findhorn and joined the other force at Tain. They took Loudon's troops by complete surprise and made 300 prisoners when they occupied the town of Dornoch. Loudon and Duncan Forbes fortunately escaped capture. This meant that they were not able to complete the necessary administration — they could not forward the names of the officers of the Independent Companies nor manning levels and in consequence, no pay could be issued.

With little ammunition left, no money and a depleted force Loudon and Forbes decided to retreat and via a devious route, reached the comparative safety of Skye. By the end of March, the

134

Lord President Forbes, Lord Loudon, Macleod of Macleod plus 900 sentinels settled in the south of Skye — there they were joined by Sir Alexander Macdonald of Sleat.

While the Independent Companies apparently did not aquit themselves at all well, they did succeed in tying up a large number of rebels in the north, including Cromarty and his 800 men from Castle Leod who was on his way to join the Prince, and allowed Cumberland time to build up and organise his forces. Cumberland, at this stage was not impressed by the action of the companies and observed: 'How negligently these Highlanders who are with us do their duty'.

Loudon's force whilst in Skye was later reinforced by the 3rd Mackenzie of Lewis Independent Company and was aided by food and ammunition supplies organised by Major-General John Campbell. His force now numbered 1300 men from 11 companies and 3 companies of his own regiment. Not all of his men went to Skye and at least two companies (the 2nd Sutherland and 2nd Mackay) were left in Sutherland to harrass any following Jacobite troops and to delay any more clansmen reinforcing Charles' army. (*See* Appendix 13).

At the end of March the two companies (Sutherland and Mackay) were involved in helping to capture arms and money which had been sent by sea for the Jacobite forces. The French ship had been forced by the Navy to beach in the Kyle of Tongue. Under Captain Hugh Mackay, the companies captured the officers and seamen of the French ship, Hazard. Denying arms and money to Charles was a telling blow and was in large part responsible for his defeat at Drumossie Moor.

So Captain Lucius O'Brien of the British warship Sheerness, was to play a vital part in the downfall of the Jacobites, when he drove the French ship Hazard, renamed the 'Prince Charles', ashore with the urgently required supplies of money and arms. At the same time, and in an effort to recover the arms and money, a strong force of Jacobites was sent north to Sutherland. It comprised some of the best fighting men, the Macgregors, Coll Macdonnell of Barrisdale, the Mackinnons and the Jacobite Mackenzies led by the Earl of Cromartie. Unfortunately they arrived too late to be of any real assistance. Also to make matters even worse, they were delayed in rejoining the main Jacobite force in Inverness by the action of the Sutherland & Mackay Companies and thus missed the battle of Culloden altogether.

This action by the 2nd Sutherland and 2nd Mackay Companies on 15 April 1746 is worthy of note. The earl of Cromartie and his considerable force now decided to run the gauntlet and join the Prince in Inverness. He and his men left Dunrobin Castle and on his way to the Little Ferry when he was attacked with great vigour by the Independent Companies under the command of Ensign John Mackay of Mudale. Cromartie was driven back by the force of the encounter with most of his followers either killed or taken prisoner. This skirmish, known as 'the Engagement of the Little Ferry' denied the Prince much needed reinforcements for the coming and decisive battle.

The Duke of Cumberland, on 8 April left Aberdeen after a prolonged training period for his army, specifically against the fearsome Highland charge. He headed a well-fed, well-armed body of men of mixed Lowland Scottish and English regiments. He reached Nairn by the 14th April and then was joined by the Munro and 1st Sutherland companies who had been stationed in that north-east area and had been fighting with groups of Highlanders who were trying to join up with the Prince in Inverness.

It was becoming increasingly obvious that the Jacobite army must stand and fight and as O'Sullivan, the Quarter Master General to the Prince's army was later to reflect 'How could you keep nine or ten thousand men together without meal or money. You could not keep them out in the fields in the season we were in . . . it was better to risque a battle.'

And so to Drumossie Moor (Culloden) on the 16th April to fight the last civil war battle on British soil.

4,000 half-starved Jacobites faced some 7,500 well-fed, well-trained and seasoned Government troops; on ground not at all suitable for classic Highland warfare and against well-disciplined artillery fire. The outcome was both bloody and inevitable. In the battle, the Independent Companies were held in reserve and only took part when a small group of them, in conjunction with the Argyll militia, delivered devastating musket fire on the flank of the Jacobite right.

The vain Highland charge into a hail of canister shot and musket balls sent a way of life into history.

While 16 English and Scottish lowland foot regiments plus 3 mounted units fought against the Jacobite Highlanders it is only fitting that no British regiment has listed Culloden among its' battle honours.

CHAPTER 14
The Prince in the Heather (1746)

An unknown Highland historian later said of Culloden: 'It was the end of the warrior society and the end of a way of life.'

Reigning Monarch
George II   1727–1760

Prince Charles retired from the disastrous site of Culloden with the cries of the wounded and dying clansmen ringing in his ears. The Lowland Scots and the English line regiments extracted a terrible revenge on the remaining Highlanders regarding, as they did, the people north of the Highland line as treasonable barbarians and therefore not entitled to humane treatment as normal prisoners of war.

'Butcher' Cumberland had won the day and his cousin 'Bonnie Prince Charlie' evaded capture in the hills and islands of the west for a period of five months, before returning to France. Prince had a price of £30,000 on his head, yet the loyalty of the clans stood firm against this enormous amount of money and there was no betrayal.

There was some controversy regarding Charles's immediate intentions and actions after the battle. It is said that he tried in vain to rally his troops and later he was to retire to Ruthven in Badenoch again, to see if his army could be reassembled. There he was joined by Cluny Macpherson and some 500 men who had failed to arrive in time for the battle. Charles had only lost approximately 1,000 men of a total force of 5,000 and with Lord Cromarty and his considerable force still intact, as were the Mackinnons who had been fighting in Caithness and Sutherland, he could virtually have made up his numbers. But the long term situation was seen to be hopeless and even Lord George Murray agreed with him — he later wrote: 'Besides our defeat, there was neither money nor provisions to give: so no hopes were left.'

Charles became a fugitive and was to remain in this situation until he was picked up by the French ship *L'Heureux* on 20 September 1746 from Loch nan Uamh in Arisaig.

The story of his fugitive life and his narrow and almost miraculous escape from the Redcoats and the Independent Companies during these five months, highlights the loyalty of his various companions and the ordinary clansmen, who risked so much to keep his whereabouts secret.

The story begins when Charles and a few trusted friends Colonel John William O'Sullivan, Alan Macdonald and Edward Burke, made their way on 18th April to the house of Donald Cameron of Glenpean, on the north shore of Loch Arisaig. At this house he got the first night's sleep for some time. Next morning he was conducted to Loch Morar where he spent the night with Alexander Macdonald, whose father had met the Prince when he first landed in Arisaig. There he stayed till the 20th. Macdonald recorded:

> He was pritty well here: he had a little meal, lamb and butter and straw to ly upon, he wanted it for he had not eat a bit of bread since he supt at Ld. Lovets the night of the battle.

He stayed with Alexander Macdonald until he left for Uist on the 26th. Before he left, on the 23rd, Charles penned a letter to all the chiefs:

> When I came into this Country, it was my only view to do all in my power for your good and safety. This I will always do as long as life is in me, But alas!, I see with grief, I can at present do little for you on this side the water, for the only thing that now can be done, is to defend yourselves till the French assist you. If not, to be able to make better terms.

This was most definitely the end of the affair.

Meantime Lord Loudon and his companies received orders to proceed to Fort William via Arisaig and Morar to ravage the country as he proceeded.

Around the beginning of May, the French ship 'Mars', arrived on the west coast. It did not find the Prince but took off some of the leading Jacobites, the Duke of Perth, Lord John Drummond, Lord Elcho, Sir Thomas Sheridan, Lockhart of Carnwath and a few others.

Its main function was to search for Charles, but it was unfortunately engaged in action by ships of the Royal Navy, the 24 gun Greyhound and the sloop Baltimore. Badly crippled, 'Mars' had to retreat and eventually limped back to France, missing Charles by just a few days. Two other French ships the 'Bellore' and the 'Hardi Mendiant' also tried at the end of April/beginning of May to trace Charles and his small party, but without success. These French ships were extremely lucky to escape as the Navy was intent on capturing the Prince —

'the sea was swarming with sloops of war, boats and yawls full of militia, vis, the Campbells (the Argyle Militia), the Macleods and Macdonalds of Skye (the Independent Companies) etc.'

The pilot of the boat to take Charles to Uist was Donald Macleod. As Donald arrived to meet the Prince he reported:

The Prince, making towards Donald, asked 'Are you Donald Macleod of Guatergill in Sky?' Yes, I am the same man, may it please your Majesty, at your service. What is your pleasure wi' me? 'Then' said the Prince 'You see, Donald, I am in distress, I therefore throw myself into your bosom and let you do with me what you like. I hear you are an honest man, and fit to be trusted.'

Before leaving for the island, the Prince asked Donald if he would take letters from him to Sir Alexander Macdonald and Macleod of Macleod, both of whom had previously refused to join the Prince when he first raised his standard at Glenfinnan, although pro- fessedly Jacobite. Donald refused saying that both chiefs were only some ten to twelve miles distant and with their Independent Com- panies ready to capture him and 'therefore the sooner he left that place the better.'

It is interesting at this stage to wonder why both Sir Alex Macdonald and Macleod of Macleod had refused to join the Jacobite cause. Jacobites they certainly were, having previously sworn that if Charles arrived with sufficient French troops, money and arms 'they would certainly join the enterprise'. As it was, when Charles arrived virtually alone, with no men, no money, no arms, both the Skye chiefs turned their backs on him. But there were two other reasons, perhaps even stronger in their way, for this apparent volte face. Both chiefs had previously been involved in a Jacobite plot to get rid of Lady Grange wife of a noted Edinburgh Jacobite, who had promised to tell the authorities of this plot in all detail. She was quietly spirited away to a remote island off north Uist belonging to Sir Alexander—Macleod was also involved in the scheme. In another escapade, Sir Alex and Macleod ('the Red Man') were both involved

139

in the kidnap and deportation of thieves and robbers to the New World. The ship 'Soitheach nan Daoine', full of 'emigrants' was driven by a strong gale and was wrecked on the coast of Ireland — the prisoners who managed to make it ashore, squatted on land belonging to the Earl of Antrim and told their story to all and sundry.

The Lord President Duncan Forbes, as chief law officer in Sutherland, was well aware of the twin episodes of the removal of Lady Grange and the lucrative practice of selling emigrants to the U.S. — however, he chose not to take any legal action against the two, but doubtless he used a little blackmail in his attempts to keep these two very important chiefs from joining the Prince. Macleod of Macleod boasted that he could raise at least 800 men for any purpose and presumably Sir Alexander could have produced the same number of clansmen, if he had so desired.

As will be seen later Charles could not have possibly escaped if Sir Alexander had been really anxious to arrest him — indeed, he actively encouraged his dependants to aid in his escape. This will be seen to be self-evident in the steps taken at a later stage of the Prince's wanderings.

So the small party left on the 26th April with Charles 'anxious to be out of the continent (mainland) where the parties were then dispersed in search of him'. After an appalling voyage in bad weather, they landed on the coast of the Long Island at Rossinish on the Isle of Benbecula (27th April).

After a few days in Benbecula, Charles decided to make for Stornoway on 29th April, and from there possibly to get a boat for Orkney and then on to Norway. They firstly went to the island of Scalpay, when Donald Macleod was sent ahead to hire a boat. In this he was successful and sent word to the Prince. So the Prince's party (O'Sullivan, O'Neill and Burke) set out to meet Donald Macleod in Stornoway on 4 May. After a day's march and soaked to the skin, they arrived at the home of Mrs. Mackenzie of Kildun, just outside Stornoway. But there was a great deal of troop activity around the town and to make matters worse, the deal to hire the boat fell through. Also the local inhabitants of Stornoway, mainly Mackenzies of Lewis, heard of the Prince's arrival and frightened that the pursuing soldiers might steal their cattle or even kill or maim some of their number, implored the party to leave at once, 'and go to the continent or anywhere else he should think convenient.'

On the 6th May off they went in Donald Campbell's boat and with six men to row. The plan was to go to Loch Broom on the mainland but the boatmen refused to cross the open sea for fear of drowning. In the meantime two British warships came sailing up the Minch and the Prince's party hurriedly set off for the deserted isle of Euirn, where they remained until the 10th of May.

Some of the Macleod and Macdonald companies under the command of Captain Alexander Macleod of Ullinish and Captain Hugh Macdonald of Armadale respectively along with some of the militia were sent to hunt for Charles in the Long Island. It was later reported that 'some of them were evidently not too anxious to find him.'

In fact there was a report sent to Lord Arbemarle (who had succeeded Cumberland) 'that for six weeks they were "appearing" searching for him.'

While the Prince was on the island of Euirn he noticed some men-of-war just off-shore. Not knowing whether they were English or French he tried in vain to bribe the boatman to sail towards the ships in the guise of a local fisherman. If the ships were French they would have made signals to them.

On the 10th May they left Euirn to return to Scalpay, but finding that their host, Donald Campbell was away, finally finished up (11th May) on Loch Uskevagh in Benbecula. There they stayed for three days under the care of Clanranald, who brought them food and clothes. Clanranald's servant piloted them to a little island on Loch Skiport but next day a British warship came into the loch. Once again Charles and his party had to move. This time to Coradale in South Uist, where they were to stay until June 5th. During his stay the Prince shot, fished and generally appeared to be at his happiest.

However, the government troops knew that the Prince was somewhere in South Uist and further detachments of the Macleod and Macdonald companies landed in Barra in early June. By the middle of June they had arrived in South Uist and also at Rossinish in Benbecula. While this search was going on, the English ships were also patrolling the coastal waters. It was obviously only a question of time before the Prince's hiding place was discovered, so on the 14th June Charles sailed to the island of Wiay (Ouia) just off Benbecula and there he remained until the 18th. From there then to Rossinish where Lady Clanranald lived but they had information that they were likely to be discovered if they remained there. Donald Macleod and O'Sullivan took him off by boat again and once more back to Coradale but the Independent Companies were only some two miles distant.

So a very hurried dash via Loch Eynort followed and there were

141

some narrow escapes from capture until they reached Loch Boisdale. It was thought that perhaps a ship could be found there to take Charles back to France, but the Royal Navy, in the shape of the 'Baltimore' and the 'Raven' made nonsense of this plan.

At the same time came the Tyral, carrying the notorious Captain Caroline Scott and a company of regular soldiers of Guise's regiment. Captain Scott's men and a landing party from the 'Baltimore' made up around 700 men. The situation became very tense and the Prince and party had to leave hurriedly up Loch Boisdale, with warning shots ringing in their ears.

From the head of the loch the best and safest escape route was across the hills to the western side of South Uist and the Prince decided to cut down the size of his party for safety reasons. So he left O'Sullivan, Donald Macleod and the boatmen behind. This left only Neil Mac Eachain, O'Neil and the Prince to make their way to a little house near Milton.

There the Prince had this momentous meeting with Flora Macdonald, who was on a visit to her brother. Ironically, Flora, his main saviour, was the step-daughter of Hugh Macdonald of Armadale who was by now a captain in Macdonald of Sleat's Independent Company. Indeed, Hugh Macdonald's Company was in South Uist busily searching for the Prince. However, Hugh was really a 'Jacobite at heart' and was said to have 'announced his movements to friends of ours so that the Prince might always have due warning of them.'

He further proposed, as his opinion was that total escape was not possible in view of the hundreds of men hunting him down and, in the words of Neil MacEachain was 'to convey him to the Isle of Skye when he as sure to be protected by Lady Margaret Macdonald'.

Lady Margaret was the wife of Sir Alexander Macdonald and a Jacobite supporter despite her husband's refusal to join the prince.

However, it was Flora who was to be his true saviour and while she initially hesitated to help Charles thinking that Sir Alexander would be implicated in the plot, she agreed to help the Prince escape.

After Flora had agreed to undertake this dangerous mission, she set out for Clanranald's house, but on the way was taken prisoner by one of the Independent Companies as she did not have a passport to travel. Luckily, and fortunately, the Independent Company in question was captained by her step-father, Hugh Macdonald. So she and her servant Neil MacEachain remained prisoner that night, the 21st June. When her step-father arrived on the scene the following morning he wrote out permission for her to travel by way of a letter to his wife in Armadale.

> My dear Marion,
> I have sent your daughter from this country, lest she should be any way frightened with the troops lying here. She has got one Betty Burke, an Irish girl, who, as she tells me, is a good spinster. If her spinning pleases you, you may keep her till she spins all her lint; or, if you have any wool to spin, you may employ her. I have sent Neil MacEachain along with your daughter and Betty Burke to take care of them.
> I am your dutiful husband,
> *Hugh Macdonald*

The passport he wrote granted full passage for Flora, her manservant, Neil MacEachain and another woman Betty Burke. So the Prince was suitably clad as 'a good spinster' and the onward plan was:

> To send his stepdaughter, Miss Florence MacDonald, to Sleet, to live with her mother till the enemy was out of west (Uist). The Prince at the same time was ordered to dress in woman's close, that he might pass for her servant maid, and Neil was appointed to take care of both.

So it was on the night of Saturday 28th June that the trio made their way across the narrowest part of the Minch. Fortunately, the night was stormy and the visibility so poor that they remained undetected during the crossing.

Just before the crossing General Campbell of Mamore (afterwards the 4th Duke of Argyll) commanding all the regular and militia forces, was on the ship 'Furnace' which was captained by the already notorious John Ferguson. They arrived with Captain Campbell of Skipness at Gramsdale only some three miles away from the Prince's hiding place.

General Campbell's 1500 men and 800 under command of Caroline Scott made a total force of 2,300 men combing the countryside — it seemed almost impossible that the Prince could escape. It was quite evident that Charles had to move and move quickly. It was certainly propitious that Flora Macdonald and the more than willing Hugh Macdonald had organised the Prince's crossing to Skye.

143

Flora would not allow O'Neil to accompany them primarily because of his foreign appearance and difficulty with the language and also because, 'She could more easily undertake the preservation of one than of two or more.'

On the morning of the 29th they made for Vaternish Point on the north-west coast of Skye. But as they approached they noticed a group of armed soldiers (sentinels of the Macleod Independent Company) and probably captained by Norman Macleod of Waterstein. They were fired upon by the soldiers and ordered to come ashore to be identified. They hurriedly changed course and made for Loch Snizort and landed just north of Kilbride.

Flora and Neil MacEachain left the Prince near the boat and set off for the home of Sir Alexander and Lady Margaret Macdonald. Unfortunately at their house was Lieut. Macleod of one of the companies and someone who was very keen to apprehend the Prince. However, Flora managed to quieten his suspicions and sending Neil back to the Prince advised that he was to be taken to Macdonald of Kingsburgh's house instead on the night of the 29th. Charles, still dressed in women's clothes as the spinster Betty Burke caused quite a stir in the Kingsburgh household with Mrs. Macdonald remarking:

> 'I saw such a muckle trollop of a caulin, making lang wide steps through the hall that I could not like her appearance at all.'

Next morning Charles left the house still dressed as Betty Burke, but he soon changed into 'Heiland cloathes' once he reached the sanctuary of a small wood nearby. Again just in time as Captain Ferguson of the Furnace came to Kingsburgh's house and after close questioning took Macdonald and his daughter prisoner. Flora Macdonald was also arrested on her way home to Armadale and taken on board the 'Furnace'. Fortunately General Campbell was also there and insisted that she was treated 'with the utmost respect'.

Meantime the Prince and Neil went overland to Portree and then to the isle of Raasay by small boat on July 1st. They only stayed two days as the island was too narrow and confining for safety. Then on to Strathaird in Sky which was Mackinnon country guided by Malcolm Macleod of Raasay. The journey was over 20 miles of very inhospitable country and the Prince assumed the position of Macleod's servant called Lewie Caw.

They stayed at the house of Malcom's brother-in-law, Captain

144

John Mackinnon. But it proved dangerous to stay too long and on the night of 4th July (Malcolm Macleod by this time was on his way back to Raasay) Charles with the Laird of Mackinnon and his son John, made his way to the south shore of Loch Nevis between Morar and Knoydart.

There they were again challenged by the forces of an Independent Company, who ordered them to land. They crossed Loch Nevis, landed on the north shore and escaped capture yet again.

From there they travelled to Macdonald of Morar's house and to Angus Macdonald of Borrodale, where the Prince had stayed on his first landing on the mainland. But by this time the ever-vigilant Captain Ferguson had burned the house, so they had to make do with a little hut on his land. There they stayed until 16th July.

Word that the Prince had fled from Skye to Morar was sent to Fort Augustus and 500 regular redcoats, along with the Munro and Mackay Independent Companies, went west to cordon off all the roads and passes from the head of Loch Hourn to Glenfinnan.

The Prince again eluded his potential captors, notwithstanding the presence of a body of troops spaced out

> 'within half a mile's distance of one another, their sentries being placed within call of one another and patrols going about every quarter of an hour to keep the sentries alert, that so his Royal Highness might be surely catched should he attempt to pass through them.'

In spite of this apparently inpenetrable barrier, Charles managed to break out of the cordon and eventually came to the cave of Coir a' Chait, which is located in the high pass between the mountains of Garbh Leac and Sgurr nan Conbhairean.

There he met the famous eight Glenmoriston men who lived by guerrila tactics on nearby military parties. They made the Prince welcome and in this cave at an altitude of 3,600 feet; he stayed there between 24 and 27 July.

On the 28th fearing capture again, the Prince and the Glenmoriston men left for an alternative cave and another 4 days stay. Again the Independent Companies were reported to be near and another move was mooted. On the 12th August they reached the head of Glenmoriston, across the river Garry by the 14th and then to Lock Arkaig in Lochiel country, where Charles hoped to meet Lochiel again at Achnacarry house. But Lochiel's house had been burned down and Lochiel was 'skulking' in the heather some 20 miles distant. So the Prince and his band stayed near Loch Arkaig from the 17th–27th August. They then set off for Badenoch to meet the hiding Lochiel, who was still lame following the wound sustained at Culloden. They met at Loch Ericht. The Prince spent a marvellous two-day spell with his favourite chief and with plenty of food and drink they talked about what might have been.

Following his visit with Lochiel the Prince was taken by Cluny Macpherson to a safe hideout near Alder Water, 'where the hut or bothie was superlatively bad or smockie'. Again a move after 2/3 days to Cluny's safer 'cage' further up Ben Alder. There he remained in comparative safety between 2nd–13th September and while Lord Loudon and his Independent Companies were only 10–12 miles away. Fortunately no one had suggested the Prince was in the Badenoch area.

At this time, the Prince received news that two French ships had arrived on the west coast — two privateers 'L'Heureux' (34 guns) and 'Le Prince de Conti' (30 guns). So the Prince set off to walk the 100 odd miles to where the ships lay in Loch nan Uamh. Retracing his steps across the country Charles eventually reached the ships on the 19th. Fortunately government information was that Charles had gone to the east coast, to gain access to the French ships and there they imposed a strict control of all maritime movements. Such information meant that the watch on the west coast was slackened off, thus allowing the Prince to escape the net for the final time.

So ended 5 months 'in the heather' and on the run from hundreds of regular troops, militia, and the Independent Companies. It is a story of amazing hardship endured by Charles, often short of food, suffering from dysentery and everlastingly attacked by the fearsome Highland midge. Lochiel's brother, John Cameron, said it all in his account of the Prince's wanderings:

> I have told you what I was witness to or informed of by such as I could absolutely depend upon. I shall only add that the Prince submitted with patience to his adverse fortune, was cheerful and frequently desired those that were with him to be so. He was cautious when in the greatest danger, never at a loss in resolving what to do, with uncommon fortitude. He regretted more the distress of those who suffered for adhering to his interest than the hardships and the dangers he was hourly exposed to. To conclude, he possessed all the virtues that form the character of a HERO and a GREAT PRINCE.

While John Cameron was obviously biased towards the Prince,

he fairly described what must have been a most difficult, dangerous and taxing time for anyone to endure.

Charles left the Scottish shore on the 20th September with Lochiel and Cluny Macpherson and arrived in Brittany on the 29th. This was truly the end of the Jacobite cause.

It is difficult to assess why the Royal Navy was so lax in sending ships to intercept the French privateers and the liaison was very poor between the Navy and the Army's variously dispersed, but active units. In September it took eleven days for the report of the French ships to travel from Skye to Fort Augustus while, in July, news travelled the same distance in only two days.

Also lax was the failure of the Independent Companies in Uist to bring news to the Royal Naval vessels in Stornoway. Their later excuse was that they did not know where the ships were anchored, although they had been in Stornoway for nearly a month. The failure to alert the navy was perhaps the main reason for the Prince's eventual escape.

Certainly the Macleod and Macdonald commanders, in particular Alexander Macleod of Ullinish, Hugh Macdonald of Armadale and to a lesser extent Donald Macdonald of Castleton, who commanded one of the Macleod companies, together with Norman Macleod of Waterstein, had a very ambivalent attitude towards the Prince and the Jacobite cause. Undoubtedly this attitude was also responsible for what can only be described as slack and pitifully late intelligence, concerning the movements of the Young Pretender and his escape to France.

When the Prince left for France this brought to an end the history of old Scotland — the tumultuous and impoverished Scotland of the Middle Ages 'loitering in the rear of civilisation'.

147

CHAPTER 15
The Bloody Aftermath (1746–1760)

Description of Roman military prowess in the Scottish Highlands, quoted by Galgacus:
Solitudinem faciunt, pacem appellant — they make a desert and they call it peace – Tacitus (c. 55–120 A.D.)

Prophetic indeed were the words of Tacitus when related to the deeds of Cumberland and his soldiers following Culloden.

Prince Charles decision to quit the country and to let down the Highlanders has been severely criticised in some quarters. It is said that he could have regrouped an army, possibly as large as the one he had at Culloden and most importantly on ground more favourable to the distinctive Highland way of fighting — that is, the fearsome Highland charge from higher ground and in terrain where the all powerful and deadly and field guns could not have been trained and manoeuvred. Certainly, a large proportion of his forces had not been committed to the battle and they withdrew in good order. Furthermore, Clan Macpherson, Macdonald of Barrisdale with his Knoydart men and the Macgregors were all fresh troops, who had been absent from the battlefield on various ploys and could more than have made up the actual battle casualties.

However, immediately following Culloden, Charles was desperately short of the basic necessities required for an extended field campaign — meal and money. Certainly, this was the opinion of his gallant commander, Lord George Murray, who had a great deal of foresight and ability in such matters.

The behaviour of the Independent Companies after the battle is hard to reconcile or understand. In many cases they must have carried out atrocities against their close relations and their fellow clansmen. Much of the mopping-up work from Drumossie Moor to Fort Augustus, scouring the hillsides on their way, was left to the Argyll militia and the Companies. However, many other reports deny this situation to a degree where the Independent Companies were said 'to have little stomach for crushing the embers of rebellion' despite the promptings of the Hanoverian Butcher Cumberland and the Dutchman, Albermarle who succeeded him as commander-in-chief. Even the Duke of Argyll had urged moderate behaviour to the combined militia forces: 'Leave devastation to the Regular forces. . . . the Militia to burn houses and possibly to murder women and children in the scuffle, I should be very tender of'.

Loudon's men, for the most part, followed this less extreme policy.

All the forces of the government, from their base at Fort Augustus, were committed to the policy of killing or capturing men, as well as destroying houses and cattle in the territories of the Jacobite clans, from Arisaig, Knoydart, Moidart, in Morar, Brae Lochaber to Mull, Barra, Uist, Benbecula, Skye, Raasay and 'wherever the Rebells can be Founde.'

For their sort of work, perhaps only acting as guides, the Independent Companies were more suitably clad than the regular Redcoats who 'were cumbrously dressed and accoutred soldiers of the line'.

In addition, the men of the Companies spoke the gaelic tongue and indeed knew many of the people they were actually seeking.

The conduct of certain commanders following Culloden, the distressing of the Jacobite glens and the subsequent 'summer's hunting' bears telling.

Among the most sadistic was Captain John Ferguson of the sloop Furnace; Captain Caroline Scott of Guises' and Major Lockhart of Cholmondley's – all three Lowland Scots in the Navy and regular Army. As previously stated, many of the captains in the Independent Companies had ambivalent attitudes towards the Hanoverian or Jacobite causes, but Captain Campbell of Skipness and Macleod of Talister were the exceptions in that they pursued the Prince and the Jacobite Highlanders with almost excessive zeal. Fortunately for many of the prisoners captured for aiding the Prince in his escape, Major-General Campbell of Mamore exerted a very benign influence on their interrogation and managed to mitigate the worst excesses whenever he was involved.

This also included his control over the forces under his command and it was noticeable that the Argyll militia and the Independent Companies were noted for their more considerate treatment of the Jacobite clansmen. Though Mamore was a Whig and a Hanoverian, he was first of all a Highlander; his militia often stood between the regular soldiers and their continuing brutality.

In July 1746 a bill was introduced in Parliament prohibiting the wearing of Highland dress. This was followed by Lord Hardwicke's

Act of 1747 forbidding Highland dress and subsequent measures to abolish the benedictary jurisdiction of the chiefs — 'A measure for disarming and undressing these savages'.

Duncan Forbes was very opposed to these strictures on the grounds that the Highland garb was the most suitable for those living and having to work in mountainous areas, with its associated harsh climate. He stated that such a ban on dress was unnecessary and that only the removal of weaponry and some control of the clan system would effectively keep the clansmen out of trouble. The proscribing of the dress (until 1782) was most cruel and petty, although in fairness it only applied to the Jacobite clans.

It was obvious that the government over-reacted to the 'Highland menace', where they were more warlike by nature and highly trained and skilled in arms, and more significantly, under the spell and control of a potentially violent chief. Where possible, Highlanders were forced to swear an oath:

> I do swear, as I shall answer to God on the great day of Judgement. I shall not, nor shall have in my possession a gun, sword, pistol or arm whatsoever and never use tartan, plaid or any part of the Highland garb; and if I do so may I be cursed in my undertakings, family and property, may I be killed in battle as a coward, and lie without burial in a strange land, far from the graves of my forefathers and kindred; may all this come across me if I break my oath.

The military patrols were maintained in the Highlands for many years in order to enforce this Disarming Act but eventually the penalties were less severely applied and in 1782 when the proscription was lifted a proclamation was sent round the glens:

> This is declaring to every man, young and old, Commons and Gentles, that they may after this put on and wear the Trews, the little Kilt, the Doublet and Hose along with the Tartan Kilt, without fear of the Law of the Land or the jealousy of Enemies.

However, much of the old attachment to the Garb of Gaul had withered and the old patterns had been forgotten. The clans were reduced in size and in influence. The Kilt was kept alive by those who joined the new Highland regiments after the disbandment of the Independent Companies.

Following Culloden, the Independent Companies were reduced

in size (by the end of June 1746) by I sergeant, I corporal and 30 sentinels, leaving a total company size of 3 sergeants, 3 corporals 1 Drummer, 1 piper and 70 sentinels. This followed the successful disposal of any further threat from the Jacobites and within six months of Culloden, the Companies and the militia were disbanded altogether. However, certain drafts taken from the companies were incorporated into Lord Loudon's regiment and sent to Flanders in 1747 but were disbanded in Perth in 1748.

During the emergency raising of the 18 Independent Companies from October 1745 to February 1746 it was obviously impossible to have them kitted out with a standard uniform in time. It is believed that initially they wore their own Highland dress and their only distinguishing mark, to show that they were in Government employment, was the black cockade and a red cross (worn saltire-wise) in the bonnet. However, by the end of the Rising, the companies were uniformed in a short red coat and long waistcoat with the brgacan an fheifidh (belted plaid), red and white hose, buckled shoes for parade and undress, cuarans or skin shoes for hill walking. To finish off the uniform, a round blue bonnet and the 'rid cros' on a black cockade.

In the year 1760, commissions were given to raise 5 Independent Companies in the Highlands under the following Captains:

> Colin Graham of Drainie
> James Cuthbert of Milncraigs
> Peter Gordon of Knockespick
> Ludovic Grant of Rothiemurchus
> Robert Campbell of Ballivolin.

These officers were to command companies of 5 sergeants and 105 sentinels each. The recruiting areas were the counties of Argyll, Ross and Inverness. It is noticeable that only two of the traditional clans, i.e. the Grants and the Campbells, supplied commanders and that the other 3 or 4 men were later from families which had not previously appeared on the Independent Companies scene.

The Companies, being soon recruited up to strength, remained in training near Perth until the end of 1761, when they were embodied and send to reinforce the Keith and Campbell's Highlanders.

Recruitment of men in the Highlands was so successful that their officers were sent back to Scotland to gather together another body of men. In a few months 600 men were assembled at Perth, where they were formed into a regiment of six companies again with 5 sergeants and 105 sentinels in each. The regiment was numbered the 101st and commanded by Sir James Johnstone of Westerhall. Apart from Major Johnstone himself, the adjutant Macreah and Sergeant-Major Coxwell, every officer and sentinel were of Highland stock.

This new regiment, Johnstone's Highlanders was reviewed in Perth in 1762 and the reviewing officer, General Beauclerk declared that: 'he had not seen a body of men in a more efficient state and better fitted to meet the enemy.'

The regiment was due to go to Portugal under the Earl of Loudon, but while waiting to embark, negotiations for peace were undertaken and they returned to Perth where the regiment was reduced in August 1763.

During the Seven Years War (1756–63) a number of unidentified Independent Companies sometimes captained by additional officers including Alexander Ross, Neil Campbell, Alexander Macdonald and John Machargh were mustered in the Highlands, only to be sent almost immediately as recruits for Lowland or English regiments. As such, they could scarcely be classified as true Independent Companies and were largely just a recruiting agency for the British Army.

So ended the history of the Independent Companies which started in 1603 and ended in 1763 covering a period of 160 years and in an era of great upheaval and violence. It virtually ended on the bleak, flat moor of Drumossie on 16th April 1746. But from it emerged the world-famous Highland regiments during the remainder of the 18th Century.

Epilogue

The nature of their country, their manner of living and their continual exercise in hunting, fishing and fowling, render them hardy, robust, enterprising and equal capable of long marches and of sustaining patiently the want of food or of rest. It is evident therefore, that the striping these men of their arms, and obliging them as it were to a new kind of life, was a bold undertaking and such a one as seemed to require an additional force: and in this case none so proper as this of the Independent Companies; for thus the arms were taken out of the hands of the enemies of the government, and put into those of their friends: this harsh law was executed entirely by their own countrymen which gave it less the air of violence, than if it had been done by English troops; and lastly it was done more effectually, for these new raised forces were able to march anywhere, knew the country, as well as those they were to follow and having legal authority were every way their superiors. — A Short History of the Highland Regiment, by Jacob Robinson, 1743.

It is difficult to assess the true value of the Independent Companies.

Opinions vary on this matter depending upon one's viewpoint. Chiefs, anxious to control a company, to have free keep for their clansmen and, perhaps even more significantly to have free military training for their followers, considered them to be of considerable importance. Many chiefs in the late 17th and 18th centuries were extremely short of money, with their estates and belongings heavily mortgaged, often to support a too lavish life-style in London and Edinburgh. They were extremely anxious to have a steady and supportable income if possible from the Crown.

Apart from any monetary considerations, the fact of having a company was also an important status symbol among the loyal Whig clans and it also underpinned their unquestioning support of the government. Sometimes, however, loyalties became a little strained and this was never more clearly instanced than in the split loyalties displayed by the Atholl, Macpherson, Mackenzie, Gordon and Fraser families, both early and late in the period 1603–1760.

153

Certainly the companies had an extremely chequered history from their inception in the early 17th century until, their final demise of their regimentation into the British Army. In the very early days of the King's Guard and the Highland Captaincies, the effect and influence of two small mounted forces properly used, paid and organised was altogether out of proportion to their size. These mobile troops, used primarily in a gendarmerie role, showed just how efficient such government troops could be and it was amazingly short-sighted of the authorities not to recognise this all too obvious fact sooner. Following 1660 and backed by the might of the Atholl and Argyll families even larger units, on foot this time, were brought into being & from all accounts showed that Highlanders dressed suitably for the terrain and led by gaelic speaking officers, had a major effect in containing, if not eradicating robbery of all types. Regular English and Lowland Scottish troops unacquainted with the ways and habits of the Highlands, were of limited use in a situation where they could not deploy their formal and disciplined method of fighting and civil control.

Furthermore the regular troops in their uniforms and boots, almost constantly soaked by rain and underfoot conditions were very dispirited bodies of men, who cared little for the local inhabitants. However, penny-pinching authorities could not make their minds up on the economies of maintaining Highland Companies and whenever there was a lull in cattle-lifting and robbery, the companies were often disbanded before they should have been. The alternative was to have recourse to punishments such as jailing or even transportation in order to keep the peace. From time to time the chiefs were summoned, so that they could be made accountable for their clansmen's behaviour: but with so many 'broken men' travelling at will between different clan areas, it was virtually impossible to enforce control without the aid of the Independent Companies.

In view of the chequered story of the Independent Companies told in proceeding chapters, it is necessary to view them synoptically to make sense of their comings and goings.

Between 1660 and 1688 some twenty companies were raised only to be stood down after a short period of time. They were completely at the whim of the ruling bodies whether in Edinburgh or London. Firstly they were fashionable and effective, then they were held to be corrupt and too costly to maintain. In 1688, to support the crown, Kenneth Mackenzie of Suddies' company suffered very heavy losses against the might of the Macdonnells of Keppoch and other clans at Mulroy. This was the final great clan battle and unfortunately Suddie was mortally wounded on this occasion.

In 1689 for the second time, a company was used in other than a policing role. The Laird of Weems' company (led by Robert Menzies, yr of Weem) was used in a full-scale battle at the Pass of Killiecrankie where they formed part of Leven's regiment (later the Kings Own Scottish Borderers) and where by all accounts, acquitted them-selves in a stalwart military fashion by warding off the terrifying Highland charge. Although forced to retreat they did so in an orderly fashion along with the remaining regulars. Initially, they had been asked by George Mackay to act solely as guides, but eventually a fully manned company of 100 sentinels assumed a more major role under general battle conditions.

In the period from 1690 to their disbandment in 1717 a further 10 companies were raised and stood down, often being used along with regular troops and acting from garrisons and/or fortified houses. Sometimes the captains had 100 men under command and sometimes only 60 in total. This number was further diluted when they were frequently used on detachment duty. They were also used in a support role during the '08 and '15 Risings, where they were commissioned to try to dissuade Highlanders, with Jacobite lean-ings, from joining in the Risings. Afterwards they featured in mopping-up operations, where they had intimate and local knowl-edge of the whereabouts of the clansmen and their houses.

A different role emerged in the years between 1717 and 1724. Four interim companies, only comprising 10 officers and 120 men in all were raised for garrison duties at Fort William, Fort Augustus, Bernera and Ruthven. Also in 1719 at the Battle of Glenshiel, the Munro company, ably led by George Munro of Culcairn, took a very positive part in the fighting: helped by their bold action to defeat the Highlanders under the Earl Marischall.

But the really momentous decision came in 1725 when a proposal initially put forward by Lord Lovat in his now famous Memorial, was physically introduced by General Wade under instruction from the King. This was to raise 6 companies properly controlled, trained and organised in order to keep effective peace in the Highlands. Some 14 years later another 4 companies were added and the whole was regimented into the 43rd Regiment of Foot, later to be the 42nd of Foot, the Black Watch or Royal Highlanders.

Then came the '45 Rising and the urgent need to raise another

20 Independent Companies (of which only 18 were formed), to fight along side the government forces against Prince Charles.

These companies, most significantly including the Macdonalds and Macleods of Skye, helped to dissuade many Highlanders from joining the Jacobites and also tied up Jacobite forces, especially north of the Great Glen. This action by the companies virtually stopped most of the vital reinforcements reaching Charles' army at Culloden. In this massive effort to raise 18 companies in such a short period of time, due recognition must go to Lord President Duncan Forbes, who single-handed bullied and cajoled the chiefs into accepting these commissions. Six months after Culloden, the Jacobites were seen to be no further threat and the companies were stood down. For all intents and purposes, this was the end of the Independent Company story. Apart from a late flurry of activity in 1760 to raise 6 more companies from clan sources, officered by leading people in the clan and used in the Highlands, the whole system of clan recruitment fell into disuse. It was replaced by a regimental system, where whole Highland regiments were recruited for the Scottish Establishment of the British Army.

The story of the Independent Companies and their importance in history depends very largely on the actions and personalities of George Wade and Duncan Forbes. George Wade's shrewd evaluation of the problems of the Highlands was contained in his famous report to George I in 1724. This report not only examined the problem but came up with the answers.

While his road and bridge-building is what Wade is most often remembered for, in the event his roads had little military bearing on the outcome of the '45 Rising and were only used by the Jacobites in their way south into England. His main importance lay in his recognition that only Highlanders from the local Highland clans could answer the inate problems of overall lawlessness and hence his recommendations to the King. He pressed for them, insisted that they were regularly trained and that their numbers had to be fully authenticated at all times. Also that they were to be regularly reviewed as to their turn-out, drill and military preparedness.

With regard to Duncan Forbes, he was born in 1685 and died an exhausted and broken man in 1747. He had been extremely active in the '15 and '19 Risings, but 1745 was to show his real value to history. Blank commissions forms were sent by Secretary of State for Scotland (Lord Tweedale) to Lord President Forbes as the person selected to choose commanders and supervise the raising of a completely new batch of Independent Companies. Andrew Mitchell (aide to Tweedale) stated:

> If your Lordship shall be able to raise the Independent Companies, so as to act before the arrival of the troops, you will have done the most essential service to the government that has in my memory been performed by any subject.

His influence on the major Highland chiefs was paramount and although he failed with Lovat, Seaforth and Cluny Macpherson, he managed to control the most influential and powerful of the chiefs and those who could have supplied many hundreds of clansmen to Charles.

His major success was to convince the Macdonalds and Macleods of Skye, both basically Jacobite in instinct, to hold back from joining the Jacobite army. Indeed, between them they furnished 8 out of the total 18 companies raised in 1745 and 1746.

The curious story is told about the Macleod companies that in order to get his men to march out of Skye, Macleod put it about that he was really recruiting for the Prince and that he even provided his men with white cockades making them think that they were joining the Jacobite cause. Similarly, with the Macdonald clansmen, there was virtually the same problem. Sir Alexander Macdonald wrote to Forbes: 'The men are as devoted to the young gentleman [the Prince] as their wives and daughter are.'

It says a great deal for the power of these two chiefs that they managed to bring their men along to serve for the government.*

The speed at which the companies were raised is notable proof of the survival of the clans military-type organisation. In spite of atrocious weather that winter, by the middle of December 1745 all the companies were mustered and all but 3 had reached Inverness.

Macleod of Macleod with his powerful clan and large estates said that he could put some 7 to 800 men into the field. It is also estimated that the Macdonalds could have produced around the same number. Such a large group of men could have significantly altered the odds in favour of Charles had they both joined the Prince.

Forbes virtually financed the payment himself for the raising and

---

*How far Forbes foresaw and encouraged the ambivalence of these commanders and their companies, can only be subject to speculation. Their actions certainly mitigated even worse terrors and consequences in the aftermath of the '45.

maintenance of the companies and he died not having fully recovered his outlay from the government. His understanding and sympathy for the Highlanders after Culloden was ill-rewarded by the treatment he received from Cumberland who considered him 'to be an old woman, who talked to me about humanity'.

Yet without his efforts it is doubtful whether the government would have won at Culloden and it is no exaggeration to say that he was 'the saviour of the Hanoverian dynasty'.

A Jacobite writer later commented:

> 'Had the Lord President been as firm a friend as he was an implacable enemy of the exiled Stuarts we should have seen instead of 4,000 men who marched into England, an army of 18–20,000 men and I am sure that James would in all probability have won back the British throne.'

Another report said that when Forbes heard that Cumberland had once referred to his services as "nor worth five shillings" he retorted: 'I thought they were worth three Crowns.'

To the Jacobites, Duncan Forbes was 'the chief object of their resentment' especially when they came back from England and it was their fixed opinion that:

> with the Macdonalds and Macleods of Skye, the Mackenzies and Frasers they might have become masters in the south had all these joined them soon enough; the failing of which they place at your Lordship's account.

In 1738 Duncan Forbes had submitted a plan to utilise the warlike nature of the clansmen by raising regiments from among the clans but this was turned down by the Government. Had his advice been acted upon it is very unlikely that the '45 Rising would even have taken place. Later Pitt, the Earl of Chatham was to get the kudos for being the first to air this idea, but the credit must surely go to this far-seeing Lord President.

When the worst of the emergency was over, Forbes wrote concerning just how effective his Independent Companies could have been in the initial stages:

> Had arms and ammunition come when they were first called for, before the unexpected successes blew up folly to madness, I could have answered it with my head that no man from the North should have joined the original force of rebels that passes the Forth.

These two men General George Wade and Lord President Forbes had a major effect on the subsequent history of Scotland by maintaining the succession of the Protestant dynasty. Their legacy was firstly the Independent Companies and then the Highland regiments.

Lastly with regard to the two Highland chiefs, Macleod and Macdonald, who supported the Hanoverian cause and who more than likely led to the Jacobites' defeat. Macleod of Macleod was for ever after known as 'An Droch Dhuine' (the wicked man) and Sir Alexander Macdonald died remonstrating with Cumberland about the treatment the Highlanders were having to suffer following Culloden. His reported statement about Cumberland after Culloden sums up his agony at the decision he took not to support Charles:

> Is it not very hard that I should be obliged to come and bow to that puppy and to kiss his fingers, whom not long ago I thought to have given a kick in the breech? Had I ever imagined that my country would have been so served I should have shewn them another thing of it, for had I raised my men MacLeod durst not have stayed at home.

On another occasion exchange of greetings revealed the arrogance of Cumberland and the proud spirit of Sir Alexander: 'So here comes the great rebel of the Isles' taunted Cumberland. Sir Alexander proudly replied: 'If, Sir, I had been a rebel, you would never have crossed the Spey'.

He died a broken man at Glenelg on the 23 December 1746 after having done all in his power to mitigate the worst excesses against the beaten Jacobites, but the Jacobite Highlanders remembered him in verse: 'Then all are pleased — Macdonald's in his grave.'

Perhaps a more fitting epitaph to this undoubted great clan chief was the reported saying when he was not given his proper place at the head of the table at a meeting of lesser chiefs: ' — wherever Macdonald sits, *that* is the head of the table'.

The whole series of Jacobite insurrections – mainly 1708, 1715, 1719 and 1745 were all doomed, in that the clans were divided in religion, politics, social mores and in self-interest. They lacked the necessary cohesion which is so necessary in any successful plan of campaign. The clans were too parochial in outlook to present a common front against the increasing power of the Monarchy.

On many occasions they came close to success, but in three battles and skirmishes of the early 18th century, they lacked the leadership and the driving force which was evidenced by the brilliant commanders of the 1640s and the 1680s, James Graham, Marquis of Montrose and John Graham of Claverhouse, Viscount Dundee.

But just how close was the campaign of 1745–46 is best described by the Elder Pitt when he said in the House of Commons on 21 April, 1749:

> If the rebel leader could have persuaded his people to have ventured a battle against the Duke in Staffordshire, or to have given him the slip, marched towards London, and fought a battle near this city, the fate of England would have depended on the issue of that battle; for if they had obtained a victory and made themselves masters of London, I question if the spirit of the populace would not have taken a very different turn.

Returning to the Independent Companies, the final verdict must be a very mixed one. They undoubtedly had a major effect in maintaining peace and order in the 17th and early 18th centuries, especially when well led and wisely used. Had they been ineffective then doubtless they would not have been raised, as they were, time and again as occasion demanded. At times, they were poorly commanded and often their numbers, boosted to collect extra payment from the government, were not as accurately recorded as they might have been. Certainly their presence as guides and interpreters proved invaluable to the regular forces. Their proper fighting abilities were only seriously questioned some 4 or 5 times – Mulroy in 1688, Killiecrankie in 1689, Glenshiel in 1719 and in one or two skirmishes during the '45 Rising at Inverurie and north of the Great Glen.

However, the least said about the almost comical episode at the Rout of Moy, the better. But later and to their credit, they showed mainly restrained and often humane behaviour towards the fleeing Jacobites and a noticeable lack of zeal in apprehending the Young Pretender especially in the Long Island. As Dr Alistair Maclean, in his book, *A MacDonald for the Prince*, stated of the Macdonald and Macleod companies that they were 'Jacobites at heart'.

Lastly, the newly regimented companies in the Black Watch, fighting a brilliant and dashing rearguard action at Fontenoy showed the real quality and mettle of the Highlanders.

The formation and the retention of clan companies in the Highlands was an extremely difficult decision for any British Prime Minister. On the positive side, it tied the chiefs and their men very firmly to the government, while keeping peace at the same time. On the negative side, it could be training and embodying a force for use by the exiled house. But eventually the common sense of such a move became so obvious and William Pitt described it thus in 1766 many years after Culloden:

> It is my boast that I was the first minister who looked for it, and found it in the mountains of the north. I called it forth, and drew into your service a hardy and intrepid race of men: men who when left by your jealousy, became prey to the artifices of your enemies, and had gone nigh to have overturned the state in the war before last (War of the Austrian Succession). These men in the last war (Seven Years' War), were brought to combat on your side; they served with fidelity, as they fought with valour, and conquered for you in every quarter of the world.

However, speaking of his recruitment of Highlanders for foreign service he was later reported to have said somewhat cynically to Lord Harwicke 'not many of them would return.' His policy served a double purpose. It provided George II and his heirs with the finest fighting men in the world but it also denuded the Highlands of manpower and so removed a potential threat to the House of Hanover.

The system of military command was second nature to the warlike Highland clansmen. It was therefore a very small step to transfer this warlike instinct from clan loyalty to loyalty for the Regiment. Lord Wavell, a former Black Watch officer was to write:

> The Highlands of Scotland have always been famous for their fighting men, They were formidable warriors indeed, matchless in endurance and courage, unsurpassed for swiftness and vigour in attack. To the fighting qualities of the old stock has been added the steadfast discipline of the regular soldier; and the Highland regiments still remain the finest fighting force in the British Isles, with a record of service which . . . shows that some or other of them have been engaged and distinguished themselves in practically every campaign of the British Army for the last 200 years. His native stubbornness, added to his regular discipline and training, has made the Highlander as steadfast in defence as any, but he has always kept the fierceness and swiftness in attack for which his ancestors were so famous.

In the mid 18th century there still existed in the Highlands of Scotland people who had changed little in lifestyle, customs, language and religion since before medieval times. This was largely due to the topography of the country, with it's almost total absence of any road system and with virtually no communication between districts in a very mountainous landscape and sea-girt islands.

The system of government was intensely local, was mainly patriarchal in kind and the various clans often were at war with their neighbours.

When the clansmen did venture far south of the Highland line, the Lowland Scots and English thought them uncouth and even barbaric, speaking as they did a language completely incomprehensible and carrying weapons of a fearsome nature.

Following Culloden, the British Government realised the potential in terms of fighting men and from 1740 onwards the Highlands supplied 27 line regiments and 19 battalions of fencible men from a variety of clans. * By the turn of the century, in the wars against France, this number was increased by a further 65 infantry battalions:

In 1746 after the battle of Culloden the fighting strength of the clans had been estimated at 31,930 by Lord Forbes and many highland chiefs were more than enthusiastic to prove their loyalty to the crown.

The breakdown was as follows:

Argyle	3,000
Breadalbane	1,000
Lochnell and other Chieftains of the Campbells	1,000
Macleans	500
Maclachlans	200
Stewart of Appin	300
Macdougals	200
Stewart of Grandtully	300
Clan Gregor	700
Duke of Athole	3,000
Farquharsons	500
Duke of Gordon	300
Grant of Grant	850
Macintosh	800
Macphersons	400
Frasers	900
Grant of Glenmorriston	150
Chisholms	200
Duke of Perth	300
Seaforth	1,000
Cromarty, Scatwell, Gairloch and other Chieftains of the Mackenzies	1,500
Menzies	300
Munroes	300
Rosses	500
Sutherland	2,000
Mackays	800
Sinclairs	1,100
Macdonald of Slate	700
Macdonald of Clanronald	700
Macdonell of Glengary	500
Macdonell of Keppoch	300
Macdonald of Glencoe	130
Robertsons	200
Camerons	800
McKinnon	200
Macleod	700
The Duke of Montrose, Earls of Bute and Moray, Macfarlanes, Colquhouns, McNeils of Barra, McNabs, McNaughtans, Lamonts, etc, etc	5,600
	31,930

Epilogue

So from the emergence of the Independent Companies and the recruitment of regiments into the British Army, arose the six principal Highland regiments which, until recently were formed and regimented during the latter half of the 18th century.

In order of their initial formation the list is as follows:

1740 – The Black Watch (Royal Highland Regiment)
1759 – The Gordon Highlanders
1777 – The Highland Light Infantry (Lord Macleod's Highlanders)
1778 – The Seaforth Highlanders (The Duke of Albany's Own Highlanders and the Ross-shire Buffs)
1793 – The Queen's Own Cameron Highlanders
1794 – The Argyll and Sutherland Highlanders (Princess Louise's)

Recent amalgamations have left only two regiments, The Black Watch and the Argylls.

APPENDIX 1
Notes on Dress and Accoutrements

From Scottish Record Office Reference BH. 2/8.

The 'Knock Notebook', 1731–33, being the account book of Sergeant William Grant, paymaster of Colonel [William] Grant [of Ballindalloch]'s Independent Company. It records receipts and disbursements, including sums paid by Colonel Grant, expenses for arms, transport, clothing and other supplies, and pay issued to the soldiers (named), with receipts. Places where money was paid or received include Ruthven, Ballimackain, Inverness, Kenmore, Stirling and Ballindalloch. Also includes:

Fo. 8 Account of spare arms, Kenmore, 5 Oct. 1732
Fos. 18–19 A love poem (in a different hand)
Fo. 28 'An list of the shoes', n.d.
Fos. 30–31 Account of plaids given out to seventy named soldiers.

(Original *penes* James McArthur, Inverourie, Kirkmichael, Banffshire)

Source Unknown
'The Board of General Officers inspecting and regulating the cloathing of the army observe: There is a peculiar cloathing for the three Highland companies in North Britain, not at all military, but like the cloathing of the natives there, that they may the better discover any designs, or machinations, against the Government, or the country, which if it should thought fit to be continued, it is humbly proposed that some particular distinctions or instructions may be given therein, for allowing such cloathing for the future; consisting of Plaids, Tartan coats, Trousers (Trews), hose, pumps, bonnets, shirts, cravats, shoulder belts, broad belts, powder horns, with belts and measures and broad swords with basket hilts; with targets and pistols over and above for the Sergeants, and how the same may be viewed since they can only be provided in the Highland countries very remote from Edinburgh.' — Privy Garden, Whitehall, February 21st, 1708–9.

THE WAR OFFICE RECORDS.

In the course of exhaustive researches at the Public Record Office some years ago the present writer kept particularly in mind Stewart's statement as to a new pattern having been assumed by the regiment in 1739–40, but found absolutely nothing which could be regarded as referring to any alteration in the tartan theretofore worn by the Black Watch Companies. The only recorded letters in which the subject of the clothing is referred to are in the following terms:-

War Office, 27th January 1739/40.

My Lord,
I am commanded by His Majesty to signify to your Lordship It is His Pleasure that you annually produce Patterns of Cloathing for your Regiment on the First day of January and show the same at Edinburgh to the officer for the time being commanding His Forces in North Britain, and when the same is approved of by him then to take care that the whole Regimental Cloathing be prepared so as to be put on the Men's backs yearly on the 11th of June being the Day of His Majesty's Accession to the Crown and the Day on which All His Foot Forces are cloathed. I am,
My Lord,
Your Lordship's most obedient humble Servant,
WILL. YONGE.

P.S. The producing your Patterns this year having been delayed for *His Majty's Approbation of the Species*, you are to prepare a Pattern as soon as possible to be laid before the Commander in Chief as above directed for his Approbation as to the Goodness.

Earl of Crawford.
War Office, 27th January 1739/40.

Sir,
I have by the King's commands acquainted the Earl of Crawford It is His Pleasure that his Lordship do annually produce Patterns of Cloathing for his Regiment on the First day of January, and show the same at Edinburgh to the officer for the Time being commanding His Forces in North Britain, and when the same is approved by him, then to take care that the whole Regimental Cloathing be prepared so as to be put on the Men's backs yearly, on the 11th day of June, His Majesty's Accession to the Crown, and the day on which All His Foot Forces are cloathed. I am thereupon commanded by His Majesty to

acquaint you with this His Pleasure, that when his Lordship doth annually produce the Patterns of Cloathing, and you approve the same, that you then signify the same to his Lordship and to me, to the end the whole Regimental Cloathing may be prepared and put on the men's backs annually on the Eleventh of June accordingly.

I am, Sir,

Your most humble Servant,

WILL YONGE

Two lengths of tartan were sewn together to form a rectangle about five feet wide and fifteen or eighteen feet long to make a plaid (Gaelic *plaide* or blanket). It was worn in the Lowlands as a cloak, often with a pattern of simple checks, and in the Highlands as the *breacan feileadh* or belted plaid, in a much richer range of pattern and colour (*breacan* means mottled or variegated and *feileadh* is a fold or pleat). Woven from tightly twisted yarn, the cloth was much more waterproof than modern tartan cloth.

There is no evidence that the Independent Companies were issued with the short red jacket which was to become regimental wear – probably not if it is true that the nickname of *An Freiceadan Dubh* or Black Watch derives from the contrast of their appearance with that of the 'redcoats'. This derivation is disputed by those who claim that the name was an abusive reference to the Companies' role of suppressing blackmail. In either case, the regiment was not known by this name in the late eighteenth century, for Boswell in his enthusiasm for all things Highland would certainly have used it in his journal when he described their arrival at Edinburgh Castle in 1775. Instead, he refers to the Royal Highland Regiment (which it became in 1758) and the Highland Watch. It was not until 1861 that the Black Watch, as an honourable distinction, was added to their title.

The corporal of the regiment in Figure 21 is based on the *Cloathing Book* and on one of Bowles's 'Mutineer' drawings (see page 34). The most distinctive feature of his dress, as a regular soldier, is of course the belted plaid of a tartan variously known as the government pattern, the government sett and the military pattern. Its origin is the subject of much controversy, as is the question of whether it was worn by the Independent Companies before they were embodied as the 43rd. It seems to have been a new tartan, and its dark blue, black and green sett, sometimes with a slight variation, became the tartan of a succession of regiments as well as forming the basis for several so-called clan or family tartans.

One very unlikely theory of its genesis is that any distinguishing overstripes were removed from the tartans of the individual Company commanders, to produce a sort of lowest common denominator; another is that it was invented from scratch because the first colonel, the Earl of Crawford, was a Lowlander. A third theory, advanced by Colonel M. M. Haldane, is that it was 'adapted from an old sett in common use all over the Highlands, since it is the basis of many tartans which only differ by additional stripes of brighter colours, and as such would be suitable to a regiment recruited throughout the Highlands'. This is perhaps related to yet another theory, that the sett, if not the colours, of the government pattern was derived from the Stewart worn since 1713 or 1714 by the Royal Company of Archers, the King's Bodyguard in Scotland.

The corporal wears a red jacket, short because the normal infantry coat would not accommodate the folds of a belted plaid. It had no collar or lapel, the buff lining and facing showing only at the throat and cuffs; a lapel was soon introduced. (Buff was a rather vague official description and ranged from cream to pale brown, to judge from extant examples.) The shoulder knot indicates his rank. His head-dress is a flat blue bonnet; its toorie may have been red, more likely blue, and it was probably garnished with a ribbon threaded through openings round the brim, which could be tightened and knotted at the back. This ribbon was later of red material, and was the origin of the familiar diced rim of the bonnet.*

His diced hose are cut from cloth, not knitted; 'plaid for hose' is a frequent entry in clothing lists. The Bowles print shows sporran (a leather pouch with an ornamental top), dirk and pistol in addition to the broadsword and bayonet, although, in the *Cloathing Book*, the private has a pouch attached to the centre of his waistbelt but no sporran, dirk or pistol. The basket-hilted broadsword was only carried, as far as infantry was concerned, by Highland troops; its name did not imply any abnormal width, just that – unlike the backsword – it was edged on two sides, designed for slashing and not thrusting. The dirk, with a blade of some fifteen inches, and the pistol were both normal Highland accoutrements as was the targe or small round shield which men of the new regiment in its early years were permitted to acquire at their own expense.

*It was usual to wear feathers of blackcock, vultures, eagles, &c., a clan badge (probably a sprig of some plant), or occasionally a piece of fur, on the left side, and to this was added the white Jacobean cockade, or the Black or Red Hanoverian one, as the case might be.

The Scottish pistol was a very unusual firearm, being of all-metal construction. It was manufactured in the Lowlands, at Doune in particular, mainly for the Highland market, although the workmanship was of so fine a quality that examples found their way to the French court. It was regarded as an integral feature of Highland dress and therefore became a government issue to Highland regiments. 'Issue' pistols came to be made in London and Leith, with wooden butts, but superbly engraved all-metal pistols were often purchased by officers. Engraved or plain, they were fitted with a catch to hang at chest height from a narrow shoulder strap. The long trigger, with a bulbous terminal, had no trigger-guard and the butt was finished in a decorative shape – fish-tail, lobed, heart and, for most Highland regiments, the scroll or ram's horn, with a pricker screwed into the butt between the incurved 'horns'. A metal ramrod lay under the barrel. The overall length of the pistol was about fifteen inches.

An excellent contemporary description of the Highlanders and their dress is provided by the following quotation from *A Short History of the Highland Regiment*, printed for Jacob Robinson at the Golden Lion Press in 1743:

'To begin with their shoes. The Highlander wears a sort of thin pump or brogue, so light that it does not in the least impede his activity in running; and from being constantly accustomed to these kind of shoes, they are able to advance or retreat with incredible swiftness, so that if they have the better in any engagement it is scarce possible to escape from them: and on the other hand, if they are over power'd they soon recover their hills, where it is impossible to reach them. The reader will easily perceive that this is one of the advantages which the Croats and Pandours have over the French troops, especially in such a country as Bavaria, which is every where intersected by rivers. They gain from hence an opportunity, first of wearying their enemy, 'till they are forced to break, and then they are sure to be knocked on the head, as finding it impossible to run away from these people. In the next place, the Highlander wears broad garters under the knee, and no breeches, but his plaid belted about his waist, which hangs exactly like the folds of the Roman garment, which we see on Equestrian statues; the reason of this dress is, to make the leg firm, and to leave the sinews and joints quite free, to preserve the wearer from any thing that may heat or embarrass him and to afford him an opportunity of extending his limbs with the greatest ease; besides this, he wears a jacket with strait sleeves, and as for his arms they consist in a fusil, a broad sword, a dirk or dagger, an Highland pistol all of steel, hung on the other side of his belt, opposite to the dirk, and a target. The use of these arms they learn from their infancy, and are extremely adroit in them.

The nature of their country, their manner of living, and their continual exercise in hunting, fishing, and fowling, render them hardy, robust, enterprizing, and equally capable of long marches, and of sustaining patiently the want of food or of rest. It is evident therefore, that the striping these men of their arms, and obliging them as it were to a new kind of life, was a bold undertaking, and such a one as seem'd to require an additional force; and in this case none so proper as this of the independent companies; for thus the arms were taken out of the hands of the enemies of the government, and put into those of their friends; this harsh law was executed entirely by their own country men, which gave it less the air of violence, than if it had been done by English troops; and lastly it was done more effectually, for these new raised forces were able to march any where, knew the country, as well as those they were to follow, and having legal authority were every way their superiors.'

Two further notes on the regimental uniform of the Black Watch are:

'The tartan, as worn by the regiment, has been the subject of much research and controversy over the years, but it has been definitely established, by Major I.H. Mackay Scobie, as the Government tartan. As such it was available to all Scottish regiments, and in slightly modified form (with coloured over-stripes, etc.) it has become the basis for other regimental and clan tartans, of which the Gordon and Mackenzie are two examples. Just as the red coat was typical of the British army as a whole, this tartan (which became one of the oldest in existence, owing to the loss of many of the clan setts after the '45 rebellion) is now regarded as almost the national tartan of Scotland.'

'The uniform was a scarlet jacket and waistcoat, with buff facings and white lace, – tartan[6] plaid of twelve yards plaited round the middle of the body, the upper part being fixed on the left shoulder ready to be thrown loose, and wrapped over both shoulders and firelock in rainy weather. At night the plaid served the purpose of a blanket, and was a sufficient covering for the Highlander. These were called belted plaids from being kept tight to the body by a belt, and were worn on guards, reviews, and on all occasions when the men were in full dress. On this belt hung the pistols and dirk when worn. In the barracks, and when not on duty, the little kilt or philibeg was worn, a blue bonnet with a border of white, red and green, arranged in small squares to resemble, as is said, the *fess cheque* in the arms of the

170

different branches of the Stewart family, and a tuft of feathers, or sometimes, from economy or necessity, a small piece of black bear-skin. The arms were a musket, a bayonet, and a large basket-hilted broadsword. These were furnished by government. Such of the men as chose to supply themselves with pistols and dirks were allowed to carry them, and some had targets after the fashion of their country. The sword-belt was of black leather, and the cartouch-box was carried in front, supported by a narrow belt round the middle.'

171

APPENDIX 2
Notes On The Highland Charge

FROM SCOTTISH MILITARY DRESS by Peter Cochrane

It has been suggested that the technique of the charge in its modern form was introduced by Montrose's ally, Alasdair MacColla, who had used it in the battle of Laney in Coleraine in 1642. Before field artillery came into general use, the critical moment for an attacking force occurred when its advance brought it within effective musket range, perhaps 100 to 150 yards, particularly if the enemy was steady, well drilled, and, by 'platoon firing' in sequence, able to produce a sustained fire. By their appearance, their war cries and their reputation, Highlanders were often able to unsteady their opponents and reduce the danger of a succession of ordered volleys, while the sheer speed of their advance carried them through the first – and often only – volley with an acceptable proportion of casualties. Their own muskets were used to fire a single volley some thirty or forty yards from the enemy and were then immediately thrown down. The Highlanders burst through the cloud of black-powder smoke, broadsword drawn, dirk in the left hand and targe on the left fore-arm, while their enemy was reloading or fixing their bayonets.

General Hawley, whose forces were overwhelmed by such a charge at Falkirk in 1746, described how the Highlanders altered formation as they charged, from line – to minimise casualties from musket fire – to bunches or clusters of a dozen or so at the moment of impact, to achieve penetration of the enemy line. It was a 'double or quits' tactic which may have been an attraction to the Highlander, coupled with its opportunities for individual valour. The charge either won a battle there and then, or it was all over; to withdraw, re-group and charge again was psychologically as well as tactically so difficult as to be impossible.

The Five Motions of the Highland Charge:

'His first motion taken descending to battle was to place his bonnet firmly on his head by an emphatic "scrug": his second, to cast off his plaid or free himself of encumbrances: his third, to incline his body horizontally forward, cover it with his target, rush to within 50 paces

172

of the enemy's line, discharge and drop his fusee or musket: his fourth, to dart within 12 paces and discharge and fling his iron-stocked pistol (or pistols) at the foeman's head: fifth, to draw broadsword and at him'

Source unknown.

One thing which had become even more evident during the '45 was the fact that a Highland charge was one of the most terrifying features of warfare. These brawny and purposeful hill-men, once they were let loose, could put the fear of God into any but exceptionally highly disciplined troops. Their rapidity of movement and the devastating swing of their broadswords, accompanied by a ferocious appearance, and the deep-throated yells of slogans were too much for most of the English and Lowland regiments of that campaign. This was proved at Preston Pans, and Falkirk, where they made a blood-soaked shambles of the regiments which tried to resist them. (Had they been equal in numbers and as well provided as the Government troops at Culloden, they might, quite possibly, have made a repetition of Killicrankie.)

APPENDIX 3
'Captain McKeinzies roll, 16th Junij 1682.'

Captain, Kenneth McKeinzie.
Livtenant, William Scharp.
Ensigne, Cristofar McDougall.
John Bogie,
William Frazer, } Serjents.
John McIntosh,
William McCloude, } Corporalls.
Robert Ailliss
William Gray } Drumeres.
Androw Hamiltoun,

Allexander Ogilvie, Allexander Hetherweick, Allexander Baine, Allexander Duncan, Allexander Mansone, Allexander Fraiser, Allexander Sunderland, Allexander Polsone, Androw Monroe, Androw Thomsone, Androw Lauchland, Androw McStiven, Archibald McCroe, Duncan Moore, David Allon, David Ross, David Donaldsone, David Tailzior, David Melvill, David Hendersone, Duncan Craige, Duncan Forbis, Donald Monroe, Donald Gunn, Duncan Tailzior, Donald McKeinzie, Donald Clark, Duncan Taise, Dugall Campbell, Dougall Livingstoune, Edward Douglass, Georg Allon, Georg Cuningham, Georg Henderson, Georg Steill, Gaven Douglas, Gilbert Dundass, Hew Sunderland, John Grant, elder, John Grant, younger, John McClean, elder, John McClean, younger, John Cambell, John McGreiger, John Greicie, John Garland, John McKeaddie, John McIntosh, John Gordon, John Camron, John Cristie, John Castella, John Chapman, John Bruice, John Robertson, John Clark, John Robertsone, younger, John McCaie, James Ross, James Peitrikin, James Frazer, elder, James Frazer, younger, James Dickson, James Merchall, James Hodge, Kenneth McKeinzie, elder, Kenneth McKeinzie, younger, Lauchland McIntosh, Neill McMillon, Patrick Lawsone, Patrick Cokburne, Robert Chisholm, Robert Adamsone, Robert Davidsone, Robert Hendrie, Robert Graye, Rorie Chisholm, Thomas Dicksone, Thomas Duncan,

174

'Captain McKeinzies roll, 16th Junij 1682.'

Thomas Leadcoat, Thomas Wilsone, William Slouan, William Forbis, William McIntosh, William Foullar, William Paull, William Robertson, William McDonald, William McViccar, William Wheallie.

	(Signed)	KENNETH MACKENZIE.
		WILL: SCHAIRP.
	(Signed)	RICH: ELPHINSTONE

(Written on parchment)

APPENDIX 4
'Role of Captain Cairnis Company, 17th Junij 1682.'

Captain, Alexander Cairnes.
Lieutenant, John Leivingston.
Ensign, Androw Woode.
John McDougald, ⎫
William Grahm, ⎭ Seargents.
William Innes, ⎫
Alexander McDonald, ⎬ Corporals.
James Carlyle, ⎭
John Michell, ⎫
Georg, Willson, ⎭ Drumes.

Abraham Cairnes, Alexander Glenny, Alexander Rosse, Alexander Drone, Alexander Paterson, Alexander Ranckine, Alexander Clarcke, Adam Widrow, Androw Kelly, Alexander McFadion, Alexander Monteth, Alexander Argoe, Cothbert Allen, Charles Gairdner, Cornilius Clarck, Douglas McFarland, Donckan Riddoch, Donald McFarland, Donckan Campbell, David Lamb, Ephraim Wilckeson, George Ranckine, Gilbert Gordone, Georg Crafoord, Georg Ashbie, Hendrie Fliming, Hendrie Pergillis, John Gibb, James Findly, James Findlyson, younger, James Wallass, James Baird, John Euelly, John Ranckin, John Martine, James Walker, James Fliming, John Shannen, John Forbis, John Frazer, James Williamson, John Mingies, John Marchell, John Campbell, James Findlyson, elder, John Grahme, John Pulline, John Crafoord, John Leng, John Yuill, James Campbell, John Watsone, John Connor, Mongow Ritcheson, Nathaniel Gordone, Patrick Forrester, Patrick Skinner, Patrick Cummine, Robert Anderson, younger, Robert Henderson, Robert Burr, Robert Jolly, elder (sic), Robert Anderson, elder, Robert Ramadge, Robert McGregor, Robert Forrester, Robert Meldrum Robert Simpson, Robert Broune, Robert Jolly, elder (sic), Samuell Dassone, Thomas McGaune, Thomas Euing, Thomas Anderson, Thomas Glene, William Joussie, William McKinzie, William McKlelland, William Scote, William Hunter, William Morgen, William

'Role of Captain Cairnis Company, 17th Junij 1682.'

Davidson, William Malcum, William Weir, William Campbell, William McDougald, William Niesbit, William Buchannen, William Litlejohn, William Torpie.

                (Signed)   ALEX: CAIRNES.

                            JO: LEVINGSTON.

                (Signed)   RICH: ELPHINSTONE.

(Written on parchment.)

APPENDIX 5
General Wade's Report on the Highlands, 1724

May it please Your Majesty,

In Obedience to Your Majesty's Commands and Instructions under your Royal Sign Manual bearing date the 3rd day of July 1724, Commanding me to go into the Highlands of Scotland, and narrowly to inspect the present Situation of the Highlanders, their Customs, Manners and the State of the Country in regard to the Robberies and Depredations, said to be committed in that part of your Majesty's Dominions; As also to make strict and particular enquiry into the effect of the last Law for Disarming the Highlanders and for securing your Majesty's Loyal and faithful Subjects, represented to be left Naked and Defenceless by paying due obedience thereto; and to inform Your Majesty of all other particulars contained in the said Instructions, and how far the Memorial delivered to Your Majesty by Simon Lord Lovat and his Remarks thereupon are founded on Facts, and the present Practices of those People; And whether the Remedies mentioned therein may properly be applied for preventing the Several Grievances, Abuses, and Violences complained of in the said Memorial. Your Majesty has farther been pleased to Command me to make such Enquirys and endeavour to get such Information, relating to the several particulars above mentioned as may enable me to suggest to your Majesty, such other Remedies as may conduce to the Quiet of your Faithful Subjects and the good Settlement of that part of the Kingdom.

The Day after I received your Majesty's Instructions I proceeded on my Journey, and have Travelled through the greatest and most uncivilized Parts of the Highlands of Scotland; And humbly beg leave to lay before Your Majesty the following Report, which I have collected as well from my own Observations, with all Faithfulness and Impartiality, as from the best Informations I could procure during my Continuance in that part of the Country.

The Highlands are the Mountainous Parts of Scotland, not defined or described by any precise Limits or Boundaries of Counties or Shires but are Tracts of Mountains, in extent of Land, more than one-half of the Kingdom of Scotland; and are for the most part on the Western Ocean, extending from Dumbarton to the North End of the Island of Great Britain, near 200 Miles in length, and from about 40 to 80 Miles in breadth. All the Islands on the West and North-West Seas are called Highlands as well from their Mountainous Situation, as from the Habits, Customs, Manners and Language of their Inhabitants. The Lowlands are all that part of Scotland on the South of Forth and Clyde, and on the East side of the Kingdom from the Firth of Edinburgh to Caithness near the Orkneys is a Tract of Low Country from 4 to 20 Miles in Breadth.

The Number of Men able to carry Arms in the Highlands (including the Inhabitants of the Isles) is by the nearest Computation about 22,000 Men, of which Number about 10,000 are Vassals to the Superiors well affected to Your Majesty's Government; most of the remaining 12,000 have been engaged in Rebellion against Your Majesty, and are ready, whenever encouraged by their Superiors or Chiefs of Clans, to create new Troubles and rise in Arms in favour of the Pretender.

Their Notions of Virtue and Vice are very different from the more civilized part of Mankind. They think it a most Sublime Virtue to pay a Servile and Abject Obedience to the Commands of their Chieftains, altho' in opposition to their Sovereign and the Laws of the Kingdom, and to encourage this, their Fidelity, they are treated by their Chiefs with great Familiarity, they partake with them in their Diversions, and shake them by the Hand wherever they meet them.

The Virtue next to this, in esteem amongst them, is the love they bear to that particular Branch of which they are a part, and in a Second Degree to the whole Clan, or Name, by assisting each other (right or wrong) against any other Clan with whom they are at Variance, and great Barbarities are often committed by One, to revenge the Quarrels of Another. They have still a more extensive adherence one to another as Highlanders in opposition to the People who inhabit the Low Countries, whom they hold in the utmost Contempt, imagining them inferior to themselves in Courage, Resolution, and the use of Arms, and accuse them of being Proud, Avaricious, and Breakers of their Word. They have also a Tradition amongst them that the Lowlands were in Ancient Times, the Inheritance of their Ancestors, and therefore believe they have a right to commit Depredations, whenever it is in their power to put them in Execution.

The Highlanders are divided into Tribes or Clans, under Lairds, or Chieftains (as they are called in the Laws of Scotland), each Tribe or Clan is subdivided into Little Branches sprung from the Main Stock who have also Chieftains over them, and from these are still small Branches of Fifty or Sixty Men, who deduce their Original from them, and on whom they rely as their Protectors and Defenders. The Arms they make use of in War, are, a Musket, a Broad Sword and Target, a Pistol and a Durk or Dagger, hanging by their side, with a Powder Horn and Pouch for their Ammunition. They form themselves into Bodies of unequal Numbers according to the strength of their Clan or Tribe, which is Commanded by their Respective Superior or Chieftain. When in sight of the Enemy they endeavour to possess themselves of the highest Ground, believing they descend on them with greater force.

They generally give their fire at a distance, they lay down their Arms on the Ground and make a Vigorous Attack with their Broad Swords, but if repulsed, seldom or never rally again. They dread engaging with the Cavalry and seldom venture to descend from the Mountains when apprehensive of being charged by them.

On sudden Alarms, or when any Chieftain is in distress, they give Notice to their Clans or those in Alliance with them, by sending a Man with what they call the Fiery Cross, which is a Stick in the form of a Cross, burnt at the End, who send it forward to the next Tribe or Clan. They carry with it a written Paper directing them where to Assemble; upon sight of which they leave their Habitation and with great Expedition repair to the place of Rendezvous, with Arms, Ammunition and Meal for their Provision.

I Presume also to Represent to Your Majesty, that the Manners and Customs of the Highlanders, their Way of Living, their Strong Friendships, and Adherence to those of their own Name, Tribe and Family, their blind and Servile Submission to the Commands of their Superiors and Chieftains, and the little Regard they have ever paid to the Laws of the Kingdom, both before and since the Union, are truly set forth in the Lord Lovat's Memorial and other Matters contained in the said Paper, which Your Majesty was pleased to direct should be put into my Hands to peruse and Examine.

The Imposition mentioned in that Memorial commonly called the Black Meal is levyed by the Highlanders on almost all the Low Country bordering thereon. But as it is equally Criminal by the Laws of Scotland to pay this Exaction or to Extort it the Inhabitants to avoid the Penalty of the Laws, agree with the Robbers, or some of their Correspondents in the Lowlands to protect their Horses and

Cattle, who are in effect but their Stewards or Factors, and as long as this payment continues, the Depredations cease upon their Lands, otherwise the Collector of this Illegal Imposition is obliged to make good the loss they have sustained. They give regular Receipts for the same Safe Guard Money, and those who refuse to submit to this Imposition are sure of being Plundered, their being no other way to avoid it but by keeping a constant Guard of Armed Men, which, altho' it is sometimes done, is not only illegal, but a more expensive way of securing their property.

The Clans in the Highlands, the most addicted to Rapine and Plunder, are, the Cameron's on the West of the Shire of Inverness, the Mackenzie's and others in the Shire of Ross who were Vassals to the late Earl of Seaforth, the McDonell's of Keppoch, the Broadalbin Men, and the McGregors on the Borders of Argyleshire. They go out in Parties from Ten to Thirty Men, traverse large Tracts of Mountains till they arrive at the Lowlands where they Design to Commit Depredations, which they chuse to do in places distant from the Clans where they Inhabit; They drive the Stolen Cattle in the Night time, and in the Day remain on the Tops of the Mountains in the Woods (with which the Highlands abound) and take the first occasion to sell them at the Fairs or Markets that are annually held in many parts of the Country.

Those who are robbed of their Cattle (or Persons employ'd by them) follow them by the Tract and often recover them from the Robbers by Compounding for a certain sum of Money agreed on, but if the Pursuers are Armed and in Numbers Superior to the Thieves and happen to seize any of them, they are seldom or never prosecuted, the poorer sort being unable to support the charge of Prosecution.

They are likewise under the Apprehension of becoming the Object of their Revenge, by having their Houses and Stacks burnt, their Cattle stolen or hockt, and their Lives at the Mercy of the Tribe or Clan to whom the Banditti belong. The Richer sort (to keep, as they call it good Neighbourhood) generally compound with the Chieftain of the Tribe or Clan, for double Restitution, which he willingly pays to save one of his Clan from Prosecution, and this is repaid him by a Contribution from the Thieves of his Clan, who never refuse the payment of their proportion to save one of their own fraternity. This Composition is seldom paid in Money, but in Cattle stolen from the opposite side of the Country to make reparation to the Person injured.

181

The Chiefs of some of these Tribes never fail to give Countenance and Protection to those of their own Clan; and tho' they are taken and committed to Prison, by the Plaintiff (who is) better satisfied than if the Criminal was executed, since he must (be) at the Charge and Trouble of a tedious dilatory and expensive Prosecution; and I was assured by one who annually attended the Assizes at Inverness for four Years past, that there had been but one Person Executed there by the Lords of Justiciary and that (as I remember) for Murder, tho' that Place is the Judicature, in Criminal Cases, for the greatest part of the Highlands of Scotland.

There is another Practice used in the Highlands, by which the Cattle stolen are often recovered, which is, by sending Persons to that part of the Country most suspected and making an offer of a Reward (which the Highlanders call Tascal-Money) to any who will discover the Cattle and the Persons who stole them, by the temptation of the Reward and promise of Secrecy, discoveries were often made and Restitution obtained. But to put a stop to a practice they thought an injury to the Tribe, the whole Clan of the Camerons (and others since by their Example) bound themselves by Oath never to take Tascal-Money, nor to inform one against the other. This they take upon a Drawn Durck or Dagger, which they kiss in a solemn manner and the Penalty declared to be due to the said Oath, is, to be stabbed with the same Dagger. This manner of Swearing is much in practice on all other occasions, to bind themselves one to another that they may with more security exercise their Villany, which they imagine less Sinful than the Breach of that Oath, since they commit all sorts of Crimes with impunity, and are so severely punished if forsworn. An instance of this happened in December 1723, when one of the Clan of the Camerons suspected to have taken Tascal-Money, was in the Night time called out of his Hut from his Wife and Children and hanged up near his own door. Another of that Tribe was, for the same Crime (as they call it) kept a Month in the Stocks and afterwards privately made away with.

The Encouragement and Protection given by some of the Chiefs of Clans is reciprocally rewarded by giving them a share of the Plunder, which is sometimes one half or two thirds of what is stolen. They exercise an Arbitrary and Tyrannical power over them; They determine all disputes and differences that happen among their Vassals, and on extraordinary occasions such as the Marriage of a Daughter, the building of a House, or any other pretence for the support of their Chief, or honour of the Name, he Levies a Tax on

182

the Tribe; to which Imposition, if any one refuse to contribute, he is sure of the severest Treatment or at best to be cast out of the Tribe. And it is not to be wonder'd that those who submit to this Servile Slavery, will, when Summoned by their Superiors, follow them into Rebellion.

To remedy these Inconveniences there was an Act of Parliament, passed in the year 1716 for the more effectual securing the Peace of the Highlands in Scotland, by Disarming the Highlanders, which has been so ill executed, that the Clans the most disaffected to Your Majesty's Government remain better Armed than ever, and consequently more in a Capacity not only of committing Robberies and Depredations, but to be used as Tools or Instruments to any Foreign Power or Domestic Incendiaries who may attempt to disturb the Peace of Your Majesty's Reign. By this Act the Collectors for Taxes were empowered to pay for the Arms delivered in, as they were Valued by Persons appointed for that Service in the respective Countries, but as the Government was to support the Charge, they did not scruple to Appraise them at a much higher rate than their real worth, few or none being delivered up except such as were broken and unfit for Service; And I have been informed that from the time of passing that Act, to the time it was put in execution, great Quantities of broken and useless Arms were brought from Holland and delivered up to the Persons appointed to receive the same at exorbitant prices.

The Spaniards who landed at Castle Donnan in the Year 1719 brought with them a great Number of Arms: They were delivered to the Rebellious Highlanders who are still possessed of them, many of which I have seen in my passage through that Country, and I judge them to be the same from their peculiar make, and the fashion of their Locks. These and others now in their Possession by a Moderate Computation are supposed to amount to 5 or 6000, besides those in the possession of the Clans who are in Your Majesty's Interest, provided as they alledge, for their own defence.

The Legislature in Scotland before the Union of the Kingdoms have ever considered the Highlands in a different State from the rest of the Nation, and made peculiar Laws for their Government under the severest Penalties. The Chieftains of Clans were obliged to send their Children or nearest Relations to Edinburgh as Hostages for the good behaviour of their respective Clans, and in default they might by the Law be put to death.

The Clans and Tribes who lived in a State of Anarchy and Confusion (as they seem to be in at this present time) were, by the very Words of the Act of Parliament to be pursued with Fire and Sword, but as the Execution of the Laws relating to the Highlands was under the care of the Privy Council of Scotland (now no longer Subsisting, who by Act of Parliament were obliged to sit the first Day in every Month for that purpose) it often happen'd that Men of great Power in the Highlands were of the said Council, who had no other way of rendering themselves considerable than from their Numbers of Armed Men, and consequently the less Zealous in putting the Laws in Execution against them. The Independent Companies raised by King William not long after the Revolution reduced the Highlanders into better order than at any time they had been in since the Restauration. They were composed of the Natives of the Country, inured to the fatigue of travelling the Mountains, lying on the Hills, wore the same Habit, and spoke the same Language; but for want of being put under proper Regulations, Corruptions were introduced, and some who commanded them, instead of bringing Criminals to Justice (as I am informed) often compounded for the Theft and for a Sum of Money set them at Liberty. They are said also to have defrauded the Government by keeping not above half their Numbers in constant Pay; which, as I humbly conceive, might be the reason Your Majesty caused them to be disbanded.

Your Barracks were afterwards built in different parts of the Highlands, and Parties of the Regular Troops under the Command of Highland Officers, with a Company of 30 Guides (Established to conduct them through the Mountains) was thought an effectual Scheme, as well to prevent the rising of the Highlanders disaffected to Your Majesty's Government, as to hinder the Depredations on your faithful Subjects. It is to be wished that during the Reign of Your Majesty and your Successors, no Insurrections may ever happen to experience whether the Barracks will effectually answer the end proposed; yet I am humbly of opinion; That if the number of Troops they are built to contain, was constantly Quartered in them (whereas there is now in some but 30 Men) and proper Provisions laid in for their support during the Winter Season, they might be of some use to prevent the Insurrections of the Highlanders; Though as I humbly conceive, (having seen them all) that two of the four are not built in as proper Situations as they might have been.

As to the Highland Parties, I have already presumed to represent to Your Majesty the little use they were of in hindering Depredations, and the great sufferings of the Soldiers employed in that Service, upon which your Majesty was Graciously pleased to Countermand them.

I must further beg leave to Report to your Majesty that another great Cause of Disorders in the Highlands, is the want of proper Persons to execute the several Offices of Civil Magistrates, especially in the Shires of Ross, Inverness and some other parts of the Highlands. The Party Quarrels and violent Animosities amongst the Gentlemen (equally well affected to your Majesty's Government) I humbly conceive to be one great Cause of this Defect. Those who were in Arms for your Majesty, who raised a Spirit in the Shire of Inverness and recovered the Town of that Name from the Rebells (their Main Body being then at Perth) Complain, that the Persons employed as Magistrates over them have little Credit or Interest in that Country, and that three of Deputy Sheriffs in those parts were Persons actually in Arms against your Majesty at the time of the late Rebellion which (as I am credibly informed) is true. They likewise complain, that many of the most considerable Gentlemen are left out in the Commissions of Lord Lieutenants, Deputy Lieutenants, Sheriffs, etc. And I take the liberty to observe that the want of acting Justices of the Peace is a great encouragement to the Disorders so frequently committed in that part of the Country, there being but one, residing as an acting Justice for the Space of above a hundred Miles in Compass.

Your Majesty's Commands requiring me to examine into the State and Condition of the late Earl of Seaforth's Estate, engaged me to go to the Castle of Brahan his principal Seat, and other parts of the said Estate, which for the most part is Highland Country, and extends from Brahan to Kintail on the Western Coast, being 36 Miles in length and the most Mountainous part of the Highlands; The whole Isle of Lewis was also a part of the said Earl's Estate. The Tennants before the late Rebellion were reputed the richest of any in the Highlands, but now are become poor by neglecting their business and applying themselves wholly to the use of Arms. The Rents continue to be levied by one Donald Murchieson a Servant of the late Earl's who annually remits (or carries) the same to his Master into France.

The Tennants when in a Condition are also said to have sent him free Gifts in proportion to their several Circumstances but are now a year and a half in Arrear of Rent. The Receipts he gives to the Tennants are, as Deputy Factor to the Commissioners of Forfeited Estates, which pretended Power in the year 1721 he extorted from

185

the Factor appointed by the said Commissioners to Collect those Rents for the use of the Publick, whom he attacked with above 400 Arm'd Men as he was going to enter upon the said Estate; having with him a Body of 30 of Your Majesty's Troops. The last year this Murchieson travell'd in a Public manner to Edinburgh to remit £800 to France for his Master's use, and remained there fourteen days unmolested.

I cannot omit observing to Your Majesty; this National tenderness your Subjects of North Britain have one for the other, is great encouragement to the Rebells and attainted Persons to return home from their Banishment.

Before I conclude this Report, I presume to observe to your Majesty the great Disadvantages Regular Troops are under when they engage with those who Inhabit Mountainous Situations. The Serennes (*sic*) in France, and Catalans in Spain, have in all times been Instances of this Truth. The Highlands of Scotland are still more impracticable, from the want of Roads, Bridges, and from excessive Rains that almost continually fall in those parts, which by Nature and constant use become habitual to the Natives, but very difficultly supported by the Regular Troops. They are unacquainted with the Passages by which the Mountains are traversed, exposed to frequent Ambuscades, and Shots from the Tops of the Hills, which they return without effect, as it happened at the affair of Glenshiels, where the Rebells lost but one Man in the (*sic*) tho' a Considerable number of Your Majesty's Troops were killed and wounded.

I have endeavoured to Report to your Majesty as true and impartial an Account of the several particulars required by my Instructions, as far as I have been able to Collect them during my short continuance in the Highlands, and, as Your Majesty is pleased to Command me, presume to offer my humble opinion of what I conceive necessary to be done towards establishing Order in those Parts, and reducing the Highlands to a more due Submission to Your Majesty's Government.

PROPOSAL

1.

That Companies of such Highlanders as are well affected to his Majesty's Government be Established, under proper Regulations and Commanded by Officers speaking the Language of the Country, subject to Martial Law and under the Inspection and Orders of the Governors of Fort-William and Inverness, and the Officer Commanding his Majesty's Forces in those Parts.

The Expence of these Companies which may in the whole consist of 250 or at most 300 Men, may be answered by reducing one Man p Troop and Company of the Regular Forces.

2.

That the said Companies be employed in Disarming the Highlanders, preventing Depredations, bringing Criminals to Justice, and hinder Rebells and Attainted Persons from inhabiting that part of the Kingdom.

3.

That a Redoubte or Barrack be erected at Inverness, as well for preventing the Highlanders descending in the Low Country in time of Rebellion, as for the better Quartering his Majesty's Troops, and keeping them in a Body sufficient to prevent or Subdue Insurrections.

4.

That in order to render the Barrack at Killihnimen of more use than I conceive it to be of at present (from its being situate at too great a distance from Lake Ness) a Redoubte be built at the West End adjoining to it, which with the said Barrack may be able to contain a Batallion of Foot, and a Communication made for their mutual support, the space of ground between one and the other being less than 500 Yards. This appears to be more necessary from the Situation of the Place, which is the most Centrical part of the Highlands, a considerable Pass, equally distant from Fort-William and Inverness, and where a Body of 1000 Men may be drawn together from these Garrisons in twenty-four hours, to suppress any Insurrections of the Highlanders.

5.

That a small Vessel with Oars and Sails be built on the Lake Ness, sufficient to carry a Party of 60 or 80 Soldiers and Provisions for the

Garrison, which will be a means to keep the Communication open between that place and Inverness and be a safe and ready way of sending Parties to the Country bordering on the said Lake, which is Navigable for the largest Vessels. It is 24 Miles or more in length, and a Mile or more in breadth, the Country being Mountainous on both sides.

6.

That the Governors, or such as his Majesty is pleased to appoint to Command at Fort-William, Inverness, or Killihnimen, till the Peace of the Highlands is better Established, be required to reside at their respective Stations, and to give an Account of what passes in that Country to the Commander in Chief of the Forces in Scotland, and to such other whom his Majesty is pleased to appoint.

7.

That Inspection be made into the present Condition of the Garrisons and Castles in North Britain, and necessary Repairs made, to secure them from the danger of a Sudden Surprize, and more especially the Castle of Edinburgh, which remains exposed to the same attempt as was made on it in the Year 1715, there being nothing effectually done to it since that time, for the security of that important place, on which depends not only the Safety of the City, but of all that part of the Kingdom.

8.

That a Regiment of Dragoons be ordered to Quarter in the Low Country between Perth and Inverness (when Forrage can be provided for their Support) which will not only hinder the Highlanders descending into that Country from the apprehensions they are under of engaging with Horse, but may be a means to prevent the Landing of small Bodies of Troops that may be sent from Foreign parts to invade that part of the Kingdom, or encourage the Highlanders to Rebellion.

9.

That for the support of the Civil Government proper Persons be nominated for Sheriffs and Deputy Sheriffs in the Highland Counties, and that Justices of the Peace and Constables be Established in proper Places with small Salaries allowed them for the Charge they say they are of necessity at in seizing and sending Criminals to distant Prisons; and that Quarter Sessions be punctually kept at Killihnimen, Ruthven in Badenoch and Fort-William, and if occasion should require at Bernera near the Coast of the Isle of Skye.

10.

That an Act of Parliament be procured effectually to punish the Highlanders inhabiting the most uncivilized parts of the Country, who carry or conceal in their Dwellings, or other Places, Arms contrary to Law; and as the Penalty of a Fine in the former Act has never been (or from their Poverty can never be) levied, it is hoped the Parliament will not Scruple to make it Felony or Transportation for the first Offence.

11.

That an Act of Parliament be procured impowering the Heretors and Free-holders in every County to assess themselves Yearly, not exceeding a definite Sum, to be applied by the Commissioners of the Land Tax and Justices of the Peace for defraying the Charges of apprehending, prosecuting, and Maintaining of Criminals while in Gaol; For, as the Prosecutor is now to defray the Charges it is not to be wondered at that so few of them have been brought to Justice, and so many Malefactors escaped with Impunity.

All which is most humbly Represented and Submitted to Your Majesty's Royal Consideration.

GEORGE WADE.

London, 10th December, 1724.

THE UNDERWRITTEN CLANS OR TRIBES WERE ENGAGED IN THE LATE REBELLION, MOST OF THEM ARE ARMED AND COMMIT DEPREDATIONS.
The Mackenzies and the small Clans vizt., the Mcras, McLennans, Murchiesons and the McLeods of North Assynt, the Mclays inhabiting the Countries belonging to the late Lord Seaforth, and all the Gentlemen and others of the Name of Mackenzie in the Main Land and Isle of Lewis, in Ross and Sutherland Shires.

The McLeods and others of Glenelg in the Isle of Skye, and the Harris, in the Shire of Inverness.

The McDonels and others of Slate or Skye and North Uist, in the Shire of Inverness.

The McDonels and others of Glengary, Abertarff, and Knoidart, in Inverness-shire.

The McDonels and others of Moidart, Arisaig, Muick, Canna, South Uist, in Inverness and Argyleshires.

The Camerons of Lochiel in Inverness-shire.

The Camerons of Ardnamurchan, Swin and Morvine in Argyleshire, and the other small Tribes in those Countries.

The McDonels of Keppoch and others in that part of Lochaber belonging to Mcintosh of Borlum in Inverness-shire.

The Stewarts of Appine and others in that Country in Argyleshire.

The McLeans in Mull, Rhume, Coll, Morvine, Ardnamurchan and Swinard, in Argyleshire.

The several Clans in that part of Lochaber belonging to the Duke of Gordon, in Inverness-shire, and those in Murray and Banffshires.

The McPhersons in Badenoch in the Shire of Inverness.

The McNeils of Barra in Argyleshire.

The Mcintoshes and other Tribes of that Name in Inverness-shire.

The Robertsons belonging to Strowan in Perthshire.

THE UNDERWRITTEN CLANS BELONG TO SUPERIORS WELL AFFECTED TO HIS MAJESTY.

	Men able to bear Arms.
The Duke of Argyle	4000
Lord Sutherland and Strathnaver	1000
Lord Lovat, Frazers	800
The Grants	800
The Ross's and Monro's	700
Forbes of Culloden	200
Ross of Kilravock	300
Sir Archibald Campbell of Clunis	200
	8000

THE TWO CLANS UNDERWRITTEN, FOR THE MOST PART WENT INTO THE REBELLION IN 1715 WITHOUT THEIR SUPERIORS.

The Athol Men	2000
The Broadalbin Men	1000
	3000

THE CLANS UNDERWRITTEN WERE IN THE LATE REBELLION AND ARE STILL SUPPOSED TO BE DISAFFECTED TO HIS MAJESTY'S GOVERNMENT.

	Men able to bear Arms
The Tribes and Clans of the late Lord Seaforth	3000
Macdonel's of Slate	1000
Macdonel's of Glengary	800
Macdonel's of Moidart	800
Macdonel's of Keppoch	220
Lochiel (Camerons)	800
The McLeod's in all	1000
Duke of Gordon's followers	1000
Stewart's of Appine	400
Robertson's of Strowan	800
Mcintoshe's and Farquharsons	800
McLeans in the Isle of Skye	150
Chisholms of Strathglass	150
McPhersons	220
	11,140

ROMAN CATHOLICKS IN THE HIGHLANDS

The late Earl of Seaforth, but none of his followers except the Lairds Mackenzie of Kilewn, and Mackenzie of Ardloch; the first has power over the Inhabitants of the Isle of Lewis and the latter over those who inhabit near Coigach and Loch Broom, which is in the North part of Seaforth's Country.

Chisholm of Strathglass and his Clan are Roman Catholicks.

Most of Glengary's Tribe are Roman Catholicks but he himself is not.

McDonald of Moidart and many of his Clan are Roman Catholicks.

McLeod of Barra and his Tribe are Roman Catholicks.

The Duke of Gordon and the most considerable of his followers are Roman Catholicks.

LIST OF THE MOST CONSIDERABLE GENTLEMEN WHO ARE WELL AFFECTED TO HIS MAJESTY'S GOVERNMENT WHO INHABIT AND HAVE ESTATES IN THE COUNTIES UNDER MENTIONED.

MURRAY
- Mr Brodie, Member of Parliament.
- Mr Ross of Kilravock.
- Laird of Grant, Member of Parliament.
- Sir Harry Innes.
- Mr Duff of Brachan.

191

NAIRN	Mr Ross, Junior.
	Mr Brodie of Brodie.
	Mr Forbes of Culloden, Member of Parliament.
INVERNESS	The Laird of Grant.
	The Lord Lovat.
	Mr Forbes of Culloden.
ROSS	Mr Ross of Kilravock
	Colonel Munro, Member of Parliament.
	General Ross
	Mr Munro of Culcairn.
CROMARTY	Mr Ross of Kilravock
	Sir Wm. Gordon, Member of Parliament.
SUTHERLAND	The Earl of Sutherland
CAITHNESS	The Earl of Caithness
	Mr Sinclair of Ulbster
ORKNEY	The Earl of Morton.

SCHEME DELIVERED TO THE KING IN APRIL, 1725.

In the Report I had the Honour to lay before his Majesty at my return from the Highlands of Scotland, I took the liberty to represent the present state of that part of his Majesty's Dominions. The Proposals contained in the said Report and those I shall now take the Liberty to mention are, in my humble Opinion, the effectual and practicable Means of reducing the Highlanders to a due obedience to his Majesty's Government.

Experience has shewn that the Measures hitherto taken have proved insufficient to reduce the Highlanders to due obedience to the Laws, and to prevent the Depredations so frequently committed on the Inhabitants of the low Country, which is a great oppression to the well affected (who are entitled to the protection of the Government) but it is of so much more importance to the State itself that the Highlanders should be disarmed, who may (if not timely prevented) prove of dangerous consequence to the Peace of the Kingdom. For, while such a number of Men who are bold, resolute and disaffected, remain in a Capacity of doing Meschief, they are ready Instruments to be employed by any foreign Power, who may attempt to Invade his Majesty's Dominions or excite his Subjects to Rebellion.

The Peace and Tranquility we at present Enjoy under his Majesty's auspicious Reign, is the proper time to apply a remedy to this growing Evil.

If the Highlanders can be dispossessed of their Arms (or reduced to the Necessity of hiding them under ground where they will rust and spoil) it will at the same time prevent the Depredations, and render it very difficult for them to rise in Arms against the Government. For, if Arms should hereafter be brought from Foreign Parts when Designs are carrying on to create new Troubles, it will be hardly possible to disperse them to the Highlanders who are scattered in so large an extent of Country, when the Forts and Barracks are garrisoned with Soldiers in the very Center of the Highlands.

Several Laws have been made to restrain these People, but they have generally failed of Success, as I humbly conceive, either from partiality, negligence or from the private Views of those who were Employed in putting them in Execution; And the Disarming Act of the first Year of his Majesty's Reign had no other effect than to defraud the Publick of a Considerable Sum of Money and to render the Enemies of the Government more formidable.

It is therefore necessary that an Act of Parliament be procured, Empowering his Majesty (or those he is pleased to appoint) to cause the several Clans to be summoned (one after another) to bring in their Arms by certain Days specified in the said Summons, after which, whoever is found in Arms (except such as are qualified by Law) should be transported to serve as Soldiers in any of His Majesty's Plantations in America, or Garrisons beyond the Seas, with a Clause making it lawful for his Majesty's Forces to assist the Civil Magistrate, and to reduce them by force of Arms in Case they assemble in Numbers to oppose the Execution of the Act, and also a Clause of Indemnity for the Soldiers who shall happen to kill or wound any of them, as in the Law against Riots and Tumults.

It is absolutely necessary that his Majesty have a power by the said Act to appoint such Persons as he shall think fit (altho' they were not Natives of that part of the Kingdom) to put the Penalties of this Law in Execution, otherwise it will render this Act of Parliament as useless as the former.

I shall now presume to give my humble opinion how the Scheme for Disarming the Highlands may be put in execution.

That three Companies of Highlanders be raised consisting of 60 or 70 Men each, Commanded by Captains.

That three Companies of Highlanders consisting of half that Number be commanded by Lieutenants.

That the Six Companies consisting of about 300 Men be compleated and Armed by the first of June in order to join the Regular

Troops at Inverness, when they March to their first Encampment.

That four Battalions of the Forces now in Scotland be in readiness to form a Camp in the Highlands.

That the Regiment Quartered at Fort-William remain there during the Summer, and supply the Barracks of Ruthven and Bernara with Garrisons.

That the Regiment of Foot now ordered to Scotland be Quartered at Innersnait, Stirling, Perth, and the Sea Port Towns on the Eastern Coast.

That the Regiment now Quartered at Berwick be ordered to send five Companies to Edinburgh and Leith to Quarter there during the Summer.

A Detachment of fifty Dragoons may be ordered to attend the Camp, a greater Number not being able to Subsist in the Highlands for want of Forage.

By this Disposition the several Garrisons and Barracks will be supplied with Men, and the Sea Port Towns provided with Soldiers sufficient to Assist the Officers of his Majesty's Customs, so that of the Six Regiments of Foot in Scotland there will remain for the Encampment four Battalions, the Highland Companies, and Fifty Dragoons.

The first Camp is proposed to be formed at or near Castle Brahan, the principal Seat of the late Earl of Seaforth, and the Vassals and Tennants of the said Earl (who even at this time continue in a state of Rebellion) may be first summon'd to deliver up their Arms. And if a promise of an Indemnity was made them for the Rents they have paid to Murchieson for the use of the said Earl, it might probably induce them to submit for the future to become Tennants to his Majesty and pay in their Rents for the use of the Publick. But if they refuse to Submit to the delivery of their Arms, they may be made Examples to others, by being treated with as much vigour as can be justified by Law, and the Act of Parliament put in Execution against them in its utmost Extent.

When this is effected the Forces may move to the next Clans who are Armed, and so proceed from one to another as long as the Season of the Year will admit the Troops to continue Encamped in the Mountains, and if no unforeseen difficulties happen, it is humbly hoped that all the disaffected Clans to the North of Fort-William and the Lake Ness may be subdued before the end of the Campaign.

That a Sixth Rate Man of War be appointed to attend the Service on the Eastern Coast, to receive on board and carry to Berwick, such of the Highlanders who shall be condemned to Transportation.

That a Quantity of Bisquit be put on board the said Ship and landed at Inverness for the use of the Parties that may be sent into the Mountains.

That Officers and Serjeants of the Regiments in the West Indies be appointed at Inverness or Berwick, to receive such Highlanders as may be sent away for Soldiers.

PROVISION OF MONEY WILL BE WANTING FOR THE PURPOSES FOLLOWING.

For building a Vessel on the Lake Ness.

For repairing the Fortifications of Edinburgh Castle and Fort-William.

For building two New Forts and Barracks at Inverness and Killihnimen, each sufficient to contain a Batallion of Foot.

For Gratuitys to such Highlanders as shall contribute to facilitate the Execution of the Disarming Scheme, Discover Arms conceal'd or Persons Outlawed or Attainted of High Treason.

For the Maintenance of Prisoners till their Tryal or Transportation.

For the Extraordinary Charge of Encampments, the Carriage of Provisions and Ammunition for the use of the Forces, and other Contingent Charges.

For the Support of the General and Staff Officers to be employed in this Service.

For mending the Roads between the Garrisons and Barracks, for the better Communication of his Majesty's Troops.

It is to be hoped that two Years will be sufficient to put in Execution the several Services abovenamed, and that the Extraordinary Expence to the Government will not exceed *Ten thousand pounds for each Year.*

APPENDIX 6

Text of the Orders for Raising the Six Highland Independent (Black Watch) Companies, dated 12th May 1725.

GEORGE R.

Order for Raising an Independant Compa. of Foot under the Commd of Lord Lovat.*

WHEREAS We have thought fit that an Independent Company be formed in the Highlands of North Britain under your Command, to consist of yourself as Captain, two Lieutenants, three Serjeants, three Corporalls, two Drummers, and sixty effective private Men: These are to Authorize you by Beat of Drum or otherwise to Raise so many Voluntiers in the Highlands of North Britain, as shall be wanting to Complt. the said Independt. Company to the above Numbers. And all Magistrates, Justices of the Peace, Constables, and other Our Officers whom it may concern are hereby required to be Assisting unto you in providing Quarters, Impressing Carriages, and otherwise, as there shall be Occasion. Given at Our Court at St. James's this 12th day of May 1725, In the Eleventh Year of Our Reign.

By His Majty's Commd.,

H. PELHAM.

To Our Rt. Trusty and Welbeloved Simon Lord Lovatt, Captain of an Indept. Company of Foot; or to the Officer or Officers appointed by him to Raise Voluntiers for that Company.

* The like Order of ye same date to Sr. Duncan Campbell of Lochneal and Colo. Wm. Grant.

Orders for Raising the Six Highland Independent Companies

GEORGE R.

Order for Raising an Independant Compa. of Foot under the Commd of Lord John Campbell.* WHEREAS We have thought fit that an Independt. Company formed in the Highlands of North Britain under your Commd., consist of yourself as Lieut., One Ensign, two Serjeants, two Corporalls, one Drum, and thirty effective private Men: These are to Authorize you by Beat of Drum or otherwise to Raise so many Voluntiers in the Highlands of North Britain as shall be wanting to Compleat the said Independt. Company to the above Numbers. And All Magistrates, Justices of the Peace, Constables, and other Our Officers whom it may concern, are hereby required to be Assisting unto you in providing Quarters, Impressing Carriages, and otherwise, as there shall be Occasion. Given at Our Court at St. James's this 12th day of May 1725, In the Eleventh Year of Our Reign.

By His Majty's Commd.,
H. PELHAM.

To Our Trusty and Welbeloved Lieut. John Campbell of Carrick, Commander of an Independt. Compa. of Foot; or to the Officer appointed by him to Raise Voluntrs. for that Company.

* The like Order of the same date to Lt. Colin Campbell of Skipness and Lt. Geo. Monroe.

Peregrine Fury was agent (solicitor) to the six Independent Companies of Foot in the Highlands on the 20th of June 1727.

From the 25th of December 1725 onwards the Independent Companies were borne on the British establishment, and paid as follows: –

1. Each of three companies commanded by captains: –

    Captain 8s. per diem, and in lieu of his servants, 2s.; total 10s.
    Two lieutenants, each 4s., and in lieu of their servants, 1s. 4d., total 9s. 4d.

Three sergeants, each 1s. 6d.
Three corporals, each 1s.
Two drummers, each 1s.
60 effective private men, each 8d.

2.   Each of three companies commanded by lieutenants: –

Lieutenant, and in lieu of his servant, 5s.
Ensign, and in lieu of his servant, 3s. 8d.
Two sergeants, each 1s. 6d.
Two corporals, each 1s.
One drummer, 1s.
30 effective private men, each 8d.[1]

LORD LOVAT'S COMPANY-

Captain	Simon, Lord Lovat.
First Lieutenant	Alexander Fraser.
Second Lieutenant	Dugald Campbell.
Ensign	Paul McPherson.

SIR DUNCAN CAMPBELL OF LOCHNELL'S COMPANY –

Captain	Sir Duncan Campbell.
First Lieutenant	Colin Campbell.
Second Lieutenant	John Fraser.
Ensign	John MacKenzie

COLONEL WILLIAM GRANT OF BALLINDALLOCH'S COMPANY –

Captain	William Grant.
First Lieutenant	Duncan McFarland.
Second Lieutenant	Lewis Grant.
Ensign	James Grant.
Sergeants	Nathaniel Grant; Peter Grant; Wm. Grant.
Privates	Arthur Grant; Donald Grant; John Grant; John Grant, *alias* Rirorie; Lewis Grant; Peter Grant; Angus McPherson.

CAPTAIN-LIEUTENANT JOHN CAMPBELL OF CARRICK'S COMPANY –

Captain-Lieutenant	John Campbell.
Lieutenant	Duncan Campbell.
Ensign	James Cumming.

Orders for Raising the Six Highland Independent Companies

CAPTAIN-LIEUTENANT COLIN CAMPBELL OF SKIPNESS'S COMPANY –
   Captain-Lieutenant   Colin Campbell.
   Lieutenant   John McLean.
   Ensign   John MacPherson.

CAPTAIN-LIEUTENANT GEORGE MUNRO OF CULCAIRN'S COMPANY –
   Captain-Lieutenant   George Munro.
   Lieutenant   Alexander Stewart.
   Ensign   Alexander McDonald.

APPENDIX 7

Text of the Orders for Augmenting the Six Highland Independent (Black Watch) Companies, dated 27th January 1727

GEORGE R.

Order for Recruiting Lord Lovat's Indept. Company.* WHEREAS We have thought fit to Augment Our Independt. Company of Foot under your Command with One Serjeant, One Corporal, and Forty Private Men, in order to Compleat them to the following Numbers, Vizt., Four Serjeants, Four Corporals, Two Drummers, and One hundred Effective Private Men, besides Commission Officers: These are therefore to Authorize you by Beat of Drum or otherwise to Raise so many Voluntiers in the Highlands of North Britain as shall be wanting to Compleat Our said Independt. Company to the above Numbers. And All Magistrates, Justices of the Peace, Constables, and Other Our Officers, whom it may Concern, are hereby required to be Assisting unto you in Providing Quarters, Impressing Carriages and otherwise as there shall be occasion. Given at Our Court at St. James's this 27th day of Janry. 1726/7, In the Thirteenth Year of Our Reign.

By his Majesty's Command,

H. PELHAM.

To Our Rt. Trusty and Welbeloved Cousin Simon Lord Lovat, Captain of an Independent Company of Foot; or to the Officer or Officers Appointed by him to Raise Voluntiers for that Company.

* The like Orders for Augmenting the Independent Companys of Foot Commanded by Colonel Wilm. Grant and Sr. Duncan Campbell of Lochneal to the Above Numbers.

GEORGE R.

Order for Recruiting Capt. Lt. Colin Campbell's Indept. Compa. of ffoot.*

WHEREAS We have thought fit to Augment Our Independant Company of Foot under your Command with One Serjeant, One Corporal, One Drummer, and Thirty Private men, in order to compleat the same to the following Numbers, Vizt., Three Serjeants, Three Corporals, Two Drummers, and Sixty Effective Private Men, besides Commission Officers: These are to Authorize you by Beat of Drum or otherwise to Raise so many Voluntiers in the Highlands of North Britain as shall be wanting to Compleat Our said Independant Company to the above Numbers, And All Magistrates, Justices of the Peace, Constables, and other Our Officers whom It may Concern, are hereby required to be Assisting unto You in Providing Quarters, Impressing Carriages and otherwise as there shall be occasion. Given at Our Court at St. James's this 27th day of January 1726/7, In the Thirteenth Year of Our Reign.

By his Majesty's Command,

H. PELHAM.

To Capt. Lieut. Colin Campbell of Skipness, Commanding an Independt. Company of ffoot; or to the Officer appointed by him to Raise Voluntiers for the said Company.

* The like Orders for Augmenting the Independt. Compas. of Foot Commanded by Capt. Lieut. John Campbell of Carrick and Capt. Lieut. George Munro to the Above Numbers.

Major Scipio Duroure was, on 24th December 1726, appointed by General Wade a Major of Brigade to the Forces in North Britain, and to take upon him 'the care and command of the Highland Companies in everything that relates to their good order and discipline and to see that they perform the several services pursuant to the orders they have or shall receive from time to time from myself or the Commander-in-Chief of the Forces for the time being'; lieutenant-colonel of Whetham's Regiment, 25th August 1734; colonel, 12th August 1741; killed 1745.

LETTERS OF SERVICE, for forming the HIGHLAND REGIMENT from the Independent Companies of the BLACK WATCH.

GEORGE R. – Whereas we have thought fit, that a regiment of foot be forthwith formed under your command, and to consist of ten companies, each to contain one captain, one lieutenant, one ensign, three serjeants, three corporals, two drummers, and one hundred effective private men; which said regiment shall be partly formed out of six Independent Companies of Foot in the Highlands of North Britain, three of which are now commanded by captains, and three by captain-lieutenants. Our will and pleasure therefore is, that one serjeant, one corporal, and fifty private men, be forthwith taken out of the three companies commanded by captains, and ten private men from the three commanded by captain-lieutenants, making one hundred and eighty men, who are to be equally distributed into the four companies hereby to be raised; and the three serjeants and three corporals, draughted as aforesaid, to be placed to such of the four companies as you shall judge proper; and the remainder of the non-commissioned officers and private men, wanting to complete them to the above number, to be raised in the Highlands with all possible speed; the men to be natives of that country, and none other to be taken.

This regiment shall commence and take place according to the establishment thereof. And of these our orders and commands, you, and the said three captains, and the three captain-lieutenants commanding at present the six Independent Highland Companies, and all others concerned, are to take notice, and to yield obedience thereunto accordingly.

Given at our Court at St James's, this 25th day of October 1739, and in the 13th year of our reign.

By his Majesty's command,
(Signed)   WM. YONGE.

To our Right Trusty and Right Well-
   Beloved Cousin, John Earl of
   *Craufurd and Lindsay.**
The following list will shew the original officers of the regiment:

* See Appendix II

1739,

Col. John Earl of Craufurd and Lindsay, 25th Oct. Died in 1748.
Lt.-Col. Sir Robert Munro of Fowlis, } do. Killed at Falkirk, 1746.
Bart.
Maj. Geo. Grant, brother of the Laird } Removed from the service by
of Grant.   sentence of a court-martial,
1746.

Captain George Munro of Culcairn, " Killed in 1746.
   Dugal Campbell of Craignish, " Killed in 1745.
   John Campbell of Carrick, " Killed at Fontenoy.
   Colin Campbell junior of Monzie, " Retired, 1743.
   Sir Jas. Colquhoun of Luss, Bart. " Promoted to be Ma-
   jor, retired in 1748.
   Colin Campbell of Ballimore, " Retired.
   John Munro, " { Promoted to be Lt.-
   Col. in 1743, retired
   1749.

Capt.-Lieut. Duncan Macfarlane, " Retired, 1744.
Lieut. Paul Macpherson, "
   Lewis Grant of Auchterblair, "
   John Maclean of Kingarloch, "
   John Mackenzie, "
   Alexander Macdonald, "
   Malcolm Fraser, son of Culduthel, " { Killed at Bergen-
   op-Zoom, 1747.

   George Ramsay,"
   Francis Grant, son of the Laird of Grant " Died Lieut-Gen. 1782.
   John Macneil, "
1759,
Ensign Dugal Campbell, Oct. 25th.
   Dugal Stewart, "
   John Menzies of Comrie, "
   Edward Carrick, "
   Gilbert Stewart of Kincraigie, "
   Gordon Graham of Draines, "
   Arch. Macnab, son of the Laird of } " Died Lt.-Gen. 1790.
   Macnab,
   Colin Campbell, "
   Dugal Stewart, "
   James Campbell of Glenfalloch, " { Died of wounds, at
   Fontenoy.

Chaplain. Hon. Gideon Murray.
Surgeon. George Munro.
Adjutant. Gilbert Stewart.
Quarter-Master. John Forbes.*

203

* In a country where so many are of the same name, some distinguishing mark besides the common appellation was absolutely necessary. I have already noticed the manner in which the people managed this in the Highlands. But, in the south, as well as the north of Scotland, districts contain many of the same name; and gentlemen are distinguished by that of their estate. In this manner, the officers in the foregoing list are distinguished. This method I must continue, so far as I know the families of different officers, as, from the number of gentlemen of the same name whom I shall have occasion to mention, it will, in many cases, be quite impossible otherwise to know what officer is meant. In all old lists of the names of Highland officers, whether regimental, or merely stating their deaths or wounds, the name of the family of each, if known, was added. By this means, the relations of these officers are now, at this distant period, able to distinguish them.

Although the commissions of the officers were dated in October, and the following months of 1739, the men were not assembled until the month of May 1740. The whole were then mustered, and embodied into a regiment in a field between Taybridge and Aberfeldy, in the county of Perth, under the number of the 43d regiment, but they still retained the country name of the Black Watch. The uniform was a scarlet jacket and waistcoat, with buff facings and white lace, tartan plaid of twelve yards plaited round the middle of the body, the upper part being fixed on the left shoulder, ready to be thrown loose and wrapped over both shoulders and firelock in rainy weather. At night, the plaid served the purpose of a blanket, and was a sufficient covering for the Highlander. These were called belted plaids, from being kept tight to the body by a belt,* and were worn on guards, reviews, and on all occasions when the men were in full dress. On this belt hung the pistols and dirk when worn. In the barracks, and when not on duty,

* This belt was the same as that anciently used by the people, and was of strong thick ox leather, and three or four inches in breadth, fixed by a brass or silver buckle in front. When the Highlanders had an expeditious journey to perform, or to run up or down a hill, they tightened the belt, which they said strengthened their loins. They also used the belt for another purpose. When pinched with hunger on their expeditions, they experienced great relief from tightening the belt. This belt was worn by old men within my remembrance, but is now entirely disused in the Highlands; latterly it has been resumed by young gentlemen of fashion, who wear it tight round the waist. In several cavalry regiments a belt or sash somewhat similar is worn.

the little kilt or philibeg† was worn, a blue bonnet with a border of white, red, and green, arranged in small squares to resemble, as is said, the fess cheque in the arms of the different branches of the Stewart family,‡ and a tuft of feathers, or sometimes, from economy or necessity, a small piece of black bear-skin. The arms were a musquet, a bayonet, and a large basket-hilted broadsword. These were furnished by Government: such of the men as chose to supply themselves with pistols and dirks were allowed to carry them, and some had targets after the fashion of the country. The sword-belt was of black leather, and the cartouch-box was carried in front, supported by a narrow belt round the middle.

In a corps which numbered in its ranks many men of birth and respectability, from character and education, those were esteemed fortunate who obtained commissions; indeed, a company at present is less prized than an ensigncy in the *Black Watch* was in those days.

The regiment remained about fifteen months on the banks of the Tay and Lyon; Tay Bridge and the Point of Lyon, a mile below Taymouth Castle, being their places of rendevous for exercise. There they were trained and exercised by the Lieutenant-Colonel, Sir Robert Munro, a veteran of much judgement and experience.

In the year 1740 the Earl of Craufurd was removed to the Life Guards, and Brigadier-General Lord Sempill was appointed colonel of the Highlanders.

---

† While the companies acted independently, each commander assumed the tartan of his own Clan. When embodied, no clan having a superior claim to offer an uniform plaid to the whole, and Lord Craufurd, the colonel, being a Lowlander, a new pattern was assumed, and which has ever since been known as the 42d, or Black Watch tartan, being distinct from all others. Lord John Murray gave the Athole tartan for the philibeg. The difference was only a stripe of scarlet, to distinguish it from that of the belted plaid. The pipers wore a red tartan of very bright colours, (of the pattern known by the name of Stewart or Royal Tartan,) so that they could be more clearly seen at a distance. When a band of music was added, plaids of the pipers' pattern were given to them.

‡ Tradition says, that this fashion commenced in Montrose's army in the civil wars as a token of loyalty to the king, and in distinction to the large and flat blue bonnets of the Covenanters and Puritans.

APPENDIX 8
Scottish Record Office – Ref. GD 248/213/8/14

An interesting insight into the varied duties expected from the Independent Companies during times of peace.

Abstract of orders from General Wade via Major Dinome to the Independent Companies.

Para 1. By order of General Wade of 28th September 1730 the Independent Companys are obliged to march with pick axes, shovells, rakes & wheel-barrows to throw off stones, sods, earth and pick out stones appearing above the level of the road, to fill up therefore the holes wt. small stones and gravall, to oppen drains etc. At four times in the year viz January, Apryle, July and October, the great Companys to clear and repair 38 miles, the lesser Companys 28 miles without pay which is a duty that noe troops in Britain are subjected to.

Para 4. By 8th article of said order, the officers are not only obliged to search for arms but to prosecute such as carry them contrary to Law without letting them know how they are to be paid of there expenses.

APPENDIX 9

Taken from a Military History of Perthshire by the Marchioness of Tullibardine (1908).

The original regimental list of the Black Watch, arranged so as to show to which companies the different officers were allotted. The companies are numbered according to the order of the captains' commissions.

	Commission dated
No. 1 Company.	
Colonel and Captain John, Earl of Crawford	25 Oct. 1739
Captain-Lieutenant Duncan Mackfarland	25 Oct. 1739
Ensign Gilbert Stewart of Kincraigie	29 Oct. 1739
No. 2 Company.	
Lieutenant-Colonel and Captain Sir Robert Munro, Bart., of Foulis	25 Oct. 1739
Lieutenant Paul Macferson	26 Oct. 1739
Ensign Archibald Macknab, younger son of the Laird of Macnab	31 Oct. 1739
No. 3 Company.	
Major and Captain George Grant	25 Oct. 1739
Lieutenant John Mackenzie of Rencraig (? Kincraig)	28 Oct. 1739
Ensign Collin Campbell	1 Nov. 1739
No. 4 Company.	
Captain Collin Campbell, yr. of Monzie[3]	25 Oct. 1739
Lieutenant Alexander Macdonald	29 Oct. 1739
Ensign James Campbell of Glenfalloch	25 Oct. 1739

[1] *War Office Estab. Books.*

[2] *Sketches,* vol. ii. p. 224.

[3] It will be observed that there are two captions of the name of Colin Campbell, two ensigns named Dougal Stewart and two named James Campbell. Owing to the fact that the family designations of the officers are not mentioned in the commissions it is impossible to say definitely to which companies the four ensigns above-mentioned belonged. They have therefore been assigned as far as possible according to local or family connection.

No. 5 Company	Commission dated
Captain James Colquhoun of Luss	26 Oct. 1739
Lieutenant George Ramsay	30 Oct. 1739
Ensign James Campbell of Stronslanie[1]	3 Nov. 1739

No. 6 Company.	
Captain John Campbell of Carrick	27 Oct.1739
Lieutenant John Maclean of Kingairloch	27 Oct. 1739
Ensign Dougall Stewart (of Appin?)	26 Oct. 1739

No. 7 Company.	
Captain Collin Campbell of Balliemore	28 Oct. 1739
Lieutenant Malcolm Frazer, son of Culduthel[2]	31 Oct. 1739
Ensign Dougall Stewart	25 Oct 1739

No. 8 Company.	
Captain George Munro of Culcairn, brother to Foulis	29 Oct. 1739
Lieutenant Lewis Grant of Auchterblair	25 Oct. 1739
Ensign John Menzies of Comrie	27 Oct. 1739

No. 9 Company.	
Captain Dougal Campbell of Craignish	30 Oct. 1739
Lieutenant John Mackneil	2 Nov. 1739
Ensign Gordon Graham of Draines[3]	30 Oct. 1739

No. 10 Company.	
Captain John Monro of Newmore	10 May 1740
Lieutenant Francis Grant, son of the laird of Grant[4]	1 Nov. 1739
Ensign Edward Carrick	28 Oct. 1739
Surgeon George Monro	17 Feb. 1740
Quarter Master John Forbes	25 March 1740
Chaplain Hon. Gideon Murray	25 March 1740
Adjutant John Lindsay[5]	25 March 1740

Captain Monro was nominated in succession to one of the former captains, whose name is unfortunately left blank. The list is other-

[1] Stewart of Garth calls him Dougal Campbell, but he appears as James in his commission.

[2] It is not stated to which companies Lieutenants Malcolm Fraser and Francis Grant belonged. No other lieutenants are mentioned for Balliemore and Newmore; they have therefore been assigned respectively to them.

[3] *i.e.* Drynie. A younger son of the Laird.

[4] See note to Lieutenant Malcolm Fraser.

[5] Garth gives the adjutant as being Gilbert Stewart (presumably the Ensign to the Colonel's Company). He probably acted in this capacity until John Lindsay was gazetted to the regiment.

wise fairly complete. It has been compiled from the 'Commission Books' in the Public Record Office, London, supplemented by original family papers and the information contained in Garth's original list.

In the 'Establishment for the Earl of Crawford's Regiment of Foot in the Highlands for 61 days from 25th October 1739 to 24th December following,' each company is stated to consist of seventy effective private men, three sergeants, three corporals, and two 'drums' – ten companies in all; and the total effective strength, including officers and men, is stated at 815. The same figures appear for 1740, when the regiment was commanded by Lord Sempill.

It is submitted that a sufficient amount of evidence has been set forth to prove the almost continuous succession of a Watch in the Highlands, on the Government establishment, from the date of the first commission to John, Earl of Atholl, on the 3rd of August 1667, to the first muster of the Black Watch as a British regiment between Taybridge and Aberfeldy in the county of Perth in May 1740.

APPENDIX 10
The Caledonian Mercury Edinburgh,
Wednesday, September 18th 1745

Affairs in this City and Neighbourhood have taken the most Surprising Turn Since Yesterday without the least Bloodshed or Opposition, so that we have now in our streets Highlanders & Bagpipes, in Place of Dragoons & Drums; of which we will be allowed to give the following Narrative of Facts as far as we have been yet able to collect them _____

On Monday last the Highland Army Stood under Arms about Corsterphin two Miles hence till about four of the Afternoon that their advanced Body marched up to attack the Regiment of Dragoons of Hamilton & Gardener & the City Companies, who Stood under Arms on this Side the Colt Bridge, a mile to the West of this City: immediately after the Dragoons etc. retired & made off down the North Side of this City towards Lieth, then turning Southward fled away for Hadington, leaving their Wives, Baggage & Tents to the care of our Magistrates, who saw the Same & the Guard that attended it Safely conducted to the Castle.

This Flight occasioned a general Consternation in this City, so that the principal Inhabitants, considering that there was no Expectation or Appearance of General Cope and his army, & that the two Regiments of Dragoons had abandoned Us, they immediately by Petition addressed the Lord Provost, Magistrates & Council to come to Some Sort of Capitulation with the Prince, in regard the City was not tenable, lest if the Highlanders should take it by storm the Conquerors might Sack, Pillage & destroy the Inhabitants.

The Magistrates ordered the fire Bell to be immediately rung to summon all the Inhabitants to attend them in the new Church & give their best Advice. They were Scarce met when a Letter was presented to the Meeting, addressed Charles Prince, Regent of the Kingdoms of Scotland, England, France & Ireland in the Dominions thereunto belonging etc. and beginning with these words Whereas we are now ready to enter the beloved Metropolis of our Ancient Kingdom of Scotland & here the Reader was stoped short. A Vote was then out what Measures were to be pursued, and as the Lord

Justice Clerk, Advocate etc. had withdrawn from the City & General Guest, at last voted that a Deputation should be appointed to go out of the Town & treat with the Prince's Army.

These Deputies accordingly went out to Gray Mills & met with their Chiefs, but did not hear that they came to any Agreement, however the Citizens delivered up their Arms into the Arsenal, & all was very quiet till about one o'Clock this Morning, when as the Gate at the Nether Bow was opening a few of the Highland Army entered thereat, & were followed by about 1000 resolute hardy like Men well armed, who took Possession of the Gate, also of the City Guard, making the Soldiers Prisoners of War, while another Detachment marched up towards the Castle and posted themselves at the weighhouse & other Places.

All these highlanders behaved most civily and discreetly, paying chearfully for what they had got & continue so to do. Hereupon the Castle fired Several Canon as a Signal, And the Garrison required that none of the Inhabitants Should appear on the Castlehill. The Prince lay in his Clothes two Hours that Night at Slateford two Miles hence & Set out Yesterday Morning for this City.

About Noon Day he made his Entry into the Abby of Holy Rood House in Highland Dress, accompanied by Several Nobility, Persons of Distinction etc. And alighting took Possession of the Royal Palace. All the rest of the Infantry to the Number of about 5000 remaining encamped in the King's Park. At one in the Afternoon the Highland Party Spread a carpet on the cross, & after clothing the Herald Purservants etc. carryed them to the Cross of Edinburgh, where with Sound of Trumpet they proclaimed the Declaration & Act of Regency, both dated at Rome 23rd 1743, the Manifesto in consequence of the Said Act of Regency at Paris May 10th 1745.

All the Publick continues their Business, nor is any Person molested or injured in Person or Property.

Printed for The Ruddiman & Company

APPENDIX 11
The Marquis of Tweeddale to the Lord President

My Lord,   Whitehall, 1st Octo^r 1745

I HAD the honour of your Lordship's of the 13th Sep^{tr} transmitted to me from Berwick by Sir John Cope; and I have the satisfaction to acquaint you, that his Majesty approves the plan you propose to follow in the distribution of the commissions, which will undoubtedly facilitate the raising of the men in the North Highlands.

The Earl of Stair has, by his Majesty's order, signified to the Earl of Loudoun, that he should forthwith repair to Inverness, to take upon him the command of the troops and garrisons from Inverlochy to Inverness, of the twenty independant companies to be raised, and of all such bodies of men as are or shall be raised for his Majesty's service; and his Lordship is desired to act in every thing with your advice and consent.

It is left to your Lordship and the Earl of Loudoun to concert proper measures for distressing the Highlanders, and for preventing their being joined by others, and in general to do what you shall think most for his Majesty's service, according as occasions may offer, or circumstances may require, either in or out of the countrys where they have been raised.

There are 1,500 stand of arms, with ammunition and proper accoutrements, to be put on board the Saltash sloop of war, which is ordered to sail forthwith to Inverness, and the Captain will take directions from you. Two months subsistence for the troops to be raised has likewise been imprested into George Ross's hands, which he proposes to send in specie by the sloop to Inverness.

The late unhappy defeat of Sir John Cope, as it must occasion the utmost distress in our country, so it gives a very great alarm here; but a very considerable body of troops, with artillery, &c. has already begun to march northward, to be commanded by Marshall Wade; and more of our troops are ordered from Flanders.

The Marquis of Tweeddale to the Lord President

I am, with great regard,
My Lord,
Your Lordship's most obedient humble servant,

TWEEDDALE.

Secretary of State for Scotland.

No. CCCCLVII.

APPENDIX 12

Military and/or family detail of 18 Company Captains. Companies Raised in 1745/46 by Lord President Forbes.

1. *George Munro of Culcairn:* Brother of Robert Munro yr of Foulis who commanded 3rd Independent Company (1714–16). George Munro served in the Highlands in 1715 in charge of men from his own clan and again in 1719 under General Wightman at Glenshiel. Led No 6 company in formation of Black Watch in 1725 and No 8 company when Black Watch was regimented in October 1739. Commanded Independent Company in 1745/46 and was shot (in error) at Loch Arkaig.
2. *Alexander Gunn (chief of clan Gunn):* Clan located in Sutherland. The patronymic in gaelic is MacShenmais (ie son of James) and pronounced in English MacHamish (however the signature of Alexander Gunn is McKemis). The chief (called the 'Chief and Captain of clan Gunn') — his men followed the Earl of Sutherland and Alexander was captain of the 1st Sutherland company.
3. *Patrick Grant of Rothiemurchus:* Acted under Sir Ludovick Grant of Grant as his chief. Had previously been a lieutenant in Lord Loudon's regiment.
4. *George Mackay:* First son of Lord Reay, chief of clan Mackay.
5. *Peter (Patrick) Sutherland:* Captain of the 2nd Sutherland company. Family history is not well authenticated. A letter written by him to Alexander Gunn (command 1st Sutherland company) is in author's possession. In his letter he is obviously being guided and instructed by Alexander Gunn.
6. *John Macleod yr of Macleod:* Son of Norman Macleod of Macleod — the 'Red man' or 'Wicked man' and chief of clan Macleod.
7. *Norman Macleod of Waterstein:* Son of one of the most important families in Skye.
8. *Norman Macleod of Bernera (Unish):* Connected in 1739 with the transportation of some 90 felons to the American colonies. Son of Donald Macleod of Bernera (the old 'Trojan').
9. *Donald Macdonald, 3rd of Castleton:* Captained one of the Macleod

companies. Great grandson of Sir Donald Macdonald, 1st Baronet of Sleat. Later rose to the rank of Colonel in the British Army. Died in 1760.

10. *William Mackintosh*: Acted under the command of the chief of clan Mackintosh, Aeneas or Angus Mackintosh of Mackintosh. Captained the Company as an Inverness Magistrate. The only non-clan captain.

11. *Hugh Macleod of Geanies*: Commanded the Assynt Macleod company.

12. *Alexander Mackenzie*: Some confusion about his antecedents. He was either 4th Laird of Muirtown and son of Roderick Mackenzie of Applecross or Alexander Mackenzie of Scatwell who married a daughter of Mackenzie of Scotsburn.

13. *Colin Mackenzie of Hilltown*: Believed to be Colin VII of Hilltown (Hilton) and brother to John VII of Hilltown who was killed at Sherrifmuir. Son of Ewan VI of Hilltown.

14. *James Macdonald of Aird*: Eldest son of William who was 3rd son of Sir Donald Macdonald 3rd Baronet of Sleat. Owned land in Aird of Trotternish in Skye. His father fought at Killiecrankie and Sherrifmuir for the Jacobite cause.

15. *John Macdonald of Kirkibost*: John, 5th son of Major William Macdonald. 1st of Aird and brother to Captain James Macdonald (2nd of Aird). Owned land in Kirkibost (Skye) and in North Uist.

16. *Hon Hugh Mackay*: 2nd son of Lord Reay. Formerly a captain in Lord Loudon's regiment. An experienced officer who had army service abroad.

17. *William Ross yr of Invercassley*: No detail obtainable from clan Ross.

18. *Colin Mackenzie*: Commanded the 3rd Mackenzie company under guidance of Seaforth and drawn mainly from the Isle of Lewis. Thought to be Colin Mackenzie of Redcastle although the Redcastle family were mainly 'out' with the Prince. Surely an example of divided clan and family loyalty.

19. *Captain Hugh Macdonald of Armadale*: Hugh Macdonald of Camuscross in Skye. Grandson of Sir James Macdonald, 2nd Baronet of Sleat. Not one of the captains listed in the original 18 but, as he did serve, his services must have been that of a replacement captain. Step-father of Flora Macdonald and who conveniently 'did not see' the Prince in South Uist and by writing a pass, allowed Flora and 'Betty Burke' to cross to cross 'over the Sea to Skye'.

Weekly Return of the Independent [Companies] Commanded by the Earl of Loudoun Dornoch March 10th 1745/6.

Companies	Officers present — Captains	Lieutenants	Ensigns	Serjts. Present	Serjts. Sick Present	Corpls Present	Corpls Sick Present	Drums Present	Centinels Present fit for duty	Centinels Sick Present	Total Effective Serjeants	Total Effective Corporals	Total Effective Drums	Total Effective Centinels	Deserted	Dead	Discharged	Left behind at Inverness etc.
Capt. George Monroe [of Calcairn]	1	1	1	4	—	4	—	2	100	—	4	4	2	100	—	—	—	—
Capt. Peter (Patrick) Sutherland [Kinminity]	1	1	1	4	—	—	4	2	73	3	4	4	2	76	—	—	—	—
Capt. Hugh McKay [Younger of Bighouse]	1	1	1	2	2	4	—	1	82	6	4	4	1	88	6	—	2	—
Capt. Alex. Gun [? of Badenloch]	1	1	1	4	—	4	—	2	71	10	4	4	2	81	—	—	—	—
Capt. Geo. Mckay [of Skibo]	1	1	1	4	—	3	—	1	89	4	4	3	1	93	3	—	1	—
Captain McLeod. Talasker	1	1	1	3	—	4	—	1	84	2	3	4	1	36	5	—	13	—
Capt. McLeod. Waterstyn	1	1	1	2	1	4	—	—	77	8	3	4	—	85	—	—	14	—
Capt. McLeod. Bernara	1	1	1	4	—	4	—	1	82	4	4	4	1	86	6	—	13	—
Capt. McLeod [Macdonald of Castleton was captain of this Company]	1	1	1	4	—	4	—	0	74	6	4	4	—	80	—	—	14	—
Capt. Wm. McKintosh [of Inverness]	1	1	1	3	—	3	—	1	57	—	3	3	1	57	15	—	11	—
Capt. Macleod. Guineas	1	1	1	4	—	4	—	1	76	2	4	4	1	78	6	—	2	—
Capt. Jas. Macdonald [of Airds]	1	1	1	4	—	4	—	1	91	—	4	4	1	94	—	—	—	—
Capt. John Donald [Kirkibost]	1	1	1	2	—	4	—	1	94	—	4	4	1	94	—	—	—	—
Total	13	13	13	46	3	50	—	14	1050	45	49	50	14	1095	41	—	70	—

APPENDIX 14

Correspondence Between Major I.H. Mackay-Scobie and Captain E.A. Campbell, concerning the Contemporary Dress of an Independent Company Private Soldier

Carbery
Salcombe
S Devon

1 Enclosure

23/9/40

My dear Campbell

I have yours of the 26th instant, with enclosed outline sketch of a figure showing probable dress of a *Private Man of the Independent Companies of 1745–7*, in his proper regimentals, some of which the Coys did not actually get until after Culloden, as you will see in my account of them, which, Baldry, tells me will be welcome for the Spring issue of the Journal, and which he is ready to work upon soon – the Winter issue being 'all set', already.

I had suggested several most suitable illus. for the above article, but owing to rising costs of printing, reproduction, etc., he says they must be limited, and probably will amount to *your sketch* and *an outline map* showing location of those clans which furnished the Companies, and including appropriate place names.

As regards *your sketch*, which will do *excellently (just the thing)*, when we have gone into certain points; I will, of course, leave to you whether *to complete it* as an *outline (line block)* illustration or, in *half tone. In colour*, it would be excellent but *doubt* Baldry being able to run to this. This being so, a line block figure would possibly be best, as those who cared could always *colour it up?* However, as mentioned, I will leave this to you, but if you desired it as a coloured illustration you might write Baldry and ask him if this will be possible? It might be worth doing this? I *would* prefer to see it as a colour illustration, needless to say. Or I could ask him?

As to the drawing, I return it, enclosed, and have *noted on it in pencil, certain suggestions, and also replied to your queries.* I suppose the waistcoat is long enough, being longer than the short cut coat or jacket? The pattern and shape of both sporan and dirk would be more as I have tried to suggest. The dirk *then* was *usually* about 16″ in blade, and also *narrow*, hence sheath would be so too, and with small narrow light mounts and chape or tip. The sheath was usually tooled, with criss-cross ornamentation.

Perhaps, *if* I may say so, the legs are a trifle 'heavy', and I have tried to indicate a *slight* 'thinning' of them, which perhaps would make them rather more in proportion to the rest of figure? I *know* you will pardon my suggestion on this point. I may be wrong.

The pistol is just about right; the rams-horn or claw-butt, however, is actually *rather more like* what I have tried to indicate on your tracing of drawing.

The top of waistcoat, at neck, might be a *little lower*, showing more of the white kerchief round neck? I think the V. der Gucht and other prints show a white neck cloth, or *is it* just *the top of the white linen shirt?*

The beret-like bonnet, as you show it, is about right, I think. The black spell cockade, however, is I think larger and more 'bow like', see the V. der G. and other prints? The red cross (saltire-wise) would show well on it, a *bit larger* than you have indicated.

The cartouche box *belt* went *over* the waistcoat, I believe, see the V. des G. etc. prints. Would the box have 'GR' on front of flap, like (if I remember right) the above prints show? In black, or yellow (metal).

Could you possibly let me have another similar tracing, so as to make sure all is in order? It would be better, and more satisfactory I think. You could also let me know in what process you complete the drawing (when you have gone into the matter, in view of what I have mentioned above)?

I suppose you will give figure a little ground to stand upon, and perhaps (altho' not necessary) some mountains behind, indicated?

We too have had a fresh influx of evacuees, including some children from London *who have already been here once*, but taken back by their foolish parents!! What a cost!

I expect Brennan has flitted from London, too 'hot' altogether!

I also had a line from Clendenin. He misses no museum at the Castle, as I do also!!

We are getting it chillier now, altho' *days* are still enjoyable on the water. The estuary is well guarded now, m.g. nests, booms, floating barrels, etc: I never thought I should ever see Salcombe as it is!! No more peaceful a place, and remote, *once*, but *now* vis-as-vis to France!

Hoping to hear further from you, and when drawing is eventually completed, with alterations, etc, it will form a *most* suitable illustration for the article, which really breaks almost fresh ground. I am so glad you could do the important illustration for it, especially as you are, like myself, of a Hanovarian clan! I am always telling people *not* all the Highlanders were Jacobite. Had they been so, the Stewarts might have returned to the British Throne, if only for a time! In haste, Yours aye

I.H. Mackay Scobie

P.S. Please excuse atrocious writing but have got a bad pen, also people are talking near me!!

Carbery
Salcombe
S Devon

2 Enclosures

7/10/40

My dear Campbell

I have your revised outline drawing of the *Private Man of an Ind. Coy. of 1745–7*. Also your First tracing of same. The former is now more in order I think, but there are a few minor items still, which I have *put in pencil below sketch*. I like expression of face in first tracing best. I have set the bonnet further down on head.

I think purse is about right now and good shape etc. As regards height, *(no lower)* but perhaps you might make curve of its clasp-top more *decided at top*, as I have indicated? As regards detail of pistol (on side shown) perhaps you have a drawing or illus. of one, so as to get the lock plate, termination of barrel in stock, ramrod-pipe, and both hammer and flash pan with its spring *correct*. I have none by me, unfortunately! The pistol strap would be fairly taunt, as it goes over shoulder, as I have indicated. I think top of waistcoat is about right now, as it was under top of coat, so far as I remember.

The dirk might be a *wee bit* lower, as at present its fastening would fold up the bottom of waistcoat? Its angle, etc, is now correct enough. Also length (total) just about right. A much longer weapon than as made now.

219

I am wondering whether, as you have now set the figure in a background, *if it would not be advisable and also add to value of the drawing*, if you could set the figure a little to one side, and *add a smaller one in probable dress before* the *military 'cloathing' was issued.* The dress (incl. shape of coat and waistcoat) would be much the same, only coat (and perhaps waistcoat) would be of tartan cut on the bias, and cuffs of coat as shown in Morier's painting of an incident in 1745, which you probably have a copy of? Certain figures in McIan's 'Costume of the clans' would help. In this figure the hose would probably be of tartan, or at least with more pattern than the military 'caddis'. If you had above details, *a target* would be *most appropriate to add* either in hand, or slung on back. The size of a target was not over 21″ in diameter. There would be room for a fair sized figure, large enough to give sufficient details? *I hope you can do this?* I *should* have mentioned it before, but only thought of it now, when seeing your second sketch, and remembering that some, at least, of the Companies did *not* get their uniform clothing until they had been *sometime in the field.* Back, front or side view would suit.

So if you *could* perhaps let me have *another sketch, like one just sent,* with present figure revised, *and* the second figure put in I should be very glad? In this second figure, it would be appropriate to show the *'cuaran' or deerskin brogues with criss-cross lacing,* which they would have certainly worn when on the hill, instead of the clumsier and heavy buckled shoes.

Morier, McIan, etc, will show you the type. If you have not got McIans Costumes, there is a Figure (in '45 kit) from this work in F Adams 'Clans, Septs' etc, which you will certainly have.

I am mentioning you in full, in my foreward or note to the article as having compiled this plate with every care as to authentic detail etc. It will be a valuable addition to the article.

So sorry to hear about Brennan. Why *do* people who *can* leave London stick there!! I trust his collection has not suffered. Please condole for me to him, when you next write. I heard from Clendenin as to his staff job. Very good. As you would prefer to do whole drawing in colour, please do so. It can be reproduced in half tone, if I can't get Baldry to reproduce it in colour. I will try to have it so done, but expense *may* preclude this. All good wishes. In haste yours aye

I.H. Mackay Scobie

Could I have both these sketches when you send next one.

Acknowledgements

Colonel, The Hon. W.D. Arbuthnott M.B.E. Balhousie Castle, Perth.
Mrs Jane Anderson, Archivist, Blair Castle, Blair Atholl.
Duke of Argyll, Inverary Castle.
Duke of Atholl, Blair Castle, Blair Atholl.
Major D.R. Baxter, Baron of Earlshall, Historian and Author, Earlshall Castle, Leuchars, Fife.
Dr. I.F.W. Becket, Dept. of War Studies, R.M.A. Sandhurst.
Dr. David J. Brown, S.R.O. Edinburgh.
Sir Donald H. Cameron of Lochiel, Achnacarry, Spean Bridge.
Alastair Campbell of Airds yr. Unicorn Pursuivant, Inverary Castle.
Mrs Monica Clough, Historian, Milton by Drumnadrochit.
Earl of Cromartie, Castle Leod, Ross & Cromarty.
Dr. A.D. Dewar, Historian, Menzies Clan Society, Edinburgh.
Professor Kenneth Fraser, Historian and Author, Tomintoul, Ballindalloch
Dr. James D. Galbraith, Deputy Keeper, S.R.O. Edinburgh.
Andrew Grant, Clan Grant Society, Aberdeen.
Dr. Alan J. Guy, The National Army Museum, London.
Dr. Eliz. M. Hallam-Smith, P.R.O, Chancery Lane, London.
Dr. Diana M. Henderson, Historian, Author and Soldier, Edinburgh University.
Dr. P.A. Hopkins, Historian and Author, Cambridge University.
Philip Howard, Literary Editor, The Times, London.
Keeper of the Public Records, P.R.O. Kew, Surrey.
Professor Bruce P. Lenman, Historian and Author. St. Andrews University.
Chief Librarian, Whitehall Library, Ministry of Defence, London.
Lumsden of that Ilk and Blanerne, Amersham, Buckinghamshire.
Norman H. Macdonald F.R.S.A., F.S.A. Scot., Historian for the Clan Donald Lands Trust.
Lord Macdonald of Sleat, Isle of Skye.
Margaret Macdonald, Archivist, Clan Donald Centre, Isle of Skye.
Dr. Alasdair Maclean (Retired Med. Practitioner and Author) Portree, Isle of Skye.
Dr. Iain Maciver, Assistant Keeper, National Library of Scotland.

The Mackintosh of Mackintosh, O.B.E., Moy Hall, Inverness.

John Macleod of Macleod, Dunvegan, Isle of Skye.

E.C.R. Macmillan, Archivist, Regt. H.Q. of the Black Watch, Balhousie Castle, Perth.

Sir Wm. Macpherson of Cluny T.D., Newton Castle, Blairgowrie.

David Menzies of Menzies, Dalbeith, Western Australia.

R.W. Munro, Author and Hon. Historian of the Clan Munro Association, Edinburgh.

Captain Munro of Foulis, Foulis Castle, Ross.

Dr. Mark Nicholls, National Army Museum, London.

Dr. Rae (now deceased) Scottish History Society.

Mrs. C.G.W. Roads, M.V.O., Lyon Clerk and Keeper of the Records, The Court of the Lord Lyon, Edinburgh.

J.F. Russell, National Library of Scotland.

The Lord Strathspey, West Wittering, Sussex.

Colonel P.S. Walton, Army Museums Ogilby Trust, Aldershot, Hamps.

Ruth E.Wilson, Librarian, Scottish United Services Museum, Edinburgh

Stephen Wood, The Keeper, Scottish United Services Museum, Edinburgh

Army Museums Ogilby Trust — Research Grant

V.M. Calder   – Layout: Typing
C.J. Simpson   – Maps: Illustrations
Dr. S.M. Simpson   – Script Correction
Maj. D.G. Simpson   – Advice: Photography
J.P. England   – Photography: Indexing: Appendices
Maj. P.J.R. Mileham   – Advisory: Editing

Bibliography

Adams F. – Clans, Septs and Regiments.

Adams Catherine & Henry – History of the British Regular Army.

Atholl, Duchess of – The military History of Perthshire.

Atholl, Duke of – Chronicles of the Atholl & Tullibardine Families. (1908)

Bain Robert – The Clans & Tartans of Scotland.

Barnes R.M. Major – Military Uniforms.

Baynes John – The Jacobite Rising of 1715. London 1970.

Baynes John & Caffin. John – Soldiers of Scotland.

Black. George F. – The surnames of Scotland 1946.

Blackmore. H.L. – British Military Firearms (1660–1850) 1961.

Blaikie. W.B. – Origins of the '45.

Blaikie. W.B. – Itinery of Prince Charles Edward Stewart. (Scottish History Society – Edinburgh 1897).

Brown James – Highland Clans (Stuart papers) Vol II.

Browne James – History of the Highlands & Highland clans 1838.

Buchan John – The Massacre of Glencoe.

Burton. J.H. – History of Scotland Vols VII & VIII. Edinburgh 1898.

Burton J.H. – Lives of Simon. Lord Lovat & Duncan Forbes of Culloden.

Burton. J.H. – History of Scotland (1689–1748) Vol I & Vol II. 1853.

Burt. Edward – Letters from a gentleman in the North of Scotland ed. Jamieson 2 vols 1922.

Caldwell David. H. – Scottish weapons and Fortifications (1100–1800).

Campbell. A. Lord – Lord – Highland dress, arms and armaments.

Campbell. A. Lord – The Children of the Mist – 1890.

Campbell. J. – A Full and Particular Description of the Highlands of Scotland – 1752.

Campbell. R.H. – Scotland since 1707–1965.

Campbell R.H. & Dow J.B.A. – Source Book of Scottish Economic & Social History – 1968.

Carman. W.Y. – British Military Uniforms from contemporary pictures.

Clark George. Sir – Oxford History of England.

Clark George. Sir – The later Stuarts (1660–1714)

Cleland. William – The Highland Host 1678.

Cochrane. Peter – Scottish Military Dress.

Cole. D.H. Major – An Outline of British Military History (1660–1939).

Cole. D.H. & Priestley. E.C. – An Outline History of British Arms (1660–1939).

Cromartie. Earl of – A Highland History.

Cunningham A. – The Loyal Clans – Cambridge – 1932.

Dalton. C. – The Scots Army (1661–1688)

Davies. Godfrey – The Early Stuarts (1603–1660).

Dickson W.K. – The Jacobite attempt of 1719.

Drummond. James & Anderson J. – Ancient Scottish Weapons – 1881.

Drummond. John – Memoirs of Sir Ewen Cameron of Lochiel – 1842.

Duff (ed) – Culloden Papers 1815.

Duke. W. – Lord George Murray and the '45–1927.

Dunbar. J.T. – History of Highland Dress Dunbar – 1962.

Elder J.R. – The Highland Host of 1678–1914.

Ferguson. W. – Scotland 1689 to the Present – 1968.

Ferguson. – Duncan Forbes of Culloden – 1936.

Fergusson. Bernard – The Black Watch – 1955.

Forbes – The Black Watch. Records of an Historic Regiment – 1896.

Forbes Robert (Bishop of Ross & Caithness) The Lyon in Mourning (ed. Henry Paton) 3 vols. Edinburgh 1895–6.

Fraser. William Sir. – Chiefs of Grant – 1883.

Frederick. J.B.M. – Lineage book of the British Army (1660–1968).

Gibson. J.S. – Ships of the '45: the rescue of the young Pretender – 1967.

Gibson. J.S. – Playing the Scottish Card.

Grant. I.F. – Highland Folk Ways.

Grant. I.F. – The Clan Grant.

Grant. I.F. – Periods in Highland History.

Guthrie H. – Memoirs (1637–1649) –1748.

Henderson Diana M. – Highland Soldier.

Hillson N. – Discovering the historical Highlands – 1959.

Hilton George – The main stream of Jacobitism – Cambridge 1954.

Hopkins. P.A. – Glencoe and the End of the Highland War (1590–1660).

Howard. Philip – The Black Watch – 1968.

Howlett. Hamilton – Highland Constable, the Life and Times of Rob Roy Macgregor.

Bibliography

Hume-Brown. P. – Scotland Before 1700 From Contemporary Documents – 1893.

Hume-Brown. P. – Surveys of Scottish History – 1919.

Innes. Thomas Sir (of Learney) – Tartans of the Clans and the Families of Scotland – 1947.

Johnston. G.H. – The Heraldry of the Campbells – 1977.

Johnston. T.B. & Robertson. J.A. – Historical Geography of the Clans of Scotland.

Keltie. J.S. – History of the Scottish Highland Clans and Regiments – 1875.

Kermack. W.R. – The Scottish Highlands – 1957.

Kinross. John – Guide to military museums – 1970.

Lang. Andrew – Prince Charles Edward Stuart – 1900.

Latham-Wilkinson. Robert – Scottish Military Uniforms – 1975.

Lawson – A History of the Uniforms of the British Army – 1940.

Lenman. Bruce – The Jacobite Clans of the Great Glen (1650–1784).

Linklater. Eric – The Survival of Scotland – 1968.

Linklater. Eric – Prince in the Heather – London 1968.

Lockhart. George (of Carnwath) – Memoirs of the Affairs of Scotland.

Lockhart. George (of Carnwath) – The Lockhart Papers (1702–1715).

Luard John – A History of the Dress of a British Soldier.

Macdonald. Angus & Archibald. M. – The Clan Donald 3 Vols (1896–1904) Inverness – 1904.

Macdonald. Donald J. – Clan Donald – 1970.

Mackay D.N. – Clan Warfare in the Scottish Highlands – 1922.

Mackay. J.G. – The Romantic Story of the Highland Garb and Tartan – Stirling 1924.

Macgregor Alasdair Alpin – The Road To Meggernie & Glencoe – 1927.

Mackenzie W.L. – Lovat of the '45 – Edinburgh. 1934.

Mackenzie. W.L. – Simon Fraser, Lord Lovat – London 1908.

Mackie. J.D. – A History of Scotland – 1964.

Maclean Alasdair – A Macdonald for the Prince – Stornoway 1982.

Maclean. Fitzroy – A Concise history of Scotland (1640–1745).

Macleod Donald Sgt. – Memoirs of the Life and Gallant Exploits of the Old Highlander – Blackie 1933.

Macleod. Olaf Colonel – Uniforms of the Scottish Regiments.

Macleod. R.C. (Rev.) – The Macleods.

Macleod R.C. – Book of Dunvegan – Aberdeen 1939.

Macwilliam. H.D. – The Black Watch Tartan – 1932.

Macwilliam. H.D. – A Black Watch Episode of 1731 – 1908.

Maidment. J. – Kays Edinburgh Portraits – 1885.

Menzies. D.P. – Red & White Book of Menzies – 1895.

Mileham, P.J.R. – The Scottish Regiments – 1988.

Milne. Samuel – The Standards and Colours of the Army (1661–1881).

Mould. D.D.C. – Roads from the Isles.

Munro. R.W. – Highland Clans and Tartans – 1987.

Murray C. de B. – Duncan Forbes of Culloden – London 1936.

Norrie. W.D. Life and Adventures of Prince Charles Edward Stuart. London 1903– 4. 4 Vols.

Petrie. C. Sir – The Jacobite Movement – The First Phase. London 1948.

Petrie. C. Sir – The Jacobite Movement – The Final Phase. 1950.

Prebble. John – Massacre of Glancoe – 1966.

Prebble John – Culloden.

Rae. Peter – The History of the Late Rebellion against his Majesty King George by the Friends of the Popish Pretender – Dumfries 1718

Ramsay. A.A.N. – Challenge to the Highlander – 1933.

Rennie. J.A. – The Scottish People – 1960.

Ross. Andrew – The military History of Perthshire.

Salmond. J.B. – Wade in Scotland – Edinburgh 1938.

Scobie. I.H. Mackay – Journal of the Society for Army Historical Research (1941–46).

Scobie. I.H. Mackay – The Argyll or Campbell Militia.

Scobie. I.H. Mackay – The Scottish regiments of the British Army – Edinburgh 1942

Skene. W.F. – The Highlanders of Scotland – 1837.

Smitherman. P.H. – Uniforms of the Scottish Regiments.

Smout. T.C. – A History of the Scottish People (1560–1830)–1969.

Stewart. David (of Garth) – Sketches of the Character, Manners and Present State of the Highlanders of Scotland with details of the Military Service of the Highland Regiments – 2 Vols Edinburgh 1822.

Stewart. D.C. – The Setts of the Scottish Tartans – Tartans – 1977.

Stewart D.W. – Old and Rare Scottish Tartans.

Stevenson-Sinclair – Inglorious Rebellion. The Jacobite Risings of 1708, 1715 & 1719–1971.

Stuart. J.S. – Costumes of the Clans – 1892.

Terry. C.S. – The Chevalier de St. George and the Jacobite Movement in his Favour – London 1990.

Bibliography

Terry. C.S. – The Rising of 1745, with a bibliography of the Jacobite Highlanders (1689–1788) – London 1900.

Terry. C.S. – Jacobitism and the Union. Cambridge 1922.

Tomasson. K. & Buist. F. – Battles of the '45–1962.

Walton. C. – History of the British Standing Army (1660–1700)

Whitelaw. C.E. – Scottish Weapons and the Scottish History of Life – 1902.

Wood. Stephen – The Scottish Soldier.

Young. Peter (Brig.) – The British Army (1642–1970).

Manuscripts

Culloden Papers – National Library of Scotland.

Regimental Rolls – Scottish Records Office. Edinburgh (*1689–91*)

Regimental Rolls.
1691–8
1717–39 } Public Record Office – Kew & Chancery Lane, London.
1760

Macdonald Papers – Scottish Record Office – Edinburgh G.D. 221.

Campbell of Mamore Papers – MMS 3733 – National Library. Edinburgh.

Jacobite Papers – Manuscripts. 1694–1696. National Library of Scotland. Edinburgh.

Clanranald Papers – S.R.O. Edinburgh.

The Red & White Book of Menzies.

Other Material

Ascarius of the Young Adventurer – London 1890.

Scottish Weapons – Scottish Art Review – Glasgow 1963.

Spalding's Memorials of the Troubles in Scotland – Spalding Club 1850.

The Black Book of Taymouth – The Breadalbane Charter Room. (1855).

More Culloden Papers – (ed) Duncan Warrand. 5 Vols – (1923/30)

Historical Papers Relating to the Jacobite Period (1699–1750) – New Spalding Club.

The Massacre of Gluencoe, being a true narrative of the Barbarous Murther of the Glenco-men in the Highlands of Scotland – London 1700.

Memoirs of the Chevalier de Johnstone – Aberdeen 1870.

The Argyll Papers (1640–1723) – (ed) James Maidment – Edinburgh 1834.

Scotland and the Protectorate – Scottish History Society – 1899.

History of the Rebellion – Chambers 7th Edition. Edinburgh 1869.

Life and Work of the Rt. Hon. Duncan Forbes of Culloden – London 1818.

Highland Papers (1689–1696) – Maitland Club. Glasgow.

Knock Notebook – Scottish Record Office. Cat. No. RH 2/8/96.

Index

Act of 1587 3, 44
Adolphus, King Gustavus 16, 31
Airlie, Earl of 98
Albemarle, Earl of (William Anne
   Keppel 2nd Earl) 141, 149
Alford 7, 55
Anne, Queen 95
Appin, Laird of 37
Appin, Tutor of 37
Argyll (Earls, Marquises & Dukes
   of) 3, 7, 12, 34, 36, 55, 58, 61,
   62, 66, 68, 69, 71, 99
Askintullie, Laird of 36
Atholl (Earls, Marquises & Dukes
   of) 12, 36, 59, 60, 61, 62, 71,
   93, 99
Auldern 7, 55
Austrian Succession, The War of
   121

Bagpipes, (The War Pipe) 31, 32,
   33
Ballindalloch, Laird of 36
Ballingoun, Laird of 36
Balnagown, David Ross of,
   Captain 82, 84
Barclay, George, Captain 72
Barrels, (4th of foot) 131
Bayne, Duncan 93
Bayne, Roderick 98
Belted plaid 20, 21
Bernera, Barracks at 101, 111, 112
Black Watch (An Freiceadan
   dubh) 23, 27, 62, 68, 101, 115,
   124, 125, 155, 160, 196–205,

207–209
Blackness Castle 112
Boyne, Battle of the 83
Braemar 58
Breadalbane, Earls of 35, 36, 57,
   86, 99
Breadalbane Men 108
Buchan, James 70
Buchan, Thomas, Major-General
   82
Burke Betty 143
Burt, Edward, Captain 8, 10, 22,
   37, 39, 117
Byng, Admiral 96

Cairnes, Alexander, Captain 70,
   176
Caithness, Earl of 66, 67, 68, 69
Calder, Laird of 36
Cambusmore 80
Cameron, Allan 97
Cameron, of Lochiel 56, 70, 77,
   92, 93, 99, 103
Cameron, Donald, of Lochiel 120,
   122, 146, 147
Cameron Highlanders 24
Cameron, John 146
Cameron – Clan 15, 55, 56, 63,
   91, 97, 99, 102, 108
Camerons of Glen Nevis 72
Cameronians 80
Campbell, Alexander of Fonab 67,
   92
Campbell, Allan Yr, of Ballardine
   124

Campbell, Archibald, of Inverawe 67

Campbell, Colin, of Glendorowell 92, 97

Campbell, Colin, of Skipness 97, 113, 114, 115, 117, 143, 149

Campbell, Dugald 124

Campbell,Duncan, of Killin 65

Campbell, Sir Duncan, of Lochnell 92, 113, 115, 117

Campbell, Duncan, of Lochness 97, 99

Campbell, Duncan, of Ochtertyre 63

Campbell, of Inverawe 124

Campbell, James, of Glenfalloch 120

Campbell, Sir James, of Lawers 62, 63, 64, 65, 66, 67, 68,

Campbell, John, of Airdes 67

Campbell, John, of Carrick 98, 113, 114, 115, 117, 120

Campbell, John Yr, of Glenfalloch 124

Campbell, John Yr, of Glenlyon 124

Campbell, John, of Succoth 68

Campbell, John, Major-General, of Mamore, later 4th Duke of Argyll 135, 143, 144

Campbell, Lachlan, of Craignish 120

Campbell, of Loch Dochart 64

Campbell, Mungo, of Lawers, Colonel 63

Campbell, Neil 152

Campbell, Robert, of Ballivolin 151

Campbell, Robert, (Rob Roy MacGregor)

Campbell, Robert, of Glenlyon, Captain 83

Campbell – Clan 13, 22, 23, 91, 117

Campbells of Strachur 44

Cannon, General 80

Cearr Iain dubh (Black John) 54

Charge, The Highland 29, 30

Charles II 7, 54, 66, 69, 71

Crawford, Lord 116

Campbell, Ronald, Ensign 120

Chattan, Clan 37, 43, 52

Chisolme, Alexander 63

Clanranald, Captain of 36, 50

Claymore 25

Clayton, Jasper, Lieut-General 118

Cope, Sir John, General 122, 124

Crawford, 20th Earl of 126, 135, 136, 137

Cromwell, Oliver ⎫
                   ⎬ 39, 48, 57, 74
Cromwell, Richard ⎭

Culloden Moor 7, 14, 16, 17, 26, 28, 30, 32, 76, 113, 135, 137, 148, 152, 158, 162, 173

Cumberland, Duke of, William Augustus 7, 16, 32, 121, 135, 136, 137, 148, 158, 159

Cuming, Alexander 89

Cuming, Alexander of Ruthven 63

Cuming, David, of Ruthven 65

Cuthbert, James of Milncraigs 151

Dalrymple, Sir John, 1st Earl of Stair 17, 83

Dalziel, John 70

Darien Expedition, The 92, 95

Dettingen 119, 121

Dirk 25

Disarming Acts 1916 (1725 & 1746) 27, 104, 107, 121, 130, 150

Douglas Regiment 16

Drummond Castle 80

Drummond, Lord John 138

Drummond, Lieut-General 57

Drumnakill 80

Dumbarton Castle 112

Duncanson, Robert, Major 83

Dunvegan Castle 42

Eight Glenmoriston Men:

John Macdonald
Alexander Macdonald
Alexander Chisholm
Donald Chisholm
Hugh Chisholm
Gregor Macgregor
Patrick Grant
Hugh Macmillan 145
Elcho, Lord, David Wemyss 125, 138

Fairfoull, Colin 92, 97
Falkirk 7, 28, 29, 30, 129, 131, 173
Farquaharson, Alexander, of Invercauld 64
Farquaharson, James, Yr, of Invercauld 124
Farquaharson, John, of Innerey 64
Ferguson, John, Captain (Navy 143, 144, 145, 149
Ferguson's Regiment (Cameronians) 92
Finlarig Castle 80
Flodden Field, Battle of, 1513 43
Foe, Daniel De 6, 15
Fontenoy 119, 121, 160
Forbes, Duncan, (The Lord President) 8, 9, 12, 99, 100, 112, 113, 122, 123, 126, 128, 132, 133, 134, 135, 140, 150, 155, 158, 159, 162, 212, 213
Forbes – Clan 91
Forbin, Admiral 96
Fort Augustus 101, 111, 112, 114
Fort George 112
Fort William 39, 101, 112, 122
Foulis, Laird of 36
Fraser, Alexander, of Culduthell 98
Fraser, Donald 134
Fraser, Hugh, of Dumballoch 93, 94
Frasers – Clan 12, 15, 22, 23, 117

Foulis, Laird of 36

Gairntully, Laird of 73
Gartmore MSS 35
George I 7, 38, 113
George II 161
Given, William, of Drymen 64, 65
Glencoe, Massacre of (1692) 35
Glengarry, Chiefs of ⎫
Glengarry, Laird of ⎬ 36, 87
Glenmoriston, Laird of 36
Glenshiel 7, 155, 160
Gordon, Dukes of 36, 73, 76, 125
Gordon, James, of Barnes 97
Gordon, John, of Glenbucket 125
Gordon, Lord Lewis 125
Gordon, Peter, of Knockespick 151
Gordon, Robert of Haughes 102
Gordon, Robert, of Straloch 20
Gordon – Clan 125
Gorm, Donald, of Sleat 50
Governor of Inverlochy – see Sir John Hill
Graham, Colin, of Drainie 151
Graham, James, Marquis of Montrose 7, 16, 36, 55, 76, 160
Graham, John, of Claverhouse, 1st Viscount Dundee 7, 76, 160
Grant, Alexander, of Ballachastell 64
Grant, Allan Yr, of Glenmoriston 124
Grant, George, Major 64
Grant, John, of Freuchie 64
Grant, Laird of 36, 56
Grant, Lewis, Major 115
Grant, Ludovick, of Rothiemurchus 151
Grant, Patrick, of Ruthven, Lieut-Colonel 64, 127, 214
Grant, William, of Ballindalloch, Captain and Colonel 93, 96, 97, 113, 115, 117
Grant – Clan 12, 22, 23, 25, 91, 102, 117, 125, 130

Grantully, Laird of 36
Guest, Joshua, Lieut-General 120
Guise's (6th of Foot) 122
Gun, Alexander 127, 129, 214
Greenock, Laird of 84

Hamilton, 4th Duke of, (James
    Douglas) 95
Hamilton, George, Colonel 89
Hamilton, James, Lieut-Colonel 83
Hardwicke, Lord 149
Hastings 77
Haughs of Cromdale 81
Hawley, Henry, Lieut-General 29,
    131, 172
Heigham, John 89
Hepburn, Robert 49, 51
Highland Captancies 52, 54, 154
Hill, Sir John 84, 85, 88, 90
His Majesty's Captains 52
Howard, Philip (The Times) 101
Huntly, Marquis of 61, 71, 98
Hyndford, Earl of 93

Icolmkill, Statutes of (1609) – Iona
    Statutes 46, 51
Innes, James, of Aboyne 65
Inverlochy 7, 55, 58
Inversnaid 112
Inverurie 160
Islay, Lord 123

James VI (Scotland): I (England)
    3, 7, 58, 71
James VII 7, 76, 83
Johnstone, James Chevalier De
    25, 28
Johnstone, Sir James, of
    Westerhall 152

Keir, Laird of 52
Keith, George, 10th Earl of
    Marischal 98
Keith, James (known as Marshall
    Keith) 103

Kenmuir's 77
Killiekrankie, Battle of 7, 26, 27,
    28, 72, 79, 80, 84, 160, 173
Kilmarnock, Lord of 125
Kilnarock, Laird of 36
Kilsyth 7, 55
King's Guard 49, 50, 51, 53, 54,
    154
Knox, Andrew, Bishop of the Isles
    50

Landross 80
Lascelle's (58th of Foot) 122
Lee's (55th of Foot) 122
Leven's 77, 79
Ligonier's 131
Livingston, John 70
Lochbury, Laird of 36
Lochiel, Donald Cameron of 145
Lochiel, Laird of 36, 87
Loch Nan uamh 137
Lockhart, George, of Carnwath
    138
Lockhart, Major (Cholmondley's
    34th of Foot) 115, 116, 117,
    125, 126, 132, 133, 155, 157,
    149
Lovat, Simon Fraser, 12th Baron
    9, 22, 36, 98, 104, 107, 113
Loudon, Earl 63, 122, 132, 133,
    134, 135, 138, 146
Lumsdaine, Robert, Lieut-Colonel
    89, 149, 151
Lumsden, George, of Perth 65
Lumsden, James, Lieutenant 89
Luss, Laird of 36, 73

Macbane, Donald, 72
Macdonald, Alexander, 138
Macdonald, Alexander, Captain
    152
Macdonald, Alexander, of
    Keppoch 37, 120
Macdonald Alexander, of
    Kingsburgh 144

Macdonald, Sir Alexander, of Sleat
120, 125, 135, 139, 140, 142,
157, 159
Macdonald, of Clanranald, 141
Macdonald, Angus, of Borrodale
145
Macdonald of Boisdale 122
Macdonald, of Barrisdale 55, 111,
135, 148
Macdonald, Donald, of Bohuntin
55
Macdonald, Donald, of Castleton
147, 214
Macdonald, Donald, of Inergary
65
Macdonald, Sir Donald, of Sleat 36
Macdonald, Flora 142, 143, 144
Macdonald, of Loch Garry 111
Macdonald, Hugh, of Armadale
141, 142, 143, 147, 215
Macdonald, James, Captain 128,
215
Macdonald, John, Captain 128,
215
Macdonald, Lady of Clanranald
141
Macdonald, Lady Margaret, of
Sleat 142
Macdonald of Morar 145
Macdonald – Clan 15, 43, 91,
122, 130
Macdonalds of Glencoe 56, 77,
83, 87, 122
Macdonalds of Glengarry 55, 122,
131
Macdonalds of Keppoch 11, 56,
72, 77, 79, 99, 108, 122, 131,
155
Macdonalds of Sleat 77
Macdonnel, Lord Aeneas, of Arros
65
Macdonnel, Alexander, of Tulloch
120
Macdonnel, Donald, of Aberarder
127

Macdonnel, Donald, of Cranachan
120
Macdonnel, Donald, of Tirnadris
120
Macdonnel, John, of Glengarry
120
Macdonnel, Ranald, of Aberarder
120
Macdonnels of Glengarry 99
Macdougal, Christopher 70
Maceachain, Neil 142, 144
Macfarlane, Laird of 36, 84
Macfarlane – Clan 44
Macfinzone, Laird of 36
Macgillivrays, Clan 72
Macgregor of Glengyle 111
Macgregor, Rob Roy 102, 111
Macgregor – Clan 44, 45, 52, 54,
99, 100, 102, 108, 135, 148
Machargh, John, Captain 152
Mackenzie, Alexander, Captain
128, 215
Mackenzie, Colin, of Hiltown 128,
215
Mackenzie, Duncan, Lieut-
Colonel 48, 93, 94, 97, 98
Mackenzie, Duncan of Castleton
65
Mackenzie, John, Lieutenant 94
Mackenzie, Kenneth, of Suddie,
Captain 70, 71, 79, 154, 174
Mackenzie – Clan 43, 91, 97, 99,
102, 108, 125, 130, 135
Mackenzie Colin, of Redcastle
128, 215
Mackay, Hugh, of Scourie,
General 28, 39, 77, 78, 79, 80,
81, 82, 84, 88, 155
Mackay, George, Captain 127, 214
Mackay, Hugh, Captain 89, 128,
135, 215
Mackay, Robert, Colonel 89
Mackay – Clan 15, 43, 91, 97, 99,
125, 130
Mackartor, Alexander 67

Index

Mackinnon, John, Captain 145
Mackinnon, Laird of 145
Mackinnon of Mackinnon 125
Mackinnons – Clan 135, 137
Mackintosh, Lady Anne, of Moy, 'Colonel Anne' 133
Mackintosh, Donald, of Kellachy 55, 64
Mackintosh, William, Vic, Lachlan 62
Mackintosh, William, Captain 128, 215
Mackintosh, Laird of 36, 124, 134
Mackintosh of MacKintosh 12
Mackintosh – Clan 13, 72, 79, 91, 99, 125
Maclean, Dr Alistair 160
Maclean, Allan, of Ardgour 50
Maclean, Hector, of Duart 50
Maclean, Lachlan, of Duart 50
Maclean, Laird of 36
Macleans – Clan 15, 43, 91
Macleans of Mull 66
Macleod, Alexander 50
Macleod, Alexander, of Ullinish 141, 147
Macleod, Donald, of Guatergill 139, 140
Macleod, Hugh, of Geanies 128, 215
Macleod, John 127, 214
Macleod, Malcolm, of Raasay 144
Macleod, Norman, of Bernera 127, 214
Macleod, Norman of Waterstein 127, 147, 214
Macleod, Rory, of Dunvegan 50
Macleod of Talisker 149
Macleod of MacLeod 125, 135, 139, 140, 157, 159
Macleod, Laird of 36
Macleod – Clan 43, 130
Macleods of Skye 122, 130
Macmartins of Letterfinlay 72

Macnab, Duncan, of Strathfillan 65
Macneil, Daniel 97
Macneils of Barra 50, 77
Macneils – Clan 43
Macpherson, Ewen Yr, of Cluny 121
Macpherson, James 97
Macpherson of Cluny 36, 125, 127, 137, 146, 147, 157
Macpherson – Clan 15, 55, 91, 148
Macrimmon, Donald 132
Mar, Earl of 7, 15, 36, 69, 73, 92, 93, 95, 97, 98
Maxwell, Henry 72
Meggernie Castle 80, 81
Menzies, Sir Alexander 77, 78
Menzies, James, of Comrie, Captain 78, 85
Menzies, James, of Culdares, Colonel 66, 67, 69
Menzies, Robert, Captain 55, 77, 78, 79, 80, 81, 82, 83, 155
Menzies of Pitfodels 77
Menzies, Castle 80, 81
Menzies – Clan 55
Middleton, Robert, Major 72
Milton, Lord, (Andrew Fletcher) 123
Mitchell, Sir Andrew 126, 157
Monck, George, 1st Duke of Albemarle, General 7, 39, 48, 55, 57
Morays (Atholl Grouping) 54
Monteith, Earl of 36, 73
Moy, The Rout of 134, 160
Mulroy, Battle of 72, 155, 160
Munro, George, of Culcairn, Captain/Major/Colonel 88, 97, 100, 103, 113, 114, 115, 117, 127, 132, 155, 214
Munro, William, Lieutenant 89
Murray, Sir Archibald, of Blackbarony 89

235

Murray, Sir David, of Gospetrie 49
Murray, Lord George 32, 103, 118, 137, 148
Murray, Lord John 36, 119, 130
Murray, James 88
Murray, Sir Patrick, of Ochtentyre 124
Murrays (Atholl Grouping) 54
Musket 25, 28
Murray, Archibald, Captain 89

O'Brien, Lucius, Captain 135
Ochiltree, Lord (Andrew Stewart) 49, 50, 51, 52
Ogilvy, Lord David 125
O'Sullivan, John, William, Colonel 29, 136, 138, 140

Perth, Earls of 73
Perth, Duke of (James Drummond) 36, 138
Philliphaugh 55
Pistols 25
Pitsligo, Lord (Alexander Forbes), 4th Baron
Pitt, Earl of Chatham 158, 161
Prestonpans 7, 28, 124, 129, 173
Pretender, the Young (see Stuart, Prince Charles Edward)
Price's (14th of Foot) 131
Privy Council 15, 58, 62, 104

Ramsays (Atholl Grouping(54
Reay, Lord (George MacKay), 3rd Baron Reay 36
Restoration, The 55
Revolution, The Glorious 57
Robertsons (Atholl Grouping) 54
Robinson, Jacob 169
Ronald, Patrick 72
Rose, Alexander 93, 152
Ross, Alexander 88
Ross – Clan 13, 91, 97, 99, 117, 125, 130
Ross, William 128, 215

Royal Scots (1st of Foot) 16, 122
Ruthven 58, 101, 111, 112, 114

Saxe, Maurice, Comte de, Marshal of France 121, 122
Scone, Lord 49, 51, 52
Scots Guards 66
Scott, Caroline, Captain (Guise's) 143, 149
Seaforth, Earls of 36, 59, 71, 82, 97, 98, 99, 100, 103, 157
Semphill, Lord, Colonel 119
Seumas An Tuim (James Grant of Carron) 55
Seven Men of Moidart 121
Sharp, William 70
Shaw, Farquhar 119
Sheridan, Sir Thomas 138
Sheriffmuir, Battle of 7, 93, 97, 99, 100, 102
Sinclair – Clan 69
Spaldings (Atholl Grouping) 54
Statutes of Iona (1609) 4, 5
Stair, Earl of 119
Stewart, Alexander, of Blair Atholl 64, 65
Stewart, David, of Garth, General 18, 20, 21, 116, 124
Stewart, James, of Arditie 55
Stewart, James, Steward Depute of Menteith 52
Stewart, Sir James, of Ballechin 53
Stewart, John, of Perth 63
Stewart, James Francis Edward 95, 102
Stewart, Robert, Laird of Ballechin 53
Stewarts (Atholl Grouping) 44, 54
Stolle, Marquis De 25
Strathglass, Laird of 36
Strathnaver, Lord – His Regiment 93
Strowan, Laird of 36
Stuart of Appin 92, 93, 97, 99

Index

Stuart, Prince Charles Edward 7, 16, 121, 122, 124, 125, 126, 137, 138, 139, 140, 141, 142, 143–145, 146, 147, 160
Sutherland, Earl of, William Gordon, 17th or 18th Earl 36
Sutherland, Peter 127, 129, 214
Sutherlands – Clan 13, 97, 99, 125, 130

Tacitus 148
Tanistry, Celtic law of 12
Tarbert, Lord 36, 87
Targe 25
Tascal Money 109
Teisdale, William 89
Thirty Years' War 15, 55
Tippermuir, Battle of 7, 55
Tullibardine, Marquis of, William Murray 'The Jacobite Duke' 7

Tweedale, Lord, 122, 125, 155

Union of the Crowns (1603) 15, 49
Union of Parliaments (1707) 12
Urquhart, Robert of Burrisyards 93

Wade, George, General/Field Marshall 10, 11, 14, 20, 37, 38, 100, 107, 112, 113, 114, 115, 118, 155, 156, 159, 178–195
Walpole, Sir Robert 123
Weem, Laird of 36, 73, 81, 84
Wightman, Joseph, Major General 102, 103
William III 7, 35, 72, 76, 80, 83, 87, 93
Wishart, George, Major 88, 89
Worcester 7